The Book of Sarahs

The Book of Sarahs

| A Family in Parts |

Catherine E. McKinley

COUNTERPOINT
WASHINGTON, D.C.
NEW YORK, N.Y.

Most names—family friends, adoption workers—are pseudonyms. Al Green and the New England Home for Little Wanderers are real, as are the names of public figures.

ISBN 1-58243-259-7

Book design and composition by Mark McGarry, Texas Type & Book Works
Set in Fairfield

Printed in the United States of America

COUNTERPOINT
387 Park Avenue South
New York, N.Y. 10016

Counterpoint is a member of the Perseus Books Group

For my grandmother, E. R. W.

For my sisters.

And for the former Brooklyn-town chapter of FMN

Contents

| Afro-Saxon |

July 1978

Scotland. This is where the whispering began.

I sat with my family in a pub in Edinburgh, anxious to warm away the sea's soak, caught in the thick sponge of my clothes. We had walked the stretch of rocky shore bordering the campus of St. Andrews, climbing to the great pier that juts out at its edge, marching to my mother's memories. She had led us out along its reach, to the point where the waves began to swallow it, wildly singing processional songs from her days as a student. My brother and I had walked behind her, pacing our steps like supplicants, our riffs on her songs rising into shouts that fell off in the booming tide. My father had lagged behind us, a tiny magnifying glass in his hand, stooping to examine what had pooled among the breakers.

Now we paused for a meal, a drink to say farewell to another point on our tour, a journey back through the McKinley narrative of

Scotch-Irish and English migrations. We sat in a far corner of the pub, to the side of a table where two men drank and blew smoke rings in a kind of dramatic repose. The men both wore heavy glasses and well-oiled afros, combed up from the collars of Harris tweed jackets. One wore a trilogy of patterned wool straight down to the tops of platform shoes. I sat and watched their quiet faces, soaking up their languor, imagining I could smell their cologne and pomade in the encircling smoke.

Suddenly an eyebrow raised in one face. The other man sat up. And the whole room seemed to shift, as if on cue. I turned with them and watched an awesome reddish, curled wig and a head, tied with a green and red plaid wool scarf in a beautiful high arch, move above the crowd. The women's headpieces framed smooth, dark faces, penciled with heavy black brows drawn nearly to their temples. Their dark-lined, lipsticked mouths moved together, offering excited greetings as they settled at the table. I sat examining the waxy-sheened, bright print dresses they wore, which revealed sweaters at their wide embroidered and laced necklines. It was an odd way to wear a sweater—on the inside—I thought. But their dresses were so beautiful and the logic of it made simple, new sense to me. Their clothes and talk sent a raucous flash through a gray and green clothed room. They were so lovely to me, reweaving the dull, familiar textures of that world, of home, where the only sight of Africa was an occasional face floating behind the windshield of a passing car, always en route to somewhere else. I had come all the way from Attleboro, Massachusetts, to get a good look at Black people.

This trip was a family return, and for me, a reprieve from turning eleven in the dulling heat and tensions of summer in Attleboro. But with every stake put down in the family's past and every new discovery, I was beginning to feel oddly cold. Sitting there, I felt weak, in the way we used it in middle school. Wussy. Soft. Suddenly self-conscious of my knit Skye cardigan and the kilt I wore, fastened at my knees with my grandmother's silver thistle-shaped pin, set with a heavy purple stone. Earlier that day, as my parents shopped for Isle sweaters in the rows of tiny boutiques in town, I had looked for the McKinley tartan among the plaids piled into the shelves. I had talked myself out of my fixation, out of the disappointment of not finding our cloth or crest after the girls in one shop put a chart of old Scottish clans in front of me, pointing to it and laughing, so that I was no longer sure of their kindness. "Are you Scottish?" they asked, looking at my family and then scrutinizing my face, different from theirs, brown like the lighter edge of an iron burn.

"My family is Scotch-Irish," I said, my voice cracking.

I tried to console myself; it wasn't a beautiful tartan at all.

Now the woman's headscarf almost seemed to be taunting me, saying, *Hey, what is this plaid anyway?*

I felt the weakness spreading as I sat watching their table, and I got up and made for the bathroom. I washed the tight stain of salt air from my face and stood looking at myself in the mottled glass above the sink. My dark, curly eyebrows had begun to thicken and spread across the bridge of my nose. Those brows, my nose—long and a bit wide and a little turned up at the same time, my brownness, and the two shoulder-length braids I'd worn since primary school had earned me the name "Pocahontas." Mysterious, exotic in those parts, the schoolyard curio. Pocahontas in Scotland, the mirror said. I took off my hat and combed out my hair with my hand. It was cut for the first time into a short afro. I'd taken the afro as my mother's defeat in the battle of caring for my thick, soft naps of hair. It was the end of Pocahontas. And it was my defeat as well—the only afro under the reign of hair spray and Farrah Fawcett-Majors flipped bangs at Willet Middle School.

My brother watched me return to the table and to watching them. He sat enjoying me from under a thick shock of white-blond bangs, angling, and then he kicked me under the table, his mouth hanging open in a moronic pose.

"Duuh! Don't stare. It's not polite, and you'll make them feel like they don't belong here."

My mother leaned toward us, whispering, "They're students at the university, I would guess. Africans. They must be Nigerians. There were some Nigerian students when I was there. And William's right—don't stare!"

But I stared so that I barely ate. I watched every shift and gesture they made, while I struggled through the questions that had been growing in me all year. When the Lutheran Church–sponsored Laotian refugee children arrived in our class, prejudice had become part of our lessons. There was talk of race riots in nearby Boston and a lot of relief expressed when it was certain that Attleboro was beyond the possible bussing zones. There was the funny confusion I was experiencing of being talked about as "Afro-American" and "Black" and "colored" and "Negro" all at the same time and knowing those things had something to do with Africa, but what exactly? And when I was able to settle that confusion, someone was there to ask another question about being "adopted," or (different from my brother) being adopted "transracially," and having Black and white "biological parents," and being "mixed race," and that other list of things all at the same time. I felt tortured by my strange status and by my isolation and distance from so many things. I watched the table next to ours. Was this the world where I belonged in bigger parts?

I wanted to cross over to them and sit in the roar of their open laughter and the ease they inhabited. Would my confusion stop then?

I was still staring; my mother hissed her schoolteacher's warning at me. At the sound, one of the men turned. He caught me deep in the eye and winked and smiled at me in a way that I thought offered so much understanding. He turned back to his friends, but I kept watching him, hoping he would pull me back with that wink again.

My father paid the bill, and as we rose to leave, the man leaned out from his table and held out his hand to me.

"Dear Lady, what is your name?" he asked.

"Ah, then pleased to meet you, Madame Catherine," he said, drawing out his reply as he dropped his head in a long, elegant nod.

I giggled at his name—Wooly? Wally?—and hurried shyly to my mother's side. He turned back to his conversation and didn't notice me looking back at them on my way to the door until the crowd in the room sealed off my view.

As we walked back through town to the bed-and-breakfast where we'd been staying, I felt rocked with an ache, an old, unspecified kind of grief that would not leave my chest. I lay in bed for hours that night, pretending to read, watching the odd sunlight in the late night sky while William and my parents pored over maps, planning our route into the northern countryside.

The next day we rose before dawn. As we drove further from the city, that ache continued to hold me. Scotland's melancholy began to drift over me. With each movement north, the desolate herds of highland cattle, the mournfulness of the often mist-covered land, the sheep marooned on the confounding pattern of hills, the collapse of peat underfoot as we stopped to stretch, walking the countryside, made me feel that I was losing my hold.

Our family travels always seemed intent on distancing ourselves from other people: packing into the Grand Teton mountains on horseback; canoeing or hiking or skiing for many days without company; weekends when we took off for the woods hoping for two days uninterrupted by the sight of other outdoorers. We traveled for several days now, stopping along the way to hike, or fish at the lakes, or walk the stone-walled edges of people's farms.

One morning we stopped at a place in the road where we could park our car and began a climb up one of the giant "stacks," the mountainlike hills that dotted the countryside. As we began our hike, my mother and I fell into our rituals of silence, comfortable together in our own heads, letting William and my father blaze the trail ahead of us. We stopped when we guessed we were about halfway to the top, and as we rested, I began one of our scouting games. I loved these games—when we imagined we were pushing through impossible terrain, and getting past it depended on my helping to read the navigational signs. I was not good at the real work of map reading, the setting of equipment, or the gauging of time and elements that William and my parents loved, spending hours at times in an intensely fixed threesome. But together with my mother like this, with my eagle eye and strength and my special sixth sense, I could chart a world of pleasure and have her all to myself.

"Is that sky or mountain?" I began, pointing at the cloudy wall of the horizon.

"It's sky, silly." She moved behind me, one arm wrapping my waist, as she pressed her binoculars to my eyes. She braced my elbow as I tried to steady and focus the glass. I felt her breath hot against my cheek, and my nose was filled with the smells of whiskey and chocolate, familiar balms against the cool air. In just that moment, as I found my sight in the tiny lenses, the etching of clouds had moved, breaking the steep, jagged line of their ascent.

"Your mountain has become smoke," she said, laughing. Then she tried to swing me around on the narrow ledge, groaning at my weight, so we could look out further eastward where the sky was uninterrupted by clouds.

"Can you see Cape Wrath? If we jump out wide from here we'll land at the very tip of Scotland!"

I looked down and saw charcoal water breaking the countless rolls of brilliant green countryside below into a thin wrist of land stretching into the sea. But with the sight of that tip of earth, and the sound of my mother's triumph for reaching this place so far from everything, an intense coldness washed over me. She stood for a while, staring through the glasses, locked in a kind of ecstatic trance.

"Mummy, why did you adopt me? Why didn't I get adopted by an African—an Afro-American—family? " I asked, wanting to pull her back to me, surprised by my own question and at the anger trembling in my voice.

At first she didn't seem to hear me, but then she sighed very deeply and dropped the binoculars to her chest, closing her jacket over them. "Well, I guess we came first. You know, we really wanted a second child; we'd waited for a long time. There were very few healthy white infants available to couples who wanted to adopt, and we were asked to consider adopting a Black or mixed-race child. And how could we have refused you?"

It was not a new question. I had asked it in so many configurations that it was no longer the question that mattered. It had become a signal of some anxiety in me—and she had begun to answer me reflexively and to try to take care of the real need more quietly. But this time my question betrayed anger, and I had called out who else I might belong to. The anger I felt seemed lodged in what I knew her answer would be. I was beginning to feel there was something wrong in what she was saying, however much she was trying to speak to a complicated thing and still preserve our "truths" and the need for clarity.

"Come on, let's not waste time," she said, with a sudden gruffness. I immediately wanted to take away the feeling of something difficult erupting between us, to pull her back to our closeness and hold her there. But she had already moved from where we were standing and was lost in her powerful stride and her excitement about what lay further up the trail. I felt something else erupt in the moment she turned from me, and every step now felt labored by my rage.

As we neared the peak, the trail narrowed to little more than a stony goat path, with an eroding earthen wall and a precipice on either side. Waves of nausea and cold sweat began to roll over me, and it seemed that space was collapsing and then opening wild around me. My breath came in ragged waves and then seemed to halt completely. I stood facing the wall, gripping dry, hanging roots, trying to feel my breath moving in me. I could not move. It was as if I had never felt space and wind like this before; I was no longer the brave veteran of our family climbs. They had moved surefootedly beyond me, expecting the baby in the family to push her last bit of strength, proudly keeping up with them. But I was caught in the fist of my anger and breathlessness several shelves of the cliff track below.

I smelled the too-sweet stench of sweat and Lady Mum deodorant from the curve of my armpits and felt the warm liquid drop from their hollow to my waist. My body trembled, and I felt that I would lose myself without the weight of my backpack holding me at the center of gravity.

I looked up at my mother now, moving closer to where William and my father rested at the bald patch of earth at the mountain's very top. She was peering through her glass, looking out again toward the sea.

I wanted the safety of being close to them. But even in my fear, I felt some exhilaration at letting go. I felt myself wanting to test the lines between where I belonged and where I didn't; where I was safe and where I was out of bounds; where they could hold me and where they would let me go. I felt trapped inside an airless space where I was left sputtering, choked with rage. Scotland had brought on something like the emotions of an asthma attack—the kind of terrible struggle you feel when your body cannot take in the air that freely surrounds you, while the people you hope will save you look on from outside, perversely gulping it in. That feeling emerged there on the cliff, and it seemed to hold me for many years.

April 1992

The verandah of the old, pillared mansion was steeped in moonlight and a humid wind shook the surrounding grove of trees with force and then retreated playfully, announcing the approach of the rainy season. From that place in the large compound, it was easy to forget the stench of open sewers and the clamor of vendors selling in the heavy, stalled traffic running alongside its edge, which told a more characteristic story of Accra, Ghana's capital city. I was at the home of a man who had left Chicago for Ghana in the early 1960s, at the end of the Nkrumah era. I watched through a door that opened on a large hall as he addressed the guests gathered there. He spoke with passion about UNESCO's efforts to restore the old slave forts lining the coast and the mission of a community of African Americans to purchase and "reclaim" some of the neglected properties not included under that plan. As he spoke, he kept cutting an angry eye toward a steward at the edge of the room who was fumbling in his attempt to open a bottle of wine. A staff of neocolonial-style maids wearing white aprons over matching batik dresses and high, elegant bridges of thread-wrapped hair—styles that in the West Africa of the 1970s approximated the social pride of the afro—moved among the crowd of African American and West Indian travelers. They were dressed with so much seriousness in expensive kente cloth despite their kente illiteracy.

I was watching this, thinking about the house's incredible beauty, in spite of what it stood for, and the uneasy, even comic, scene we created, although all around me, people seemed enormously content. I was thinking about the way the ugliest contradictions can be gracefully contained, how rapture and melancholy can sit side by side.

I had come to Ghana to celebrate my twenty-fifth birthday. I was hoping to strengthen a connection with a place that had held my fascination so thoroughly since childhood—a connection deeper than my attempts to read my way through African literature, my few close friendships with West Africans, my involvement in the anti-apartheid movement, and "Buy Africa" consumerism had forged.

During the summer that my family journeyed to Scotland, Alex Haley's miniseries *Roots* re-aired, a year after it had set fire to national television. I watched the episodes night after night, while William and my parents retreated to the basement, consumed with building a bright yellow, two-seat kayak that they were hoping to launch in a local Labor Day race. From time to time, one of them would pass through the living room and pause behind my chair to watch snatches of the program. I sat rigid through each hour, powerfully in love with the images on the screen, feeling my sense of isolation and my longing for Black company begin to grow and overwhelm me. I began to nurse a nearly consuming anger for my family's indifference toward people (ultimately me) they were supposed to care about. At times that anger felt so overwhelming, and so unanchored, that I imagined dashing myself, dramatically, like a bolt of fire, down the basement stairs.

But the story narrated by *Roots* was also working on me like a kind of balm. It helped me to understand the specificities of "African" and "Afro-American" and "Negro" and the many complications of naming and history that I was so confused about. And in the absence of the actual story of my own birth heritage, it nurtured my imaginings of who my own Black people were, how I came to be a part of my adoptive family, and where I fit into The Story of Race in America. At the same time, the legacy of the trans-Atlantic slave trade—the ancestral and cultural dislocation through slavery—became an allegory for my own burgeoning sense of loss. Black people at home, in Attleboro, Massachusetts, seemed as elusive to me as Africa was for most Black Americans, and my racial roots were as elusive as my actual family roots were. And this was where I began to make a way through my questions about racial belonging and adoption, both of which were complicatedly entangled in my thoughts and emotions. For many years, Africa came to represent some extreme location—the ultimate reach, a solid landing beyond what felt like some formless suspension—where all that I sought could be attained.

Now I was twenty-five and I was in Ghana. I had arrived back in

Accra that afternoon after visiting the forts along the country's middle coast. For the past few days, I'd been traveling with two women, magazine editors I knew from the new life I was making in New York City. I had recently left graduate school, and I was working as an editorial assistant in book publishing. I had been surprised to discover them on my flight to Accra, and we'd made plans to meet up before the end of our trip and travel together a bit. We had arrived at the town of Elmina early that morning and walked through the bare fortress of Elmina Castle, happy to find only crews of workmen there. We followed a group of men as they walked into the belly of the fort, seeking shelter from the already blazing heat. They chose one of the narrow holding rooms and stretched out on the ground. A little further down the passageway, a small team worked with kerosene lamps, scraping away several inches of cement-like ground that covered original cobblestones. The ground turned muckish black as it was removed. As we looked on, one of the men explained to us that what they were removing was centuries of packed-down feces and body waste. They would clear it away from all but half of one room, where it would be left as part of a museum display.

I felt sorrow in that instant that I had been trying not to give in to. I had been trying to temper my almost Negritude-brand romanticism about Africa with my more usual cynicism. I had traveled to the forts armed with the knowledge that they were becoming a lucrative wailing wall. I'd heard about Ghanaian women and men sometimes being sent down into the castle's bowels to sing and reenact the terrors of the forts for tourists before the collection plate was passed. And as soon as we had parked our car, we had been met by a cavalcade of beggars and children offering, as if it were an original school essay, neatly transcribed pages making the same Pan-Africanist plea for

African American and African solidarity. I had suspected it would not be worth it to come there and *feel*. But there was something too terrible about those workmen relaxing in that cell and about what was being scraped from the floor.

I turned to leave the room and saw a man, bare-chested, in threadbare pants, filthy from his labor, crouched near the doorway, devouring in fingerfulls a thick sticky ball of kenkey and tiny, pungent fried fish. I felt dizzy and a little sick from all the associations of senses and the lack of air. I walked quickly back along the corridor, following the trail of sunlight, blinking back tears.

As we stood in the courtyard looking out at the Gulf of Guinea through the cuttings in the wall that had once cradled cannons, trying to shake off our queasiness, a young Ghanaian man and woman, led by a museum guide, walked over and stood a little to our side. They were carefully watching us. I began watching them just as intently.

The guide greeted us, and after we exchanged introductions, we fell in with their tour. Soon, the young man turned to my friends and began to explain to them that he was a university student and that he was doing research on trans-Atlantic slavery and was interested in African Americans visiting Ghana.

"Do you feel an ancestral connection to Ghana?" he asked. He attacked the matter with his whole body, and his companion and I were literally pushed to the side. He was not purposefully rude; he was preoccupied with a question he thought they could answer for him.

"I think I'm a Sahelian woman, myself," I said, wanting to play with his assumptions.

He turned to me when I spoke and said, "Ah, but you are a German?"

"German? She's American. She's a Sister! She's a Black woman!" my friends answered in surprise.

"Oh, I thought she was a German," he said, looking carefully at my face, the soft naps showing at the edges of the scarf I'd tied on my head.

"Obruni nkaw nkaw!" laughed one of the workmen who was passing, listening to us. I knew from my tiny understanding of Twi that he was saying that I was yellow like a yellow plantain, a "white" person, an "obruni"—the name thrown at any person with lighter than dark-brown skin or any person of any color from the West, or anyone who is not a native-speaking Ghanaian.

"Ah, you're half-caste," the student said, with new authority.

And this launched us into an argument about race in the Americas and race in Africa, and the heavy persistence of a colonial history that allowed him to use "half-caste" so easily. While they debated race through me, the "half-caste," all of my private rages and insecurities, and my perennial sense of illegitimacy, descended on me.

I had been feeling painfully conspicuous in Ghana, so much so that many mornings, I would linger in my room at the guesthouse where I stayed, preparing myself to meet the world outside. As soon as I emerged and moved onto the streets, I could feel people's stares, their quiet, intense watching. It wasn't everyone on the road that noticed me, and no one was unfriendly, but being in their focused eye unnerved me. People would call out, "Obruni!" or "Blufono!" ("Eng-lishwoman!"), and the words felt like they were echoing everywhere. They became the only things I could distinguish in the languages spoken around me. Children I met on the road would sing out their English lessons,

Obruni,

how are you?

I'm fine! Thank you!

Several times, people had passed me in the narrow corridors of the markets and brushed their hands along the length of my arm or grabbed my hand—the touch so delicate and quick that it was ghost-like. I would turn to react, and the person would be steps away from me, moving on as if I'd passed them unnoticed. I felt the touch of my old classmates in Attleboro, who would dig into my head with their knuckles, chanting, "Rub a nigger for good luck." It was schoolyard play for them; their aggression was carefully masked. Now, where I kept expecting hostility to erupt in those glances and songs and touches, people would offer warm grins and laughter that had no trace of malice and made me feel like my anger was cruel.

This odd, offending warmth was bringing back a powerful sense of the outsidership that I had often felt at home. In Attleboro, as I moved about town, I would feel the pressure of people watching me. I would imagine that I was dangerous in a hundred ways (I was a Black Panther, I was MLK, I was a notorious whore) as I passed amongst the white teenagers and adults who wore their disaffection like their blue factory Dickies, heavy metal t-shirts, leather hats and Harley gear. They stood in bands at McDonald's, at the zoo, near the school yard, in the town Commons, in front of head shops, against the memorial statues in town. "Hey, nigger—or are you one of them I-ranians?" they would call. My street encounters in Ghana stirred up all of that discomfort, even without the sense of threat.

Attleboro was a small factory town twenty or so miles west of Providence, Rhode Island. My parents moved to Attleboro in 1966 with my brother, whom they'd adopted just a year before, when they were living in Scotch Plains, New Jersey. My father had a new engineering job at the Texas Instruments plant, and my mother started teaching history in a neighboring town soon thereafter, pounding dates and decisions into the heads of kids mostly destined for rote factory work. They settled in Attleboro, happy to escape suburbia, happy to live in a "real town" (a place where everyone lived *and* worked, my mother explained), where they could have a sense of community, enough land to garden, and a patch of woods to roam in. They would have preferred a proper farm, but they decided that it would not be fair to young kids to opt for a completely rural existence. So we lived out their great homestead fantasies in a weathered Cape house on "the Hill," a few blocks of haven from factory grit (Attleboro was Jewelry Capital, USA—home of the companies that made America's school rings) and poverty that radiated up from the center of town where clothing mills and industrial stacks rose as high as the Roman Catholic church towers. Our house sat amidst obsessively manicured homes, bordering the swampy woods that met the Bungay River. The river passed just a short walk behind our house, organizing the nearby line of factories. We left our yard untended, almost as a defiance, it seemed. It became more deeply ensconced in plant life over time— the lawn gone to seed, run over by weeds and wild flowers; the once-prized rose bushes at the front yard's edge grew wild, mauling the cedar fence they grew along. The rock garden at the side of our house became a harbor to snakes taking refuge from a neighbor's AstroTurf lawn. In the backyard, my parents raised chickens and kept hives of honeybees, in defiance of the city's zoning laws.

I thought of us as a newfangled Addams Family, living a '70s and '80s drama in a madcap house, moving about unconscious of the gawking crowd. I was the tortured, seeing one. I felt uncomfortably linked as my parents' not-quite-Black, not-white adopted daughter to a host of curiosities that set us apart from everyone. My father, tall and lanky and balding, withdrawn in quirky shyness, played our off-stage ringleader. My mother, with her thin, straight, boyish body, her hair capped under a railroad conductor's hat, was a familiar figure, moving about in an old Plymouth station wagon—often with the canoes loaded on top—or on her bicycle on the way to the grocery store with the red buggy trailing behind, or on roller sneakers (years ahead of the rage) with one of our succession of odd family dogs running alongside. William gained repute in our corner of town by riding his unicycle through the streets, practicing his juggling as he rode. Or, trading whatever he was tossing for his trumpet, he would ride through the neighborhood, belting out "Reveille." He became an infamous trumpeter, playing at all of the official town celebrations from third grade until he left home for college. He was the "sissy-fag" bandleader, the Drama Club "queen," the tall, beautiful, blond, blue-eyed boy who wasted all that power carrying sewing boxes home for the nerdiest girls. He advanced through Attleboro's public schools with sheer guts and abstracted vision, and a refusal to ever strike someone, coming home defeated in every fight.

I was William's adopted sister. (No one really thought of him as someone in the same position.) My parents' adopted child. And as I grew older, I often felt—internalizing people's quiet suggestions—that I was the welfare kid, my father's little whore, my mother's sign of having been with Black men. How else could that world understand our connection? I felt like I was the angry but sweet-faced sign of something discomforting and illicit in a very Catholic place, where being a child of divorce or a member of a single-parent home was the far side of difference. But all of the dangers of who we were seemed mediated by the protections of our class and our being a "good," if agnostic, family.

I remember my mother once calling a woman who lived down the street from us a "fucking swamp Yankee" when a neighborhood friend appeared to tell me that the softball game was off because the woman had just announced that her children "weren't allowed to play with niggers." There were not enough people for a second team. There was embarrassment in my mother's half-hearted slur. She never talked this way. But she was angry. She came outside and played pitch with us. And that was the first time I noted where the real lines of class were drawn between us and our neighbors, who were, if they would admit it, mostly one generation off immigrant ships, up from bench work, hiding now behind vulgar displays of middle-class consciousness. They stooped to bigotry. On the other side were my fiercely frugal parents, with their educated reserve, their better politics, and their blue bloodlines.

The writer Anatole Broyard explained so perfectly his own predicament in a family where the lines of race were similarly complicated: "Anyone who saw me with my parents already knew too much about me." I felt a similar loss of privacy, of being out of control of how others saw me—a self I didn't always understand and was struggling to present with some authority. With the rest of the McKinleys able to escape the most critical fallout of my parents' choices concerning adoption, I increasingly felt a sense of being outside the protection of family.

The discomfort of living like this, in the place we did, and our growing remove from each other as the years went by, led me to increasingly elaborate deceptions. I wanted to throw off people's gaze and the conspicuousness of my anger about being who I was, where I was. I was fighting a deep sense of shame for being Black and white and an adopted child, a bastard. Every posture and every choice I made began to feel like a defiance or an apology.

If you asked almost anyone who lived in Attleboro in the 1960s through the 1980s, when I left there, whether there were any Black people living in town, they would tell you, no. If you went to City Hall today, they would cite that a hundred or so Black people lived there by the 80s and then admit that the count probably included some Portuguese. The reality that I lived counted Black people so small in number that they remained shadowy and unseen. For most of the twenty-five years our family lived there, the most visible, enduring sign of integration was the result of my adoption and, some years later, the adoption of a Black "bi-racial" boy, Christopher, into an Irish family—old-timers in town, who were my parents' political friends. We will be remembered because, being children, attending Attleboro's schools, being McKinleys and Crosbys, we became as thoroughly integrated as we could be.

A few people might remember Mr. Henderson, who worked for a time in the factory where my father was manager, or the man who came and did quite well at the YMCA, moving up to lower management by the late 1980s when folks would have finally been comfortable with him there. For most, the closest thing to someone "colored" were the Vietnamese and Laotian refugees who arrived in the 1970s, the Portuguese greengrocer who worked at the fruit stand downtown, or Mr. Shang, the laundry man, whose old, bare-bones laundry and dry cleaning business was closed down under the cruel pretense of rezoning the downtown. Years later, in 1986, Mr. Shang would win two mayoral terms, with my mother, a loyal customer, championing his campaign. By then, Attleboro was slowly changing, and Christopher, my fellow transracial adoptee, and I had both left for the big city, while my parents began packing up to move to Vermont to start a life as farmers.

In actuality, there was a Black church in Attleboro. John Wesley African Methodist Episcopal Zion Church was there, less than a mile from our house, tucked away at the bottom of the Hill on a street that made a queer corner behind an abandoned jewelry plant on the Bungay River. In the middle of rows of decaying two-family houses, the weather-beaten, gray-shingled church stood, proclaiming itself with an old, hand-stenciled, buckled wood sign. The church had been built in 1873, when the railroad had run regularly through town, bringing a community of Negro porters and railroad workers, foundry men, masons, and domestics to join the local potato farmers and dairymen. That history was mostly invisible by the time my parents moved there. My mother had known about John Wesley A.M.E. Zion for years through her various political associations. But I was almost through junior high school before she thought of the church as a possible help to me, and I was introduced to the six or seven extended families that came from outlying towns to worship there on Sundays.

I was still feeling an awful, full-blown sense of alienation that evening at the party in Accra, and I remained on the verandah, watching our host and the partyers revel in the air of good fortune. After a while, a woman came and stood by my side. She was wearing blue jeans and a tie-dyed t-shirt covered with a bright-red, embroidered Guatemalan shawl. She had silver, shoulder-length dreadlocks and a face that seemed chiseled with sadness. Then she held out her hand to me and introduced herself as "Rhae," and her quick, pretty smile obliterated the lines of age. She seemed in that moment like a genuine trickster, like the Spider herself. I liked her immediately.

I felt a familiar anxiety as soon as she asked, "Where are your people from, baby?" More than anything, the question is the pre-desegregation generation's way of marking your tribe (Boston, Harlem, Louisiana, Los Angeles-by-way-of-Houston, Detroit, Nutbush, Tennessee—African American nation-states). It's an easy question, passed among strangers seeking easy affiliations, but sometimes it barely masks people's curiosity, or their discomfort with not being able to immediately place me among the familiar.

Are you all Black?
A Latin sister?
Which side is the chocolate on?

The question always made me feel like I was being asked to expose more than I wanted to. For most of my life, questions people were fond of asking, such as "Which one of your parents is Black?" required an answer I didn't have. I would have to explain something more intimate than I cared to or fall back on a repertoire of lies I told to mask that I was from Attleboro, Massachusetts, which wasn't on that tribal map, that I was "mixed" and that I was a transracial adoptee. If I started by offering just a piece of that truth, it always invited curiosity and more questions, and in the end I felt terribly exposed. I'd had too many conversations like that—where people would walk away in the end, on the heel of unwanted editorials, usually without having revealed anymore of themselves than a first name.

For a long time, until I was in my late twenties and well into my search for my birth family, I practiced lying. I hid my adoption fiercely, until some terrifying moment of truth (*Your parents are here!*) collided with the elaborate lies I'd perfected for so many years. Most people, despite their curiosity, really wanted me to affirm the politics of the "one drop" law of Blackness. It was easier to shrug and say, "I'm just Black." They would take it just like that—comfortable that you hadn't troubled the baseline assumptions about who any of us are.

I told Rhae I was from "a small town just outside of Boston," and she asked me if I was related to the McKinneys from Haverhill— "Oh, you said *McKinley!*"—and she went on to tell me something about herself. She had left home for Ghana in the early 1980s with her husband, who was a well-known sculptor. She had worked as a museum administrator in Chicago for many years. Now she was "retired" and was working on a book and "earning chop" as the secretary for the 31st December Women's Movement, an NGO headed by Nana Rawlings, Ghana's then First Lady. I listened to her talk about surviving Chicago and Los Angeles in the Black Power 1970s and her decision to expatriate and face a whole new set of disillusionments and contentments. She was smart and full of funny irreverence. I stood with her for a long time, lost in her storytelling.

She began to tell me about a project she was working on, interviewing Ghanaian children from mixed marriages. Then she paused in the middle of a thought and said, "Now, what's your story?" I don't know if it was Rhae's easiness, or my enormous need for a friend, or if it was that something in me had shifted in two weeks of exhausting emotions, but I found myself telling my story with the details and honesty that I had not shared even with my closest friend.

I started to talk, and as all the awkward language of race and adoption spilled out, she said, "Child, sit your hips down. Let me go get us a glass of wine!"

Rhae listened as I told her about how I'd grown up and about how being in Ghana was pulling up all of my most difficult struggles. She listened carefully to what I was saying and told me about her own discomforts, which had persisted even after a decade of living there. They were quiet affirmations of what I'd shared with her. She talked about living through so many generations of changing Black political consciousness and coming to Africa to become an "obruni" and slide back to some of the worst colonialist understandings of nationhood and race and color. "But really, it's difficult for most Black folks to swallow our myth-making and our stubborn need to be a part of this world, and to know everything about Black folks, and let some other people set the rules—right or wrong. That's too uncomfortable."

We talked until the party nearly emptied out and it was time, as Rhae said, for her "to get back home before my dogs and my husband don't want to let me in." I told her that I would be going back to New York the next morning. "Well, I'm the last of the real letter writers, so give me your address so that we can stay friends. My husband would love to know about you too," she said.

As I left her, I felt truly happy. I had opened my mouth and told someone the truth. And Rhae's quiet listening, and her sense of humor about Ghana and about my struggles, had eased my melancholy.

On the flight home, I was thinking about Rhae, and I found myself lapsing into an almost reflexive fantasy: *Maybe Rhae is my birth mother. Maybe that is why she was so interested in my story and wants to keep in touch with me.*

I let myself drift around in this: how and when she might reveal to me that she was my mother; how I would return to Ghana, and how being there would now be easier for me; what kind of man a woman like Rhea would have had a baby with. I traveled through a skein of fantasies. Then I caught myself and felt a flood of punishing shame. Just before I left for Ghana, I had bought a book, a suite of short essays called *Lying,* by Sissela Bok. I had seen it in a bookstore, just as I was starting to think about how many people I lied to as if it were a reflex, the price of hiding huge parts of myself from so many people, and how that hiding mushroomed so that I wasn't always certain when and to whom I'd revealed my/these different incarnations. It was a book that examined, in a hard-boiled way, questions of private and public ethics and mental health. And it was a book that was in some ways sympathetic to the liar, so it seemed both appropriately punishing and kind. It was a pocket-sized paperback book, and it reminded me of the Christian *Daily Word,* alternately admonishing and a kind of ready place for the Believer to turn to for affirmation. I kept opening it and putting it down. I wasn't ready to read it, but I carried it, even on my trip, as a reminder and a sign that I was trying to get a handle on myself.

Only a few months before, I had thrown away a photograph that I had kept for almost ten years of a woman I did not know who I imagined was my birth mother. I had seen her only once—just long enough to take a photograph. A brief encounter and a photograph had fed many years of imaginings that gave life to some wonderful lies.

I took the photograph during the spring that I turned fifteen. I was then a day student at a private high school in Providence, Rhode

Island. I had seen an ad in a Providence daily for a Black Liberation Day festival that was being held just after school would let out for the summer. By then, our car pool would be on recess. My parents and William were away each weekend in Vermont clearing land they had just bought to start a Christmas tree farm. I had just staked my independence from farmwork and toolshed squatting on weekends and holidays. I stayed alone in the house and swallowed my loneliness by reading and working double shifts at a nursing home to collect overtime pay.

I was at home without a car or a driver's license, or good public transportation—just my bicycle. I had made the nearly thirty-mile back road journey to Providence with my mother, and I was thinking about doing that the weekend of the festival. But at the last minute, I learned that a neighbor was going to be driving there for the day. We left very early that morning, and after I was dropped off, I sat in a coffee shop near Brown University for several hours, waiting for the nearby row of bookstores to open. Then I visited each one—a ritual from the days I had waited for my mother when she'd attended summer classes at the college. I found a used copy of Ntozake Shange's novel *Sassafras, Cypress, and Indigo* on the sale table in one of the stores and bought it. It was a book that I'd had my mother borrow once from the university library and then mourned not being able to keep or find again. Then I walked some miles across the city to the park where the festival would be held, excited by all my good luck.

I took the longest route so that I could pass through the side streets that housed the heart of Providence's Black community, look at the life taking place on people's porches, in corner stores, and in barbershops, and take in that world for a while. I had on big, heavy gold hoop earrings, and my hair was freshly cornrowed. I had convinced my mother to shell out $60 and devote one Saturday to travel-ing to a salon a few towns over that had been recommended by a temp nurse from Sierra Leone who had just been transferred to the rest home where I worked. We had arrived at the salon without hair extensions—the main ingredient—and had to drive another hour to Roxbury and back with one of the girls from the salon before sitting for four hours of hair-styling. I had just traded Levi's for Lee jeans (the girls from the public school across the street from mine had schooled me on what was "fresh" for Black girls), and I wore my red New Edition t-shirt tucked into the jeans with the requisite (red) belt and matching (red) Adidas. I was full of myself that day. I felt that I finally had a stake at really belonging, a feeling that was only a little less powerful than the yearning that was driving me.

When I arrived at the park, I saw a woman in the row of vendors lining the walkway. She was selling cloth that was spread around her on the lawn. The cloths were very beautiful—a deep indigo blue—and their intense color roused some feeling in me. They were the color of a Danskin tie-dyed outfit my godmother had bought for me when I was in second grade and that my teacher had said was very African, showing me off to the class. For the next few days, at recess, my friends and I had played "African Queen." I started to feel some of that second-grade pleasure, and the longing that its fleetingness stirred in me. The cloths made me think of the Ntozake Shange book, and Indigo, the hero I dreamed of being: Indigo, with "the moon in her mouth," who made dolls that she imbued with powerful spirits and was content with as company, and her brilliant mother who conjured an intoxicating, fantastical Black girl's childhood for her. The woman selling the cloths wore a dress made of the same blue, and she sat with her legs spread out in front of her on the grass, ivory bracelets clacking as she sewed and talked with the woman beside her. Her skin was red-brown, and she had long, thick black hair and tiny almond-shaped eyes in an oval face that was not unlike my own. I stood and stared at her for a long time, thinking, *Is this my mother?* She caught my eye and smiled. I could not find any way to respond. She turned back to her sewing, and then she must have felt me still standing there and looked up at me again. I felt ashamed, and I got myself together and moved on. I joined the crowd and listened to the drumming and the political speechifying and imagined that I was my own version of Indigo, the Black girl who was never lonely, with the perfect mother and the moon in her mouth, just sitting at a Black Liberation Day festival in Providence. Each time the speakers and performers broke, I walked back along the rows of vendors and made wide circles around the woman's spot on the lawn so that I could watch her. When I noticed it was getting close to the time I'd have to leave to meet my ride home, I approached the woman again and nervously snapped a photograph. Walking back across town, I stayed lost in my fantasies. I felt dizzy with happiness from being comfortably anonymous in a crowd of Black people, sporting my symbols of belonging.

I put her photo in a frame that I hid from everyone at home until I went off to boarding school that September. The daily commute to school in Providence had begun to wear all of us out, and my parents thought I might finally need to be in a more diverse school, so we'd agreed on this solution. The 2 percent Black student body at Northfield Mount Hermon School in western Massachusetts provided my first stake at a Black community beyond the Sunday community of the John Wesley A.M.E. Zion Church, which I had joined a few years earlier. My mother and her sister had attended Northfield, and in some unexamined way, I guess it was a means for my parents to try to solve my social aches and still keep me aligned with the world of my family. I was happy enough to go away—I had spent two summer sessions there and had enjoyed the place. But as I went off to school, I began nursing an anger at my parents for trading me, for "giving me up," instead of reconfiguring their own plans. The choice had been boarding school, not a move to a more diverse community. The need for Black and brown people was my own; it was not a conflict for the family. When I arrived at Northfield, I placed the photos of my family in a drawer and the photo of the woman on my dresser. I called her Mattie, a name I'd read in those narratives of Southern childhoods where the archetypal Black mother was recast again and again. I'm sure that the anger toward my family made Mattie even more attractive. And in some way, I relished the hurt that Mattie's photo would cause my parents—the way she came and so easily killed them off.

Mattie stood up to the ever-elaborate stories of who she was and why we were apart. An adoptee's boon is that she can imagine and reimagine herself into any life. But outside of the life of my fantasies, Mattie became a protection. As I made more and more friendships with other Black students, who were fighting in their own ways the intense alienation of our fancy prep school, I joined them in trading battle cuts as we policed a strong Black line of social identity. I knew that the one-drop rule assured me membership in that community. Our number was so small, who could afford to cast off a ("phoney" was the word we always used) half-breed? But I knew I needed a definite sign of my legitimacy. I knew that old saying, *Mama's baby, papa's maybe*. Mattie was the sign.

Although my stories about Mattie barely concealed the truth, the people I showed her photo to told me again and again how much I looked like my "mother." My parents came only at the beginning and end of each school year, and when they came, I told my friends and dorm-mates that they were my guardians. It was easy for people to accept that. So I decided to take Mattie to college, where the stories continued to spin, changing with the new ideas I had about myself and about Blackness and with new social pressures. I had put her photo away by the end of my first year of college, but I hadn't dislodged the *need,* and the photo stayed among my things long after that.

I was sifting through all of this history as I recrossed the Atlantic, lost in the dead space of the flight. I kept thinking about the stubbornness of my imaginings and the toll of lying.

Just five months before, I had received the first pieces of my official adoption narrative, and what I had learned stood uncomfortably in defiance of my fantasies. One day, provoked by my persistent melancholy, the ungrounding of leaving school, I had called my mother and tried to ask some of my questions about my birth history that we had not spoken of since I was in my early teens. We talked over the sound of the ragga music booming in the street outside my Brooklyn apartment and the sheep wailing in her Vermont living room. (She and my father had wired the sheep pen to pipe barn noises into every room of their new home. They were keeping vigil; it was lambing season.) I listened deliberately as she answered the questions I had called to ask her. "The agency that handled your adoption is the New England Home for Little Wanderers," she said. "I will be glad to send you their address. Certainly, if it is helpful to you."

I listened to her funny formality. She must have long anticipated this moment, maybe as long as I had taken to ask the question; or maybe her aloofness came from her distraction with the barn.

Later that week, a familiar Mead standard envelope arrived. In her schoolteacher's hand, my mother had written the name Mary Steed, L.C.S.W., Adoptions Coordinator, and an address for the agency. Her letter was full of caution: a request would take time to answer, and there probably would not be much information to share. She reminded me that the laws of closed adoptions kept the agency from giving out anything but "non-identifying" information. She thought I should be prepared for only a very cursory reply. She and my father had also been told very little: "I've shared everything I know with you." She was offering me all the help she could give. I knew that her letter was also saying, *You are on your own.* My parents had often stressed to my brother and me the importance of independence and of responsibility for our choices. We were also taught to not stand in the way of each other's desires. She spoke of these principles so often that her insistence became a litany underscoring my loneliness. It seemed to me then that this code took us all further and further outside of each other's care.

Her letter went on into her familiar recasting of news: spring snowfall, and the prospects for maple sugaring; how Christmas tree farming was ruining their backs; a be-kind-to-city-folks-they-feed-our-economy seminar for locals they'd taken in exchange for a season lift pass at Mt. Snow. Folded with her letter was a clipping on "Black Awareness" events held at a local community college. She'd written across the top, "You see, we Vermonters do try!" I have a box of letters like this. They came weekly after I left for boarding school and in my first years of college, and they still turn up in my mailbox sporadically. They are unchanging—short notes on a folded page of Mead tablet.

Practical. Never risking any deep admissions or preciousness. They let me know that she and my father are holding down the fort. Nothing has moved, inside or out.

After I received her letter, I wrote to Mary Steed at the New England Home for Little Wanderers. I did not give a lot of thought to what I was doing. I simply wrote the letter, feeling protected in some way by the limits my mother had reminded me of. A form letter arrived a few weeks later, along with some pages that outlined the Massachusetts state adoption laws and an application to complete if I wished to continue with my request. The letter explained, as my mother had, that the agency could give me only "non-identifying" information about my birth parents and possibly some details of the circumstances leading to the adoption. To find out more would require the consent of my birth parents, which meant that they would have to initiate their own search for me. The agency or the state could not notify one party of the other's desire for information or a meeting without a court order, and a court order would not be granted unless there was an absolutely compelling and persuasive need—along the lines of a medical catastrophe. Like unmanageable mental illness or a need for bone marrow, I imagined.

I decided to call Mary Steed and pretend that I was making my first contact with the agency. I asked her to explain the process and regulations around searches, and in a very officious, smoker's voice, she elaborated a bit on what the letter had said. She told me that she could send me the application I'd just received, and if I liked, I could attach a letter requesting that the agency contact me if my birth parents also initiated a search. She explained that the letter would be placed in my file in the agency archives until it was matched up with letters from my birth mother or father. She must have anticipated my frustration, because she then told me that I could also gamble with the courts. "If you try, you can get the names of those judges in your jurisdiction who have reputations for sympathy to open adoption records, and then try to time your petition with the cycle of their court."

After we hung up, I filled out the form and wrote the suggested letter. I did it all without much feeling. I put some narrow hope in what the request for non-identifying information might give me, but my desires and the whole idea of getting something meaningful were too abstract. It was like dumbly fishing for a prize card in a cereal box.

After a year and a few notes to prod the agency, I received a reply.

10 December 1991

Dear Ms. McKinley,

In response to your recent letters, most recently on 7 September 1991, I am enclosing the information you requested about your Birth Parents. The information provided here is non-identifying. As you know, the sealed records can be opened only by court order. Should you wish to pursue this option, your adoption was finalized in the Bristol County Probate Court.

Your Birth Mother was a twenty-two-year-old white, Jewish woman, who is described in the record as being 5 feet 2 inches tall, and weighing about 125 pounds. She had dark curly hair and brown eyes. She had graduated high school and completed a nursing program and was working as an L.P.N. just prior to your birth. Her health history reports that she had no allergies or history of serious illness in the family. Her maternal grandmother had diabetes mellitus, which had responded well to medication.

Your Birth Father was an African American man, in his forties and a Protestant. He is described as being 5 feet tall, with dark brown skin and eyes. He was working as an interior decorator and enjoyed art as a hobby. He was reported to have been in good health, though there was no further background provided on his family. The records show that your Birth Father was married to another woman, and that he was unwilling to provide support for your Birth Mother's baby. She was unable to support a child on her own and elected instead to relinquish you for adoption in order to provide you with a stable, two-parent home.

Your Birth Mother's parents were Jewish, both high school graduates, and both reported to have been in good health. Your grandmother was described as being of medium build, and she worked as a bookkeeper. Your grandfather was 5 feet 7 inches tall and worked as a supervisor in a clothing factory.

. . . Please feel free to contact us if we can be of further service. I apologize for the delay in responding to your request . . .

Sincerely,

Jim Wideman
Social Work Intern

I read the letter so quickly that I scarcely took in the details. Then I put it back in its envelope and hid it in my suitcase with the photo of Mattie. Both the photo and the letter were things that I felt I couldn't relinquish, but my suitcase felt like a container of shame. I did not like the story the letter had on me, or how it disturbed the foundation of my fantasies. I mistrusted everything it said. The New England Home for Little Wanderers. The name itself was the sign. I considered the letter to be like that cereal box prize—a disappointing little token in return for my patronage—and I stubbornly put it out of my mind. I didn't talk to my mother about contacting the agency again, and I continued to keep in my order for a birth mother like

Mattie with the "Spirits of the Search for Birth Family." I had no room in my imagination for a white birth mother; I just excised that from my mind. I wasn't looking to go back into the water I was treading with my family. And the complication of a Jewish family—the fact that there was another dimension of challenge to my identity—felt excruciating. Sometimes I thought a little about what had been written about birth father. *An interior decorator. Enjoyed art as a hobby.* I thought about how interesting a father, a Black man who would have been born in the 1920s, who made a living as an interior decorator in the segregation era, might be. I wondered if art could have only been his "hobby." Was he an *artist?* These details pricked my imagination, but I wasn't ready to reorder it for this father. If I did, I'd have to come back to the possibility of being Black and Jewish.

I thought about this letter again on the flight home. I watched the movie screen in front of my seat switch between a flight map and airline ads. I was surprised to see that the plane was headed northwest and that we were nearly flying over Scotland. My mind roamed from the letter to that summer in Scotland and back to my problems with lying, and then I felt the line of my imaginings shift again.

Maybe Rhae recognized some part of my story, or calculated what I'd told her and was going home to talk to her husband. She wasn't my birth mother, but perhaps she had figured out that her husband was my birth father. I thought about the little she'd told me about him. He was in his sixties; he was an artist; she had mentioned some connection he had to Boston; he'd had a previous marriage to a Ghanaian woman and they'd had a son, and he had daughters in the States; he and Rhae had never had children together. She had almost seemed to be insisting on something when she said he'd be happy to know me.

Then I caught myself. This was a *sickness.*

My thoughts raced to my friend Henri. Henri and I had been roommates in 1985 during our first year at Sarah Lawrence College. We had met for the first time at an open house for accepted students the prior spring. At first sight, Henri had been an intolerable reflection of me. She was very light-skinned, and I knew that she was vulnerable to people's gaze as they played the inevitable racial guessing game. I often imagined people toying with our images in their heads the way *Ebony* magazine had looked at racial perceptions once in the early 1980s. *Who Is Black?* was the caption above the rows of variously hued and configured faces laid out over several pages. The reader made guesses and checked the answer key at the back of the magazine. I recognized so much of myself in Henri's soft, close-cut hair—not nappy in the classic sense, but equally resistant to straightening and "white people's" combs; her preppy, formal wool suit and small wire glasses; and her somewhat tentative, self-conscious assertion of a Serious Black Woman self behind all of this. When I saw her, there was none of the eager excitement I felt connecting with some of the six or so other entering Black students. I hated something about her simple *presence,* like just the fact of her skin.

Henri approached me at the reception with friendliness that shamed my anger, and before the day was over, I had exchanged addresses with her, telling myself that I was being polite. She wrote to me early in the summer. The person I met on the page began to slowly break through my still-hardened reluctance toward her. In her first letter, she wrote that she was "a Black bi-racial woman" and had grown up on the southside of Chicago in a Black adoptive family. Her forwardness about this startled me, and my discomfort became that much more intense. I started to close off to her again, but something in what then felt like the unspeakableness of what she was sharing and in her struggling language eventually won out. *Black bi-racial woman.* Someone else was fighting to put words to something. I had only met two other "bi-racial," transracial adoptees—Christopher, from Attleboro, and a guy in boarding school who also ran on the track team, but he and I had hardly spoken. When my brother and I were very young, my parents took us to some of the Boston-area Open Door Society meetings where we played with other transracially adopted children and their siblings. This led to a few play dates. But all I can remember clearly of that was the inexpressible resentment I felt toward those kids and toward my parents for forcing us to be comrades. When Henri started to write to me about her passion for Black women writers (it turned out we had both chosen Sarah Lawrence because Alice Walker was a graduate) and sent me clippings of poems and postcards of writers I also loved, I could not resist her offer of friendship.

Later that summer, she wrote to tell me that her mother had died of pancreatic cancer. A few weeks later, her father had suffered a massive stroke, and she had begun nursing him. Suddenly I could feel my attachment to her; I was terrified that she would not start school in the fall. But a few weeks later she wrote to say that she would be starting school on time in spite of what had happened at home. We continued to exchange letters the rest of the summer. Each time she wrote about her mother's death, I felt pulled closer to her by her drama of lost mothering and what I imagined was also a liberation from the constraints of her adopted family. I also felt a kind of jealous fascination with her having a real person—a Black mother at that—to mourn. As she told me more about herself, I realized that we had a bond of outsidership within our families as well. Her brother was also adopted, but he was her adoptive father's nephew, and he looked like the family. He was dark brown–skinned like her adoptive mother, so he easily passed as her son. Although her adoptive father was very fair-colored, Henri looked very different from all of them and was an obviously "bi-racial" child, which marked her as illegitimate in some way. Something in this placated my jealousy.

On the first day of school, Henri and I agreed to meet at an appointed time at the main gate of the campus. But even before that, as I entered my new dorm room, I found her there waiting anxiously for me, unpacking her things with a band of aunts and cousins who had driven with her from Chicago. It turned out that we had both sent in our housing forms with notes requesting Black roommates, and the dean's office, a little worried but cowed by these instructions, had put us in a room together. So for the first year we stuck closely together and threw attitude at the white kids, who were 96 percent of the college. We signed up for a lot of the same classes and made tag-team Afrocentric arguments, dated hard-rock Black men who were friends, hung out together in Harlem after classes, pasted photos of Black women writers on our walls (she put up one of Alice Walker with her half-Jewish daughter, Rebecca, riding behind her in a bike seat, and Henri swore it might really be her), ate Jamaican patties, and listened all night to Prince. We began to organize a new Black student organization, called Harambee, and among Black and white students alike, there began to be a lot of speculation about whether we were "reverse racists," and how two very yellow girls could have ended up the way we were. But despite my intense, growing connection to Henri, I still wrestled with my anger at how uncomfortably she mirrored me. And when I watched her huge extended family surround her with visits and every long-distance gesture they could offer,

I was consumed with jealousy for all that love and Henri's place amongst them. My own family was proud of me and supportive, but very much from afar.

My jealousy made me hang even tighter to my lies about Mattie. Now, even after seven years of friendship, visits to each other's families, many intense conversations about adoption, and our incredibly intimate talks about living in our yellow skins, I had not stopped lying to Henri about Mattie. I let her think that Mattie was just removed from me—by illness, by my adoptive parents' desire, by her own benign abandonment.

Now, as I thought about my battle with lying, I thought about how absurd and how sad it was to still be lying to her. I decided that I would call her when I got back home and make a giant step toward saving myself.

I was standing in JFK Airport when I called her and told her: I lied. Mattie is not my mother. I do not really know who my birth parents are. I've started to search, and I've found this little bit, I said, telling her about the adoption agency's letter. I am going to really start to look for them now. She said, "Really? Dang. You still look like Mattie." And then she, who I was sure had been infinitely more honest, told me about some of her own lying ways. I stood there shaking with exhaustion and giddiness, proud of myself, and so grateful for my friend.

| My Twenties |

Summer 1992

Not too long after I returned from Ghana, I retrieved the letter from the New England Home for Little Wanderers, and I tried to read it without flinching. For a moment, I decided the story was kind of interesting, but then my old discomfort returned, and my feelings sidled into questions and blame.

I called my mother one afternoon, worked up with suspicion. More than a year had passed since she had given me the agency's address; she must have thought I was satisfied with just that little bit, because we hadn't talked about it again in all that time. Or was there something she was avoiding? The information that the agency had given me was so *basic* —wouldn't they have shared it with my parents? How could they have let me reach twenty-five without telling me these details if the non-identifying information was in fact true?

"They probably told us that your father was Black," my mother said after I'd read the letter to her. "Maybe they told us some of the other things, but there was never enough significant information to tell a real story."

I listened for signs that she was covering: "Well, no, I never knew that your birth mother was Jewish. Or maybe we were told this, but—I don't remember now. And anyway, it wouldn't have mattered. We are not Jewish. We are nothing—you know I've never had any use for religion. Your father and I have always thought it was important that you and William knew everything that we knew. We didn't want to keep any secrets..."

I started to have my doubts—not about the letter or her honesty—but about my own memory. I was the one who lived outside the laws of truth-telling and reality. About my adoption, and every other thing it seemed, my mother did not lie.

For a long time after we spoke, I tried to pick apart the past to quiet the nagging feeling that there was some hole in both of our memories.

I thought about how my mother had encouraged me to develop relationships with some of the few Jewish families in Attleboro. There was a small Jewish presence there, mostly an elite of shop owners and professionals. The commercial center of town had a strip of little shops, and one long-established family owned a large part of that property. They owned London's custom store and tailor shop for men, and the other London's, which passed as a small department store, and a women's dress boutique. The stores brought an air of gentility to the downtown with their selection of Izod shirts in nearly every color and middle-rack designer clothing that only a few people could afford. And there was a small, beautiful synagogue at the border of town, a few hundred yards from the new crematory, nearly hidden in the tuck of grove that was rounded by the curve of the car ramp onto Interstate 95.

I went to school with the London kids. Jodi London and I were in the same classes from fourth to eighth grade. We had a friendship laced with rivalry, uneasily forged by our lead in the classroom, our parents' political life among Attleboro's liberal elite, and our exoticness, which we were both uncomfortable with, but which afforded us a kind of protection. (She looked very Semitic, which was not Attleboro's ideal, but she was very pretty and had a head of thick, long, kinky, truly golden hair that for many people suggested things biblical.)

Jodi's mother and mine had been members of Attleboro's chapter of the League of Women Voters. They had served together on a committee that had spearheaded a fair housing initiative in the mid-1960s, a few years before my parents adopted me. The committee had made a pledge to foster racial integration in Attleboro. They joined with other chapters in and around Boston and brought prospective Black homebuyers and renters to Attleboro, helping them to obtain mortgages and leases while they tested for red-lining and other acts of discrimination. My mother remembers that they could not convince many Black people to settle in town, and they had learned very quickly about the real estate market's treacheries. After two years, Attleboro's color line had not moved a fraction, and the committee's efforts were exhausted. My mother used to tell me her civil rights battle stories. She would try to explain the kind of hope she had felt then and I would question what I saw as her terrible liberal naiveté, her activism at the fray. "History is a foreign country," she would quote, and I would hear her voice choke a little before she would turn away from my angry ribbing.

My parents were very close to another Jewish family from this circle. In our last years in Attleboro they had been our neighbors. The husband was a son of Italian immigrants who were Holocaust survivors. His wife was Polish Catholic and had converted to Judaism when they married. Our families used to ski together, and they were very nice and always interested in me. When my mother and I went to Washington, D.C., to attend the 1983 Martin Luther King Jr. "I Have a Dream" anniversary march, he and their daughter, who was a few years older than me, joined us. We rode to Washington overnight in a fleet of buses that had been organized by the Providence chapter of the National Urban League. Our bus was filled with members of a welfare group led by young white socialists who acted like they'd staged a coup just getting their constituency on the bus. There had been something important to my mother about our traveling with these friends—more than just our old camaraderie. But it had been lost on me. I spent the night fantasizing about being on that earlier freedom ride, while my mother talked to me about history between fitful periods of sleep.

Was there something more in my mother's thoughts than a sense that we were sharing a revisitation of some important history? It always seemed like there was a quiet pressure for me to connect with that family. Connecting was easy; I liked them very much. But I always felt like there was a vague equation being figured out when we came together—like something important was being added up—but it was never clear just what it was. My brother moved casually through their lives, without that pressure, without really connecting to the ideas of our parents' liberal political world at all.

Had my mother known my birth mother was Jewish? Had she not told me this to protect me in some way—to keep my identity struggle less complicated? Was she afraid that if I knew I was both Black and Jewish, there might be a larger distance between us? What my mother was saying now, as we spoke about the letter, was that my birth mother was a Jewish woman, but she was "white," and that—unlike faith, or faithlessness, which were choices—kept us part of each other.

Maybe my parents had told me I was "half Jewish" in those early years of explanations, and I had not been able to take it in, or maybe I had put it out of my stubborn head. I still scour my memory at times to see if that is possible, and it seems it might be. Sometimes I can feel hints of this: I remember attending the bar mitzvah for our neighbor's son when I was in middle school. It was my first time inside a synagogue, and there was some heavy, uncomfortable significance about being there, but I cannot draw anything more from those feelings or even remember what the bar mitzvah was like. Perhaps my feelings came from the fact that I was witnessing something "different" and, in such a Christian town, "unsanctioned." Maybe it was some fear of a part of myself—perhaps even the Jew in me.

There's an interesting irony in this and the way my mother eventually worked to connect me to Black people. One evening when I was in junior high school, she came home and told me that she had found me a certifiable Black community. She taught then at the high school in Norton, a town that bordered ours. Norton was smaller than Attleboro, more rural, with pockets of houses surrounded by cornfields and turkey farms. The two biggest features of town were Wheaton College, a small women's college, and a weekend flea market, celebrated as the biggest on the eastern seaboard. And what Norton also had was Black people, at least five or six families. Any two of these families might be related, which explained how the town achieved what might be considered a critical mass. And on top of this was a seasonal Black presence: in the summer the community swelled a bit with Cape Verdean laborers who worked the farms. The few miles between Attleboro and Norton put the town just a bit closer to Boston and the small cities that radiated out from there. Most of the settled Black families were originally Southern transplants who had moved from Boston to escape the city grind. In Norton, they could commute easily to the city and neighboring towns, afford a "start-up" house, and still have something like the Georgia farm. Norton had some attraction for Black people in those years that Attleboro never achieved.

My mother had had a few Black students in her classes over the years, and after teaching two or three successive siblings, she had worked up tenuous relationships with their parents. One evening she pulled aside someone's mother at parent-teacher conferences and told her that she had a Black daughter who needed support and community. Then the invitation came to join them at church. The church was John Wesley A.M.E. Zion in Attleboro.

My mother came to John Wesley with me the first Sunday. I immediately fell in love with the old church, with its punchy smell of mold and collard greens cooked in the basement kitchen, its water-stained ceiling, the groaning floorboards, and the worn velvet pew cushions and battered hymnals inherited from a Baptist church. She and I stood self-consciously at the call to guests, and I announced my entry to the six or seven families who made up the tight but often quarrelsome congregation. My mother went to church with me a few more times, and over the years she would come for holiday programs and special revivals, but she decided that the church was mine. Being neither a colored woman nor a woman of God, she took herself as an intrusion and left me to my people.

I endured stockings and dresses and Sunday school for the opportunity to pass the building's old signboard on that bend of Leroy

Street where the church stood, and proudly enter "the African corner," a name playfully adopted from the segregated pews of the pre-A.M.E. movement Protestant church. And so that I could do it all again midweek, I joined the tone-deaf choir, singing to a wheezing organ anchored by the Morrow sisters' lovely, near full-range trio.

The church elders looked after me with humor and a mix of pity and kindness, offering gifts of hair oil and stockings for brown-skinned women and gentle attempts to socialize me. When I hit the right notes or was in perfect rhythm, or at least stepped in the same direction as the choir or acted like I had the right kind of home training, the elders would exclaim, "Oh, you're so colored!" Their voices rang with triumph and encouragement, as if I were a baby trying to get myself up on two legs. They wanted to get me right with Black people and, above all, the Lord. I loved the singing and the testifying of the Baptist contingent that crept into the somewhat staid A.M.E. worship. I did feel rapture there. But I was there less for God and more for the spirituality of Blackness. And I was studying it so fervently that what I lacked in religiosity seemed to be overlooked.

I made fast friends with the kids my age, who were as restless and as edgy in their circumstances as I was in mine. I won points with them because they liked my mother, whom their older siblings had assured them was a "cool white lady," a teacher who cared and who taught history with some politics and humor. They recognized her toughness—as a fighter and a disciplinarian. She admired their intelligence (many of the Black students of Norton High School had been at the top of their class), their fortitude in a tough town, and their willingness to fight like hell to leave, which was different from so many of the other kids who were sliding toward the local factories or jail.

Church clannishness spilled over into school and work competition during the week, and I had to pay attention to what happened when I didn't see my church friends and learn how to walk the lines of allegiance between families and factions. I still remember with amazement how the congregation split and rejoined over and over again, testing John Wesley A.M.E.'s faith. But the stake in an institution close to home counted for a lot. And the chance to hold power on the usher board and to make important decisions concerning the community, where they might have been shut out in larger city-side churches, carried everyone a long way. I walked the minefields carefully, somewhat glad to be a few degrees outside. On breaks between church services and dinner on marathon Sundays of worship, I would invite the church youth home for snacks while their parents worked out their quarrels. We would walk in a small posse to my house, all of us dressed to the nines. I felt this huge pride, aware of my neighbors watching us, worried that my parents were away in Vermont at the farm.

Soon there were invitations to people's houses and to the world of Black people beyond Attleboro. We traveled for revival meetings and picnics and to visit church members' extended families. There was an invitation to join Jack & Jill, that hatefully elite Black social club that the choir director was trying to get us involved in. (My invitation curiously died, and my mother and I figured out many years later that it was because Jack & Jill was organized through the membership of the mothers.)

My mother connected tangentially with other parents, seeing them when she chauffeured me to their houses. They talked about school affairs and their gardens and exchanged vegetables and honey and eggs. But the deepest social advance I remember ever being made was talk between my mother and the father of my closest friend, Penda, about going in on rearing pigs. My weekend life as part of John Wesley remained almost completely separate from my life at home and at school. The walk of less than a mile to John Wesley often seemed like a huge journey to a secret meetinghouse.

It was interesting that my mother hadn't made a similar bid for me with the synagogue. But Jewishness hadn't been in our consciousness then; it had been pushed aside by my Blackness, by the New England Home for Little Wanderers's record keeping, perhaps by my parents. And perhaps by me. I often think about how I would have *been* Jewish, except that I am Jewish. Or how I would have *been* Black and Jewish, except that I am, and how I would have held my tiny stake in two small, mostly marginal, seemingly antithetical religion-based communities. And how would I have also lived in the third world that is mine, the world of the WASPy, agnostic McKinleys?

The search for my birth family, when searching became a conscious act, involved five years of fits and starts and tunneling through what seemed to be dead ends. After my trip to Ghana, I committed myself to finding my people. At first, I turned to all of the conventional means. Every year since my junior year in college, I had been renewing my registration with the International Soundex Registry, a well-known organization that attempts to unite adoptees and their birth families through the use of their database. Like my pursuits with the New England Home for Little Wanderers, filling out their form, sending in the same unchanged details, satisfied something but kept me protected by the improbability of success.

In 1992, I registered with them again. Then I dug out the files I had begun in college when I did a research project on the history of transracial adoption. In it was a list of organizations in Massachusetts that offered support for adoptees and their biological and adoptive families. Years before I had written letters to the five organizations on the list, asking for search assistance and information about groups or social networks for transracial adoptees. I'd kept each group's brochure and the five replies, all of which said that although they had some transracially adopted clients, they did not have formal networks or support services. At that time, the racial dimension of my adoption seemed paramount. Race had so thoroughly defined how my adoption was arranged and legally defined, how it was labeled and referenced—in my family, in the courts, at school, in the doctor's office, and in people's imaginations, and this reality marked—even if at times only subtly—every experience I had. There were adopted children, such as my brother, who were free of public curiosity and scrutiny—and there were *transracial adoptees,* who could never escape it. I wanted search support that would pat attention to this and normalize transracial adoption. I became deeply discouraged by these organization's response.

I'd also been frustrated by the vagueness of the search help the groups described. None of the organizations said they actually performed searches. "Search support" was most often dependent on attending regular meetings, which seemed more like group therapy sessions. I mistrusted this completely. And the meetings would have been impossible for me to attend since I was living in New York City. But now I telephoned each organization and asked about their services again. Their answers had not changed, but this encouraged me to look into similar groups in New York to see if they could at least put me in touch with other transracial adoptees or an agency or private investigator who were familiar with Massachusetts law and agencies and could help me to get a little further through the maze.

A few months after I made some contacts with New York City adoption groups, a friend all but dragged me to a meeting that was held by one of the big national organizations working to ensure a wide range of legal protections and "adoption liberties." Rita was not an adoptee, but she saw my accumulating anger and melancholy, and she was one of those rare people who are willing to intervene just when everyone else is ready to retreat. We paid our $15 meeting fee and sat in a roomful of about thirty people, while a social worker, an adoptee himself, led a support group for those searching for their birth family. Everyone in the group was either at some terrible dead end or, like me, just beginning. The group leader listened to people's frustrated stories and stressed again and again the importance of people's *feelings* during the process, as opposed to material discoveries. I felt uncomfortable listening to the repertoire of tearful narratives. Each confession was punctuated by this man's clinical prescriptions, laced with the language of recovery and new age spirituality. I was learning a bit from people's accounts of how they were searching, but it was also very evident that New York's adoption laws were much more liberal and flexible than the system in Massachusetts. Whatever they lacked, the big New York agencies had much better post-adoption social services, and adoptees had access to small but critical details that could lead more quickly to contact with a birth parent. In some cases, people had been able to gain access to their birth records and their original names. But as I listened to people talk about little victories, I was struck by how everyone seemed oddly invested in the mystery and the difficulty of searching. In all that I was hearing, and somewhere in my own thinking, there seemed to be some attachment to the burden of discovery. The burden is very real, but it made me wonder a little if I was more attracted to the impossibility and the idea of being a victim of the system than to finding an actual person.

As the meeting continued, and people came and left the group, the discussion was taken over by two quite angry and emotional birth mothers. The women talked about their incredible guilt over relinquishing the Black sons whom they had been searching for and how that guilt was cobbled to problems they'd had in the past with drugs and alcohol. At times, one woman was almost screaming as she expressed her pain. Rita sat with me, deeply affected by what she was hearing, full of compassion. I was almost paralyzed by sadness and discomfort with their purging. Rita and I were the only Black women in the room. When I'd introduced myself, I had said that I was a transracial adoptee. As the women talked, I felt my old fear of not being able to control how others perceived me. Of being the Racial Reminder. I was waiting for the room to shift, to become Everyone's Spectacle, implicated in these women's stories. But the women luckily held everyone's attention until the meeting ended.

Afterward, Rita told me that she had learned a lot, even about herself, and offered to go back to the meeting with me again. I told her that I hadn't liked any part of it. I didn't see how these meetings could help me to find anyone. I never went back again.

I began keeping my adoption files on my desk so my intentions would stay fueled. And I started to slowly read some of the literature on adoption for the first time since college. I went back to the psychosociological studies, but they held the same frustrations I'd felt before. The data and speculations about Black adoptees' social adjustment issues were deeply flawed. The studies had mostly been conducted in the early 1970s, during the peak years of transracial adoption, and they depended on observations of young children and interviews with new adoptive parents. These studies lacked the narratives of those who had come of age and could elucidate a post–Black Power, post-segregation transracial adoptee's consciousness. I went back to Joyce Ladner's *Mixed Families,* the only book on transracial adoption written by a Black scholar. She was also an adoptive mother. It had been given to me in college by my very first Black teacher—a beautiful, young, formidably intelligent sociologist. And for the first time, I began to tentatively read other adoptees' search narratives when I stumbled across them. The racial dimensions of adoption and transracial adoptees' stories were mostly absent, or they were conventional and as flat as a piece of news reporting. Still, there was something encouraging in these stories about searching, even the most tragic of them. They made it clear that it was possible to actually find someone.

I followed some of the stories' leads on how to search, and that led me to make closer contact with Mary Steed at the New England Home for Little Wanderers. I started to call her from time to time, using the letter I'd written requesting contact with my birth parents as an excuse to check in. She always knew who I was when I called, which raised my hopes just as it was always followed with complete officiousness. I usually hung up feeling angry, utterly in need of a social worker friend. I wanted to challenge her, but I was also afraid to reveal my anger and maybe jeopardize the small hope that her mildly interested duty held out to me. Over time, she seemed to soften incrementally. She sometimes offered me the names of private investigators or other adoption support groups, and some warmth occasionally crept into our conversations. I'd follow up on her suggestions, but each contact would take his or her own time replying, usually offering only a tiny amount of promise, and often requiring outrageous fees. I'd feel so disheartened that it would be months before I approached someone again. Several years passed like this. It was a slow trail in the beginning, through phone calls and networks and adoption conferences where I gathered an overwhelming, mostly useless collection of references and business cards from social workers and psychologists, agencies for Black adoptions, activists, policy heads, lobbyists, handwriting specialists, and psychics.

I started to look at legal avenues. I played with the idea of hiring a lawyer, and I contacted several of the adoption policy heavies I'd met. A few of them were on the faculty at Harvard, and they knew the inside of the Massachusetts legal system. Some were quite interested in issues of race and adoption, so they were happy to talk to me, and they gave me advice and legal referrals. The legal costs were staggering, and two of the lawyers I spoke to said that unless a case could be made for a mental or physical health crisis, petitions to open individual adoption records were more effective as a means to challenge the system and test the courts in the struggle to reform closed adoption laws. In the end, I rather half-heartedly sought help from a friend, a constitutional rights lawyer, who drew up what I now know was an inappropriate and naive affidavit. The motion came back a few weeks later stamped DENIED.

These are the follies of adoption. Somewhere in the literature on searches, a person suggested that adoptees request a copy of their birth certificate to see whether a clerk will perhaps overlook a detail that should have been omitted, or send a copy of the original, pre-adoption-amended certificate, or one that might reveal some other clue. I imagined something like the government Freedom of Information Act (FOIA) documents, where classified information is struck out of documents with a black marker. I had worked in a law firm for a period, and I remember sitting with an attorney going through the supporting documents for a prominent civil rights case, holding papers to the light, looking for clues to the concealed information, hoping they might appear, like watermarks on bills. You try to gauge the letter spaces—the number of characters in a name. Maybe you catch the top hump of a "B" (or is it an "R"?) or identify other letters so that you can begin to make guesses. You start with the vowels, like a crazy "Wheel of Fortune." Or perhaps a whole crucial word bleeds through. Suddenly you have your name.

Henri was also searching now, and she had had this kind of good luck. On a visit to her agency, she had been given a copy of a page from her file that had her birth mother's last name on it. I was ready to give it a try.

The certificate that eventually arrived was the same as the one my mother had, with Catherine Elizabeth McKinley on it and my adoptive parents' names listed as my parents. But where the certificate my mother had read "Color: Colored," this one said "White." I tried a second time, and this time a copy arrived that designated me as "Colored" once again. I put them up on my bulletin board and tried to enjoy the ironies of being the alternately "colored" and "white" child of two good Scotch-Irish WASPs. It had the shades of absurdity of sitting in front of the mirror, trying to define the parts of me that were Black and the parts that were Jewish. Every time I looked, it was the same dumb face looking back at me.

For a long time, my search took place at the level of discovery of a social and creative world that nourished my efforts and that would, in time, support what I found of my family.

Not long after my trip to Ghana, a British literary review crossed my desk at work, and I saw an ad for a book, *In Search of Mr. McKenzie,* by Isha McKenzie-Mavinga and Thelma Perkins, two Black British sisters who were the children of a Russian Jewish woman and a Trinidadian father. The sisters had grown up with only the shadow of a mother, and they had been separated from each other in welfare homes and in foster care until they were reunited as adults. The book was a chronicle of growing up and struggling with identity parallel to their separate searches for their elusive father. I ordered a copy from the publisher in England, and when it arrived I read it in one sitting. It was the first book I'd encountered that told a story about transracial adoption and fostering apart from a very few picture books and young adult novels, like John Neufield's *Edgar Allen,* which were often heavy-handed with "feel-good" intentions that I felt completely cold to, even when I was a child. The distance between these stories and my own made me feel rigid and resentful of them. I was overwhelmed by this story; it seemed to legitimize all that I felt about my own struggle for answers to my past.

The sisters' search for their father had seemed impossible, even though they knew several details about him. They never found the man—he had died—but they traced his Pan-Africanist political legacy in England and in the Caribbean, and as they searched, they found each other and other siblings. They also made peace with the mother they had known only from a great distance. I wrote to them when I finished reading the book, and within what seemed like only a few days, I received a reply. They invited me to share my own story and my search efforts with them.

Then, a few months later, a collection of Scottish women's writing was sent to the editor I assisted. I flipped through the book and discovered a writer named Jackie Kay, an Edinburgh-born, Glasgow-raised Black poet who had grown up transracially adopted. Her poems were about adoption, and as I looked into more of her work, I read about her intense love for her Scottish adoptive mother and her alienation from the birth mother she reunited with. I wrote to Jackie Kay, and a few months later she returned my letter with a copy of her beautiful chapbook, *The Distance Apart,* and a note inviting me to keep in touch about my own explorations. My community was now growing well beyond Henri and me.

Then, in November 1992, the writer and activist Audre Lorde died. I joined a committee to help organize a memorial service for her at St. John the Divine Cathedral in Manhattan, and I volunteered to host people who would be traveling long distances for the service. At the memorial I was introduced to two Afro-Germans, Renata and Faustie, who had traveled from Munich and were part of ADEFRA (Afro-deutsche/Schwarze Frauen), a Black German women's organization that had grown alongside the creative and political work Audre Lorde had done over the years she was in Germany undergoing treatment for cancer. Renata and Faustie stayed with my roommate and me for a week after the service. One night we invited a group of other women from ADEFRA and some of our own friends to dinner so they could meet. We all stayed up drinking and talking late into the night. Then I learned that Renata and Faustie had African American fathers—servicemen who had been stationed in Germany. Renata was in her early forties and had grown up in foster homes. She had searched for her parents some years ago and had been able to trace her mother to a tiny village outside of Munich with the help of the Catholic church. Renata told us that a priest from her mother's local parish had called her mother for a meeting, hoping to reunite them. When her mother arrived, she had spit at Renata and scratched and hit her and damned her for coming there. The priest discovered and told Renata much later that her mother had been an active member of the Nazi party. She claimed that she had been raped by a U.S. soldier.

Faustie had been talking about leaving for New Jersey the next day, and she explained to us then that she was going to meet a half-sister—her father's oldest child—after several years of exchanging letters. She told us about her white German mother's marriage to a soldier stationed in Germany after the war. Her father had returned to the U.S. when she was two years old, and she had grown up in a small city in West Germany with several younger, white half-siblings. Her mother had never heard from her father after he returned home. Faustie was now in her mid-thirties. Several years earlier, she had gone to the U.S. Salvation Army for help in finding her father, which eventually led to a brief, disappointing visit in Illinois. Now she was trying to get to know his extended family.

After everyone had gone home, Renata, Faustie, and I stayed up talking, connecting our stories, and the stories of other ADEFRA women. They told me that nearly every summer, many of the women in the group traveled to the United States to keep a sense of connection to African Americans, if not to their actual families. Others traveled regularly to West Africa and the Caribbean—wherever their missing Black family originated. Faustie and Renata's experiences, like Jackie Kay and Thelma Perkins and Isha McKenzie-Mavinga's, were in some ways closer to mine than those of most African Americans—maybe even more so than my friend Henri's. We shared the experience of being raised in extreme isolation from other Black people, and we had all made efforts to patch together a Black identity from books and imaginings and journeys. We were all the children of

African American men's segregation-era sexual crossings of racial lines, which had created a whole international community. And we had all framed our searches around the need to recover a missing Black father.

When Faustie and Renata talked about their frustration with the way Audre Lorde had become the icon of Black women's consciousness—spoken of as the Great Mother and the inveigler of Afro-German politics—and with the way that American racial politics were written over their own, I understood them. I, too, was looking for a way to find my own story within the larger story of African Americans, but I felt worn out from trying to cast myself within the very narrow conventions in narratives of Blackness of that era. I was an African American woman without any discernable roots, with barely any melanin, with a Jewish birth mother, adopted into and raised in a WASP nest. After I began to connect with these women from Europe, I started to see myself within a broader story.

After Faustie and Renata returned to Germany, they sent me a copy of a book called *Farbe Bekenan,* a collection of personal stories by several generations of Afro-German women. It was written in German, so I could understand only the narrative of its photos, but I knew that many of the women were writing about growing up in painful social isolation, without their Black families, and often without family at all. I was happy with the simple existence of the book, and the women's faces, with their very German Blackness, reassured me somehow.

New York City is a mecca of "mulattas," of half-breeds of every kind. I used to sit in the Village and in Soho and watch them on the street, tracing the stories of all of the other yellow girls I had begun to encounter by the end of my twenties. I used to wonder whether New York City was more productive that way or whether "mulattas" migrated there hoping to disappear into a certain order of varied brownness. But even in the mix, I could see that we seemed to retain a kind of hyper-self-consciousness, a desire to fade and yet be *seen*, moving in and out of people's flashes of perception about who we were. Perhaps I was projecting my own feelings, but there was something in these women's body language that seemed familiarly studied, anticipating people's gaze—the by-product, I am sure (because now so many of us talk about it), of being imagined as especially different, good or bad, and often the Only One.

There's a kind of classic "mulatta" scene I've encountered again and again in the United States and in Europe, Africa, and the Caribbean. For some reason, it always happens at the beach or at a pool. You can go for days without seeing any evidence of racial mixing, or even any Black people if it's someplace even a little bit elite and in the West, and then you go swimming and you inevitably see the "bi-racial" kids being trotted out with their funky, overgrown hair. Everyone watches them with this immense pleasure, as if they are an emblem of something (something different to each person, I'm sure), and they go out of their way to pet them. I don't know too many yellow girls who don't have the photos from those holidays. I see my yellow sisters on the street recasting those scenes again and again.

I was beginning to take sensuous delight in "mulattas," which I'd never allowed myself to do when I was first meeting the women of the yellow African diaspora. I had always thought of "mulattas"— unless they were the Halle Berry/Dorothy Dandridge/Jane Kennedy polished pin-up girls who represented another side of Black people's self-deprecating ideals—as funny looking, even ugly. Just as when I first met Henri, I felt a certain self-loathing in the company of people who reflected me—feelings many people don't expect from "mulattas" or light-skinned Black people. There has not been any popular story of a post–Black Power "mulatta's" self-hatred. No yellow girl's *The Bluest Eye*. But I had learned self-hatred very well. I knew that for Black people, loving one's color—God forbid it being "too dark" or "too light"—was socially punishable. I knew that there was a post-1970s distinction between the light-skinned Black woman and the "mulatta" that persists. One has social swing, and the other bore a (white) taint. There was currency in one, shame in the other—although shame has a currency all its own.

I remember one of my earliest lessons in this area: At the end of a Sunday service at John Wesley, a few months after I had begun attending church, the pastor told the members of the congregation to turn to the person on their right, and to hug and kiss them and say, "God loves you, Sister or Brother So-and-So. And I love you, too." I had always feared these moments; I wasn't big on shows of affection. I could barely get "I love you" from my mouth. But I also loved the chance to be hugged by My People. I was sitting at the end of a pew that day, and at the pastor's cue I got up and crossed the aisle to greet a little boy named Zachary. That should have been easy. He was six or seven years old, and he was adorable in his usual uniform of a three-piece white suit and tie. I bent and kissed him, and then he wiped his cheek in disgust and turned to his mother and said, "I don't want no white lady kissing on me."

Zachary had a sister who was adopted. She had long hair that was always curled in perfect ringlets and tied with too many ribbons, and skin with an almost otherworldly smoothness and glow. She was like a poster child for a hatefully frilly, over-delicate "mulatta" child, in a family of strapping, work-worn, dark-skinned Georgia women. I was *whipped* by what he said. I was already so thin-skinned, feeling very vulnerable in my new community. I started to bawl; Zachary's mother slapped him. The preacher came over to see what was wrong, and I got tears and snot all over his robes as he held me. "Whatever your background is, you are one of us, and you are never God's stepchild," he said, and then he tried to give us all a lesson on Black people being wonderfully different, before he had Zachary apologize to me. I left church early and couldn't stop bawling for the walk home, and I cried on and off all weekend, angry with my family for being away.

I had one close friend from church, Penda, who was my mother's former student at Norton High School. As soon as we met, it was as though we had made a kind of unspoken pact. Penda was her own spin on Diana Ross, with pretty, dark brown skin, long, pressed hair, a face set with big wide eyes, and skinny, expressive, flailing arms. She was smart—on the way to being the school valedictorian—and was hoping for a Diana Ross-in-*Mahogany* trajectory out of Norton. She was self-confident and funny, and she became my champion, even riding her bike the seven miles to Attleboro to let anyone who was threatening me know that I could call out my ass-kicking Black sisters. We would spend hours on the telephone between church weekends, laying elaborate plans to sneak off to Boston on Saturdays, discussing the centerfolds in *Jet* ("We're finer than that!"), and reading articles and poetry to each other from the issues of *Ebony* and *Essence* we shared before my mother collected the subscription order cards.

I started to think Penda could hang the moon for me. We would pull out everything we knew for each other—she from her Georgia low-country family and the rows and rows of paperback romances beneath her bed, which her father eventually got so fed up with that he burned. (It nearly killed her because she lost copies of the only two published Black Harlequins.) I would dig into my book knowledge of Black people and tell her how to handle her father, a tiny, bullish man whose brutality needed punishing just like Alice Walker's character Grange Copeland. She would tell me what to do with my mother, who made me hold a job and do so much at home that escaping to Boston was difficult. We joked about plantation work and started to call my mother Miss Ann.

Penda hadn't been in church on the Sunday that I was called a "white lady," but she'd heard all about it on the wires. She called and invited me to sleep over at her house the next weekend and go to church with her and her sisters. "Forget Zachary," she said. "No two ways about it. You're real light, but you are Black. 'Light, bright, damn near white,'" she half-sang. "But you're a sister. Look at how fair my mother is; look at how high yellow the preacher's wife is."

Well, no one could argue with that. Then she said, full of what I loved in her, "You just have to learn how to do something with your hair. Anyway, you'll be pretty when you're older. Not all yellow girls are pretty, now—don't be getting a big head 'cause you're pink." I took all of what she said as assurance. But Zachary's words also stayed right beside her encouragement.

Penda and I spent a lot of time together dreaming and getting each other ready for when we could leave and commence our real Black lives away from Attleboro and Norton. In the meantime, we were seeking opportunities to practice for that freedom. After school on Fridays, on the weekends my parents were away, Penda would feed the pigs, call me just before she let her mother press her hair, bribe her baby sister to do her chores, and meet me on her bike at the ice cream parlor near the lake—a midpoint between our houses— before we rode to my place. My parents and William would be leaving for Vermont by early evening, and we'd plan to get there after they had left. On Saturday mornings I'd call in sick at the nursing home, and she would dress me up like a proper Black girl while she played out scenarios with the boys she was "talking to" in Boston. She would practice her kissing, pressing me up against the wall in my bedroom, fueling my impossible, shame-filled crush on her. We would plan for the ten o'clock train, ride to town, and hide our bikes with the Pastor's son, and then we'd walk almost another mile to the train station and travel forty-five minutes into Boston. My afro would fall by the time we reached the city, and she'd pick it out again on the train platform. Then we'd walk around Boston and talk to all the groups of boys who claimed they were New Edition.

Penda would deliver her best Diana Ross vivaciousness in Boston, and I followed her, feeling immobilized by inadequacy next to her dark beauty and her confidence. She was like an *Essence* cover girl with "Black, Bold, and Beautiful" tagging her image. I was trying to master her Black-girl-ness—her attitude and phrases, adopting the pitch of her mother's Geechie tongue. It was not so much a problem of learning the words and syntax of a Black vernacular—I had got all of that from my reading—as the sound and posture. Penda could deliver herself like Marsha Brady, and Black people would laugh at her ("Girl, you think you're cute with your rusty black behind!"), but they knew she was part of them. I would stand quietly and try to hide behind the props she'd dressed me in, with my hand on my hip, saying *Ummmmmm hmmm* (as in "Girl, I know what you're talking about") over and over again. It sounded like *Hmmm?* in my mouth, and people would repeat themselves and then get impatient with me and say, "Why are you laughing and asking me to repeat myself all the time?"

I would share my insecurities with Penda, and she would coach me. My heart would be screaming, *Can I depend on you, Penda? Can you carry me through this complicated world?* There were times when I would doubt her, when her tolerance for my bookishness and shyness would wane, but then she would do something hugely reassuring—like the time she called me about the sandy-haired, blue-eyed, pass-for-white model who made the cover of *Essence,* breaking the monopoly of dark brown women that were part of the urgent cry for "positive images." The cover brought an angry outcry from readers. "We have got to write letters to the editor! We can't have this! We'll write one together and sign it "Black Salt" and "Pepper."

I could depend on her.

As I met other "mulattas" in New York in my twenties, I began to let myself love our skin—the flatted browns, and darker browns, and ivories and yellows. I was beginning to enjoy the oddities of how we were configured: a WASPy boyish face and a Black woman's waist and behind; brick red nappy hair against near-white skin; sandy blond, naturally straight Caesars; nearly lavender cat eyes; no bridge in the nose of an otherwise Semitic face. Whiteness showed in these women, and I still felt some discomfort, but at heart I liked the sense of disrupted expectations. I liked our crazy hair and being able to laugh at the trouble of having some nappy patches and some bone-straight ends amongst curls—all on one head—and the ultimate problem of not really knowing how to take care of it and style it, having grown up, as many of us did, with our white mamas. And just when I thought the jokes we told on our mothers might not be fair, a white woman with her brown child would stop me on the subway or in a store and ask nervously—illiciting affection, annoyance—if she could look at how I had fixed my hair and who my hairdresser was.

As I was meeting these "mulattas" I would always remember my struggle with Henri. I was trying to let myself love my yellow sisters with the same passion I'd felt for darker-skinned Black women, the passion instilled in me by Penda and the *Essence* girls, my library of Black characters, and the women at John Wesley.

During my final year in college, I fell in love with Noir, a graduate student who taught me and Henri African dance. I began to question whether I was a lesbian and began waking up to another complication that had quietly troubled my identity struggles and my feelings of outsidership. Over the next several years, as I made my way into gay communities in New York, I realized that I was meeting more and more transracially adopted "bi-racials." I was even lucky enough to find my comrade from Attleboro, Christopher, in a men's bar in the West Village one night. Suddenly it seemed I was a part of what we could actually call a critical mass of "trans-bi" girls—the name we began to use for ourselves, playing on the language of the queer community and on our contested racial and family identities.

In 1994 I met Vanessa, another trans-bi girl who was born in Illinois and had grown up in a white adoptive family in rural Ontario. Vanessa had been reunited with her white birth mother while she was in college, and a few years later, the relationship had wound down to angry silence. When I met her, she was beginning to search for her birth father, working with very little information because her birth mother had played cruel games about his identity. At the same time, Vanessa was slowly reapproaching her birth mother after almost four years. Henri, who had been in graduate school in Atlanta, had just moved back to New York with her husband and was on the verge of finding her birth family. Henri and Vanessa became two spokes on the wheel driving my search, as I shared their progress step by step.

One day Vanessa and Henri and I decided to incorporate our threesome, and we began calling ourselves Friends of the Mulatta Nation (FMN). We were helping each other to find a sense of humor about our predicament. We would make lawless jokes about our birth parents and the treacheries of our muddled identities and, for Vanessa and me, our white families. Vanessa bought us packs of Little Debbie's brand Zebra cookies to celebrate, and she presented us with a Certificate of Mulattahood, with Thomas Jefferson's famous pseudoscience of race, the Theory of Hypodescent, which mathematically figures the blood equation of the "mulatta," the octoroon, the quadroon, copied on the back. Then Vanessa started to take the FMN newsletter to press, writing down all of our jokes and inventions: Mulatta Yom Kippur. The Mellow Yellow Awards to Outstanding Mulatta Personalities. "If You Ain't Nappy, Don't Front the Edges" and "Afrocious Hair Watch" were our headliners. There were media watches on Mariah Carey's morphing commercial Black identity and personal ads that read:

> Treach! Are you my Daddy? My mom's white, hip, and with the band.
> I have your eyes and a special way with the ladies. Can you help me?
> Am I really Naughty By Nature? —Transracial in Trenton, P.O. Box
> #1212, c/o FMN.

The newsletter always signed off:

Any complaints? Write me at Massa's. Signed, In the Name of
Jasmine Guy.

One Christmas, Vanessa made us honey-brown t-shirts with
MULATTA across the front, and A BIG HOUSE PRODUCTION™
on its back. There was a shirt for every day of the week. It took some
time for me to wear them outside of the house, but when I did, I got
some funny responses. There were people who asked whether it was
an announcement for a new movie. There were "mulattas" who were
uncomfortable with it, Latinas who got the humor quicker than anybody else, Black people who asked for one, Black people who were
angered by it. Some of my Black friends thought the shirt expressed
despicable, even dangerous, politics, akin to the multiracial box on
the census, but I reminded them that in subtle ways, they had been
calling me all kinds of half-breed names all along.

I was finding the deep eroticism of yellow, as Vanessa and I
worked our way into a love affair. I loved her parchment-colored body,
and when I lay next to her, or when people admired us together, I felt
the beauty of my own body settling into my consciousness for the
first time. I was feeling guilty about reveling in it. I could not imagine
ever being able to act like I knew I was cute — Penda's warning had
stayed with me — or to hang out with my girls and swoon out loud:
Girl, she's a yellow hammer! Could people hear that and understand
that it was a remark that was totally mindful of history and the social
warfare of colorism and also recognize that it's a yellow Black girl's
revolution, too?

When I would hang out with Vanessa, I would drift into Technicolor-like daydreaming. My old home movies would suddenly play. The childhood memories I'd excised would roll out, at first in jumpy, fitful images that would eventually relax into a lucid stream. I'd be eating Thai food with her, and the smell of mulch from our backyard in Attleboro would fill my nose. Or I'd walk into a room and see the corner of the living room in our old house. The name of a bird would suddenly come into my head. Or I'd step out of the shower and recall the bruise of cold air when the zipper on the tent was opened in the morning. Some noise would recall the eerie beauty of a loon's whooping cry across a glass-still lake before folding beneath the surface. Then I'd drift off to sleep remembering paddling on the Bungay River, seated in the safe, steady place on the floor behind my mother's seat at the bow of the canoe. Vanessa, with her ice hockey playing, her hip-hop and country music, and her Canadian-trying-to-cross-the-border-to-where-the-other-African-Americans-are Black girl self reassured me.

I could share things with Vanessa from that storehouse of memory, without shame or faltering, and I realized it was probably the first time I had ever done this. Vanessa was the first person I'd brought my whole self to. She was allowing me to be a Black woman full of contradictions; with her, I could admit my anger, and also reveal my love for, the people I had left behind.

The spring of 1989, when I graduated from Sarah Lawrence, signaled a break with my family and a break in my memory—the final push in my attempts to find a comfortable identity, an achievement that seemed dependent on forgetting parts of myself.

At graduation, the campus was bristling with tension. Six weeks earlier, Henri and I, part of the lead of Harambee, the group we'd started our first year in college, and eight other students who made up Concerned Students of Color, had occupied the college administration building. We were eventually joined by more than 150 other students. The occupation was our parting shot in a four-year struggle to get the administration to look at admissions practices, hire more than the two tenured Black faculty members, advance the school's curriculum, and intervene in the rising racial harassment on campus.

We'd had a heady last semester, and we were high on the image of ourselves as Black radicals and the power of our actions. We had paralyzed the college for a week and received national media attention, and at the end of the takeover we had been assured that, among other things, six full-time tenure-track Black faculty would be hired over the next few years, a pledge the college actually fulfilled.

I felt strong and proud among Henri and my friends as we marched in our kente cloth–draped gowns, raising our fists high in the air as we took our diplomas from the president's hands. But when the ceremony ended, as I walked across the lawn to find my family, I felt myself buckling. For four years, I had managed to hide the fact that I was transracially adopted from most everyone at school except Henri and a few of my beloved teachers. I had played the radical, the uncompromising watchdog on concessions to white people or white institutional power. Now my family was going to tell a different story about me on the final day. So when I stood in front of my mother and father and William and my grandmother, I felt a wall of shame and anger rise. They were open-armed and smiling on the other side. I hugged them each uncomfortably, looking around to see if anyone important to my myth-making was watching. Then I relied on an old ruse — something I'd perfected since I was a child. I spent a little time with them and then looked for an exit, hoping to lose myself in the crowd. I snared a teacher who had advised me on my adoption research, and as soon as she and my parents were talking comfortably, and my grandmother had found a place to sit down and rest, and I saw William making friends with some of the theater girls, I ran off and joined someone else's Black family.

I would circle back to the McKinleys when it seemed like a safe moment, and my grandmother would convict and hang me with her eyes. If the rest of my family were hurt, they didn't let me know. My parents seemed quietly conscious of the pressures and the shapeshifting I was struggling with but it was never outwardly confronted. They were always cautious about "intruding" on the communities I was part of. Whenever they crossed into my other worlds — at John Wesley A.M.E. Zion, at boarding school and at college, and during my junior year when I studied in Jamaica — they always came for short visits, maybe just for an hour or two, even after considerable travel, once or twice a year. They would reason that the dog, the farm, never let them leave for long. We always met somewhere on the periphery of where I lived, and I took it as an offer of some kind of understanding. Perhaps they felt they were helping to protect me. But it was curious and ultimately sad, because these places — especially my very liberal schools — should have been some of the safest places for us.

Later that afternoon, after their car was packed with my things, and we were saying goodbye until I would go home to Attleboro the next week, my mother handed me an envelope. She had written me a letter that tore at my shame.

26 May 1989

Dear Cath-

It's pretty early on your graduation day. The dogs got me up to take them out. While everybody else is asleep, maybe I can say some of the things I probably won't say very well later today. So often we let the big ones go by.

You have done so very well! Against heavy odds you have found a path that lets you live in a divided world with divided allegiances and still become a productive, in fact, creative contributor. You've emerged from an unusually complicated adolescence into personal, emotional, and intellectual maturity with tremendous promise for your own future satisfaction and valuable contributions to make to our troubled society. And you love and are loved by a wonderful, various group of people.

Dad and I are terribly proud of you. We love you more than we'll probably be able to tell you today (I'll cry) and we wish you ever more love and happiness and success.

Take good care of yourself—and phone home.

Love,

Mom

My mother did not know how much I was hurting. Maybe graduation had let her see something more of me. Through that whole year she had been my champion, coaching me and sharing the victory of our campus struggles. In her eyes I was growing ever more sophisticated and adept at moving between worlds. The truth is that I felt like I was moving about in an airless room, foreshortened on all sides.

It seemed that there was no place that my different worlds met. In the previous eight years at schools, where I was never part of more than a very tiny Black and Latin student body, I had never had any significant white friends. I had led a highly social and yet isolated life at school, superficially friendly all around, but keeping most everyone at a great emotional distance. I was hiding my family, where I came from, and my sexuality from most everyone—from my friends, from the teachers I respected, even from Henri. I was too much or too little of what I needed to be for every community I tried to join, and I was too afraid of being excommunicated to risk greater non-conformity. But the concealment and the lying, the sartorial adjustments, and the emotional dishonesty I thought was necessary had actually pushed me further and further outside. Meanwhile, my parents and William stood in a world that was completely white; they had never sustained even a casual relationship with a Black or brown person.

I had a graduate fellowship to Cornell, a coveted summer job, the triumphs of the sit-in. But no one seemed aware of how much I was fighting terrible depression, feeling the effects of a severely fragmented self.

At the end of the month, my parents were retiring and moving from our house in Attleboro to become Christmas tree farmers in Vermont. I was happy they were leaving Attleboro, happy to be able to finally wash my hands of the place, but I was also losing my childhood home, the anchor of my memories, however intent I was on forgetting my roots there. It was fine for me to reject home and hold it at arm's length as long as I could reclaim it when I needed to. Now, with this move, I felt the split between me and my family, which had been threatening for so many years, finally set in.

For many years, going home to Attleboro, or to my grandmother's house in Connecticut, had become difficult for me to do. When there was a call to go home, I would find myself stalling, missing trains, traveling days later than I had arranged. On the journey there, I would feel such a terrible loneliness. I would feel that I was about to lose who I was and everything that had been so hard-won—my identity, my place in other worlds—in just that little physical distance. We often had family gatherings at my grandmother's house, and the first whiff of those Fairfield County commuters and the housewives returning from Manhattan shopping trips, uncomfortably sharing the train cars with the mostly Black and Latin laborers, would set off a powerful rage. When the train arrived in Stamford, I would take a taxi to my grandmother's house and wait to see what version of the familiar conversation the usually Black driver would have with me when we turned into the private lane she lived on.

> Do you work here?
> No, I'm going to see my family.
> I thought only white people live up here.
> (*So, do I answer,* You got it! *or wait and watch him crane his neck to see who comes to the door?*)

> Do you work here?
> Yes.
> How did you get this job?
> It's been in the family.

> Do you live here?
> My family lives here.
> Oh, Black people live out here?
> Yes./No./Are you surprised?

The shifting and negotiating didn't always change much inside of my grandmother's house. The spring before I graduated from college, we'd thrown her eightieth birthday party at her house, and I had been mistaken for the coatroom help—once I was tipped—by more than a few of my grandmother's friends. At the party, my mother gave my grandmother an album she'd made of photos that friends and family had sent her as remembrances. Included among the photos were images of my grandmother smiling in blackface at a sorority fête. When I protested, no one in the family had been willing to acknowledge that there was something wrong with that, that even if it was just "the times," maybe those photos didn't have a place in that album now. The party was a kind of unusual, vulgar encounter, but it exposed what was always there—a refusal to face uncomfortable truths if it meant upsetting what seemed like a more important sense of family "peace." It was this history that undergirded my rage toward my family.

My anger would tinge my visits with them. They would return it with distraction. They were never pulled from their usual intense pace of work—work invaded everything—so that holidays were spent tending the yard, or the birdfeeders, or repairs on the house. William would rejoin their familiar intense threesome, going over projects and plans. They seemed to never relax from workday rituals, and conversations seemed focused on the universe of their toils. I would find a place to hide in my books or visit with my grandmother. She had always been my friend, but more and more, our conversations would quickly tip into fights, as I struggled with my rage and she struggled with her incomprehension of me. We usually fought at the level of disapproval of my hairstyles or of what I was wearing ("Do you think you're an African?" she'd say if I wore even braids or bright colors). I often felt like a not-too-friendly organism that joins a larger body, the host accommodating, not bothering too much the about the effects of the invasion, leaving the thing to nurse undisturbed.

When it was time to leave, I felt the promise of relief. My mother and I would ride in silence to the train station, or she would use that time before we parted to focus some of her attention on me. We'd have awkward conversations about very little, but when my train would arrive and I'd turn to leave, my mother's eyes would fill with tears, and it seemed like I was waiting for that moment to allow myself to feel something like love or a connection with her. I would quickly turn back and hug her again, always feeling guiltily conscious of how we looked to the people on the platform, conscious of being seen with her by other Black people. Then I'd board the train, and from my seat I'd watch her stand there crying, her body, usually strong and lithe, suddenly unbalanced. She would look frail and vulnerable in a way I never experienced her, and I would feel a kind of smug satisfaction. I felt mean and powerful in a small, despotic way. When I arrived home I would call her, and we would say warm things about the visit and relax back into our usual weekly check-ins.

With my parents' move to Vermont, it seemed as though a very final, pronounced line had been drawn between us. It was different than the boundaries I had drawn in the past, acting against the surety that they would still be standing right there no matter how firmly I drew and redrew the battle lines.

In Attleboro, those lines were drawn like this: In our house, I built a haven for myself, constructing my bedroom the way I thought it would have been if I had grown up in a Black family. My shelves were filled with Black books, replacing the artifacts of a former self— the dolls from my grandmother's travels, the complete Laura Ingalls Wilder boxed library, the collections of Scottish verse, the Peterson's guides to wildflowers and the seashore. I stowed them in the crawl space under the eaves of the house and moved my mother's copies of

The Black Child: A Parent's Guide, the SNCC freedom movement songbooks, Amiri Baraka's *The Dutchman* and *The Slave,* the row of James Baldwin paperbacks, and Stokely Carmichael and James Hamilton's *Black Power* out from between the Rachel Carson and Thoreau and Henry Beston books, the trail guides, and my father's engineering manuals in the den. I covered my walls with clippings from *Essence* and *Ebony* and turned up the dial on the "civil rights station" (read: Black radio, aired only on late night and Sunday slots, picked up from the Boston airways) to let everyone know who was living there. And I put a ban on my room. My father, who was my ally, if only for his silence and quiet amusement at my lobbies against the family, was the only one allowed in, and only so that he could tend the African violets he grew on shelves he built into my bedroom windows. I liked the flowers; they were African, despite how suspicious they seemed to me, sitting in the living room of every old white lady in town.

The three feet of landing at the top of the stairs marked a great divide between me and the rest of the family. My brother's room, across from mine, was done over patriotically, with white walls and red and blue trim. I had helped to pick the American flag curtains and bedspread from the Sears catalog, and my mother ordered him a red, white, and blue shag rug. The rest of the house was filled with the outdoors. Gear catalogs and wildlife magazines piled the tables and shelves and tops of toilet tanks; a spectacular assortment of containers and thermoses and utensils, NASA tubing to ration and pack food for our excursions, insect repellent, ski wax, fly-fishing gear, bicycle tire gauges, seed packs, cork and cat gut and kayak patch was in every kitchen cabinet or drawer. Dried foodstuffs, iodine tablets, a snakebite kit sat on the shelf above the liquor stash. There were shells and bones and feathers, moose horns found in a glacier in the Grand Tetons mounted on the wall, snake moltings and rattlers, porcupine quills, and owl pellets on the fireplace mantle, on the corners of living room tables, and the edges of bookshelves. In the hutch with the china, you might find something rotting in a covered dish. And always there was a hint of my parents' upbringing and its expectations: *The New Yorker* magazines, a piece of furniture or a painting, a fussy something, the Abercrombie & Fitch clothing in a closet full of overalls and Sears & Roebuck farm wear.

Other lines were drawn this way: My parents and brother had developed an interiority, a language and an emotionality expressed through nature that I wanted them to extend outside of that closed world. As we moved about in our lives in that house, different longings and a different material life were possessing me. I had an argument with all that obsession about the woods and bird watching, fly-fishing, animal tracking and nature conservancy.

When we sat together at meals, I would imagine that I was at a table with the characters from my books—maybe Indigo was eating gumbo by my side and M'Dear was asking me about school. William and my parents would eat and watch the suet sacks hung outside the window, a pair of binoculars and a journal they used to record the birds that came to feed on the table between them. I would sit there, imagining I was Zora Neale Hurston, anthropologist, and create my own catalogs: He smells this way because he is white; I feel this way because I am Black; she burns her chicken and doesn't use pepper because she is not my Black mother.

I remember sitting at the dinner table one evening—it must have been early in high school—cataloging my grievances with them in just this way. My anger got the best of me, and I went after my brother over whatever I felt was one of his recent sins of ignorance or his currying of my parents' favor. I cannot remember what the matter was, but I do remember that part of his response was "because you're half-Black," and that I launched all of the artillery of my rage at him.

"I am BLACK!" I shouted. "In America, if you have one drop of Black blood, you are BLACK!"

"Well, you don't have to . . . ," he stammered.

"Don't tell me what to do! I don't have to do nothing but STAY BLACK AND DIE!"

William didn't understand anything about my anger, or what I was saying. I felt that connection between us that made us brother and sister sever a little bit more.

The Black world was like Mars to him. He didn't know any Black people, not even my friends, and in those years—the early 1980s—in a place like Attleboro, not even television or the radio or pop culture allowed much acculturation. Our lives became increasingly remote even as we moved through the same house. The previous summer we had been together at a summer program at the boarding school I would later attend. We ate lunch in the same cafeteria every day, but we hardly interacted in those six weeks. I stuck to my Black friends, and he moved with the Frisbee and drama crews, and when we passed each other, we said a few friendly things and moved along. I remember on the last night of the session, before we packed up to go home, my brother came to give me a message from my mother and found me sitting with my boyfriend and his sister. My brother was being friendly and trying to exercise some "cool." He said, "Hey, boy . . ." to my boyfriend in this affected redneck-sounding voice, and I knew that if he went much further, he was going to get stomped on.

He had no idea that he had crossed a serious line, even when it seemed like time had stopped and then went on fast forward.

"What did you say, cuz?" my boyfriend said, And everything started to rumble.

"William, you are so fucking ignorant! Forget, him ya'll. He's my brother, but he doesn't know any better," I said.

Other people were standing by, waiting so see what would happen. My boyfriend was backing down.

"Damn, Cathy, your brother is fucked up," he said, shaking his head.

"That's your *brother?*" Stefan, one of the student leaders, was listening to us and started shouting. "You are not William McKinley's sister! You are not William McKinley's sister!" His mouth was actually hanging open.

My brother and I were standing next to each other, and everyone was adding up our differences—his white, blond, preppy figure, and me, brown-skinned, hair in cornrows, and dressed in a Lee outfit like my friends from Trenton. I almost couldn't breathe because I felt so leveled from different sides.

I know that I was crying the next day when I told my mother what had happened. "I'm surprised at William. I'll talk to him. But you and your brother are different—you don't have to have the same friends or the same interests. You just have to respect each other. William has his trumpet, and you have your Black activities . . . ," she said, with some desperation.

I needed her to step in and make our worlds a little closer. I did not want to give up my family's world. I wanted to be Black, to be a part of a Black world, and I wanted them to share in that world wholly. Instead, I was feeling more and more like they were homogenizing as

McKinleys, and I was an appendage to their lives. I was fixed on my outsidership and how I didn't belong, and he was daily perfecting his McKinleyness—working on projects with my parents, applying to the college they had attended, being a good son. In my rage-distorted lobbies, I was begging all of them to see that the McKinleys were a white *and* Black family, and that demanded that they be attuned to particular things.

So, when my parents began to pack up the house in Attleboro, I felt that their move to start a life as farmers was a signal of some final undoing between us. I went to visit them in Vermont a few weeks after they had moved. The time I spent with them was filled with the waves of sadness that had begun at graduation. I remember moving in circles around their new house, sifting through the boxes where all of our life in Attleboro had been stashed. I found my father's old steamer trunk full of darkroom equipment and hundreds of old slide boxes and photos, and I settled down on the floor next to them, trying to distract myself from the racing panic I had been feeling in my chest for several weeks. As I worked my way through the trunk, I found an envelope with photos of me with a boy about my age—were we seven?—lying next to me buried in sand. The photos framed our faces, with green and red sweatshirt hoods making bright, spongy liners between our deep, sun-browned faces and the sand trapping our heads.

I called my mother and handed her the pictures. She looked at them curiously. "I don't know who that is. Oh, well, that must be Jimmy," she sighed. Jimmy, my cousin. My mother's sister's adopted child, who had stood in the same brown relief against our family as I did for two or three years and then disappeared. I can still remember the call that came one evening when I overheard my mother and her sister in Kentucky talking about Jimmy being "sent back." Later, my mother explained to me and my brother that my aunt and her ex-husband had decided to give up being parents to Jimmy because single parenting was proving too hard. When they had divorced, my aunt took *her own* two children (it was never said this way, but the truth of it was evident) and left Jimmy with her ex-husband. Her ex-husband was battling alcohol abuse. Jimmy had "problems with his feelings" and was acting out, and the situation had become too difficult.

I remember feeling frightened by his being "sent back" and what it revealed about the adults' feelings: there was a difference between your kids and your *own* kids. It had always seemed like William and I and the cousins were treated with a sameness in everyone's affections, but now it seemed like distinctions could be drawn. And the absence of my parents' outrage—or maybe they'd just hid it and tried to explain what had happened to us without judgment—betrayed their covenant of Responsibility, No Matter How Difficult It Is. It made me afraid for myself. I didn't really understand why alcoholism or divorce made it hard to be someone's parent; It was all around us. I knew that Jimmy was no different from me, and not even so different from William, since we were all adopted. The only difference was that Jimmy came "late"—when he was four years old. I was beginning to feel confused by all of this and by the waffling I was seeing in adults' ideas. Sometimes they were insisting that to be Black and transracially adopted was a special thing. (Didn't my school principal pull me into the teachers' lunchroom, which was in itself a great privilege, to show me photos of her adopted Black granddaughter?) But now it looked like being Black and transracially adopted was also a special problem.

The photos, and my mother's slow memory and lack of emotion, became a flash point for all of the feelings that were overwhelming me. I started to go at her, and I remember her her eyes narrowing the way they do when she's angry. "I'm tired of all this race business," she said as she walked out of the room.

I know that her words were more a sign of exhaustion from the changes we were all undergoing, but I let them punctuate my sense of being utterly lost to her and to any sense of family. I sat there for a long time, feeling my chest hollow out, while my old struggle resurfaced—wanting protection and wanting to let go. I decided to take her words at face value. I thought: *I cannot love you. I cannot love white people. They cannot love me.* She could be tired and turn her back. I was going deeper in.

For the rest of my visit we barely talked, and then I left to return to my job in New York before leaving for graduate school.

This is when I decided that in some way what I now had was freedom to remake myself. And this was the beginning of my decision that my search for my birth family would be everything by way of a remedy to my sense of loss.

1994

I had never thought that I might have had a name other than Catherine Elizabeth McKinley. But one day Henri told me that she wanted to add Nicole, which was the name she found in her adoption records, back into her name. *Nicole.* I thought about that all day.

Vanessa had been named Jocelyn.

I envied them knowing their birth names. I envied them so many things. A hospital feeding chart. A Black mother. A chance to meet a birth mother, even if she messed things up. A piece of paper with her signature. Black adoptive parents. A *name*.

I had never thought to ask Mary Steed whether she knew my birth name. I guess I never thought that I might have been given one. I imagined that my birth mother would not have thought to name me or that she wouldn't have had time, or maybe even the right. If she had named me, wouldn't I have been told, maybe even in that first letter from the New England Home for Little Wanderers?

I decided to call Mary Steed.

"Your birth mother named you Sarah," she said when she called me back that afternoon. "I cannot tell you a last name, but as you know, your mother was of Jewish persuasion."

Sarah. I hated that name. I thanked Mary Steed and hung up the phone.

My mother, the historian, named me for Catherine the Great and Queen Elizabeth, although Elizabeth was also part of her name and her mother's. "Those are slave names," I told her, full of Malcolm X, when she explained that to me in high school.

The name kept moving through my head. *Sarah.* It seemed so odd and disconnected—from me, from this woman who had birthed me. Rather than adding flesh to her, and to me, everything seemed to flatten again into the abstract.

But then I remembered: when I was in junior high school, I had added Sarita to my name. It was a new spelling of Syreeta, who sang with Billy Preston on a hit that was at the top of the civil rights station charts. Sarita was a new mark, soulfulness to undercut my white girl's name. Throughout high school, I wrote Catherine Elizabeth Sarita McKinley, or the initials C.E.S.M., on everything. I remember explaining even in college that it was the name I had kept from the mother I was separated from, and I didn't drop Sarita completely until I left graduate school and was moving to New York, trying to start over the right way.

Sarita means "little Sarah" in Spanish or Portuguese.

Had I ever been called Sarah? I had to have been called something before I became Catherine. Perhaps three months in foster care was long enough to absorb Sarah into some part of my subconscious.

Learning my name changed everything. Not so much in how I saw myself, but it changed my relationship with Mary Steed. If this information—the name I was given by my birth mother—was in my files, and she'd shared it without hesitation when I'd asked, then what else was there that the law didn't prevent me from knowing? It's strange to me now that I never directly challenged her on this, but it says so much about how powerful she seemed and how little I felt entitled to. Discovering my name made me feel a little more assertive, and I started to call her more frequently, as questions came to me. One year a boss, who greeted everyone in the office on Mondays with our weekly horoscopes, gave me an astrologist's reading as a birthday gift. I couldn't tell the astrologist my time of birth, so I called Mary Steed. "You were born at 4:14 A.M. in Boston Lying In Hospital, which became Brigham Women's Hospital, which you know is now closed. Other details—let me see. APGAR scores were 8, 9, and 10 taken at 1, 2, and 5 minutes after birth. Your parents seemed to have had a meaningful relationship."

Then a tease: She told me that she had my original birth certificate in the file. "It is unusual for the agency to have the birth certificate. And most often the birth father will not be listed on it, unless the couple was married." She spoke as if she were confiding.

I listened to her, weighing what she was telling me. I was always looking for a nod that it was time for us to end the game. I'd heard stories about agency workers casually dropping a detail, or letting something accidentally slip, or making a referral to someone outside the agency, stressing that the adoptee follow through. Then that someone would offer them a page from a file, or a name, as they collected a fee. But when I asked Mary Steed if she could tell me anything more, nothing in her answer suggested help. She was suddenly hurrying to get off the phone.

Before we hung up, I told her that I would be traveling to Boston for a writers' conference the next month. She seemed pleased, and she invited me to visit her at the New England Home for Little Wanderers with uncharacteristic warmth.

I spent the morning before my appointment with Mary Steed wandering through Boston, working my way toward South Huntington Avenue, trying to reconnect with the city that had been the setting for so many of my imaginings about *my people* and for my early attempts at entering a Black social world. I went back to some of the places where I'd hung out with Penda. I hadn't spoken with her in many years and didn't even know how to find her anymore. The city seemed alien to me. It had been more than six years since I'd been there, and it was difficult for me to think of all the ways I was a Boston child.

South Huntington Avenue was longer than I remembered, and I was worried that I wouldn't find Mary Steed's office in time, but the old stone building appeared, set back from the road, gray and institutional in the ways I imagined. The sign for the New England Home for Little Wanderers gave the place an almost comedic air, like an unoriginal Yankee riff on a Charles Dickens story. This was the same building my parents had visited in 1966. Although I shouldn't have been, I was surprised when I entered the building to see Black and Latino staff moving through the hallways and posters and brochures about the agency's services that featured Black and brown children. This was the predominant face of child welfare since the mid- to late 1950s. But it was still difficult for me to reconcile this reality with my awesome sense of isolation and of being a pioneer. I kept staring at the posters as I waited for Mary Steed at the reception desk, imagining my face on one of them. It could so easily have been there.

I was surprised to meet a woman well into her sixties. The cigarette smoker's dryness of her voice had somehow masked her age. She was tall and trim and wore a neat, plaid wool suit with a WASPy self-possession that reminded me of people in my parent's pre-retirement world. On our way upstairs to her office, she gave me a tour of the agency. We passed an alcove on the first floor of the building that led to a meeting room, and she stopped and told me, "This is where the old nursery was—it is the place where you most likely would have met the McKinleys." I thought that maybe I should have felt something significant then, but the whole place made me feel numb.

In her office, we made small talk for a while. I started to feel that I rather liked the woman. But I also felt an urge to get up and smack her for being so dependably polite and yet of so little help to me. I nursed this feeling as we began to talk about my search. I was listening to her ideas about hiring a private investigator when someone came to her door and called her. She got up in the middle of a thought and left to go down the hall. I wondered whether my file was there on her desk. Was that what kept holding her glance? Would she purposely give me this chance to just get up and look at it? Could she sit there and casually chat with me knowing there was only a desk between me and the file that I wanted so much to see? When she had these kinds of meetings, did she ever think she might be putting herself in the way of the violence I sometimes felt was about to push my hand? I sat there frozen in my chair, wondering whether she was giving me permission to look. So far she had acted like my ally in her own funny way, but she had not offered subterfuge of any kind.

She returned before I could resolve the questions racing through my mind.

"I think you are taking all of the right steps, Catherine, and I wish I could be of more help. I'll let you know if I get any leads on a good investigator." She flipped through some papers in front of her, going back over old details with me, apologizing again for not having anything more to offer. I'd only been there for ten minutes, and the conversation seemed to be ending. I felt like I was being played with, and my frustration began to overwhelm me, and there were tears welling up in my eyes. I didn't want to cry in front of her. I thanked her and stood up, saying that I had to make it to another appointment.

As she accompanied me downstairs, she said, "If you would like to try to file a court petition again, you might have your therapist attach an affidavit saying that you are in therapeutic treatment. Your birth mother's health history would give sufficient reason for a court hearing about opening your files. You told me that you have had bouts of depression. Your birth mother was hospitalized close to your birth for what the records say was psychotic and depressive illness. I wish I could tell you more."

As soon as she said this, that first letter from the agency ran through my head: *Her health history reports that she had no allergies or history of serious illness in the family.* I stood quietly near the reception desk looking at her, not really knowing how to respond.

Afterwards, I walked for miles—all the way across town to my hotel—feeling a familiar numbness climb down from my head into every limb. I didn't know what to think about Mary Steed or the agency's wacky rules of disclosure, or what I was supposed to do with this new bit of information. I had no idea what "psychotic illness" was or what it really meant in relation to my birth mother. I felt a little frightened too because, as Mary Steed reminded me, I had fought depression. Before this, it had just seemed like a disposition, an *affect,* in the clinical sense. But lately the familiar melancholy, the cast of isolation, seemed to be enveloping me more and more, as if it might actually have a deeper hold on me.

I called Mary Steed when I got back to New York. I told her that what she had told me was worrying me. It was new and totally surprising information. Didn't she realize this?

Before I could continue, she said that she had been thinking more about my situation and had gone back to my files.

"It appears that there was a forced termination of your birth mother's parental rights—I cannot tell you precisely why—but the Massachusetts Department of Child Guardianship was somehow involved with the adoption before you came to us. I would like to check into this further with an adoptions supervisor for the state. You might qualify for state agency search assistance, which could make certain kinds of help available to you that you might not otherwise be able to get." She promised that she would call me back as soon as she had more details and apologized for her crypticness.

I hung up feeling more worried about what she was saying about my birth mother. This new story was so far from the narrative I had been piecing together, and the lack of specificity of "psychotic" and "depression" alarmed me, but the drama of it was also becoming slightly appealing. A mad Jewish birth mother. It reverberated nicely with the legacy of Bessie Head—a tortured, genius writer born of a Black father and a white mother who, under the cruelty of South Africa's system of apartheid, went mad in the wake of delivering her Black daughter. I was baffled by all of the erratic changes between one conversation with Mary Steed and the next, but I also felt my hopes of *maybe really getting somewhere* open for the first time.

The FMN girls and some of my other friends were trying to get me more comfortable with the Jewish bit. It wasn't Jewishness, really, that I had to get comfortable with; it was the fact of having this new dimension to integrate into my imaginings and my fragile sense of a new self.

What did all of this being Black and Jewish actually mean?

One of my friends gave me a children's picture book about Ethiopian Jews celebrating the Holy Days as a Hanukkah present. Another friend gave me a copy of Hettie Jones's *How I Became Hettie Jones,* her memoir about becoming the "white Semitic mother of Black children." (Inside the cover my friend wrote, "Because you've read too much damn LeRoi Jones!"—joking about the man who is now Amiri Baraka, Hettie's brilliant but frighteningly reactionary Black nationalist former husband). I felt like I was back in middle school, being handed my heritage through books all over again.

The FMN girls pointed again and again to other African Americans with Jewish heritage: Lani Guinier, Rebecca Walker, Anna Deveare Smith, and Walter Mosley—all people in the public eye. But what was I going to do with them? Being Black and Jewish never became a defining point in their public contributions. "Take them like this," my friend Tola, a Nigerian-Irish-Puerto Rican who is the comedic doyenne of mulattresses, obsessed with "types" and phenotypes, said laying out all of their photographs together. "See how classically Black and Jewish you are—different from the American WASP/Black mixes, different from the European WASP/Black mixes," she said. "Ya'll look a little afflicted. If you never get anywhere with the People for the Little Wanderers, you still have some kind of identity papers. You know your mother really has to be Jewish." It was kind of interesting to look at all of our faces. There were some themes there, but then if someone lined up some photos of Arabs or South Asians or Latins, the case might also be made for my similarity to them.

My friend Rita, who had accompanied me to my first adoption support group meeting, had been given an invitation from her father, who owns an art gallery, to the opening of "Bridges and Boundaries," an exhibit at the New York Jewish Museum. This was in 1992, not long after the explosion in Crown Heights, and not long after I faced up to the letter from the New England Home for Little Wanderers. The exhibit chronicled the similar social and political history of African American and Jewish American. That night, as Rita and I crowded into the vestibule, then made our way through the museum, I tried not to stare too obviously at the gatherings of Black and Jewish families: Jewish women and Black men, Black women and Jewish men, and their children. There was something stunning about them—not just their presence but the way they seemed powerful against the backdrop of the exhibit, the fancy opening party, and the old New York wealth represented by the building we were in. But then the people I saw were powerful. Rita whispered editorials to me as we strolled through the exhibit: they were mostly elite families, intellectuals and artists, politicians and business people, and some proper socialites. I began to feel like a hungry interloper.

I imagined how much saner it might have been to grow up in New York City, alongside progressive and maybe even radical Jewish and Black communities, to have both parts of your family present as a kind of psychological protection, and to have your personal history made plain. I imagined that no matter how difficult it might have been to walk between these two worlds, it would have been easier than the confusion and denial of growing up adopted and part of neither community. I started to feel sorry for myself—and I began to feel resentment toward everyone around me.

Rita and I walked through the exhibit, looking at the fascinating documents of Black-Jewish history. There was "Hymie Town" Black nationalist hyperbole set against Goodman, Schwerner, and Chaney martyrdom. There were photos of concentration camps among others of lynching, Martin Luther King's writings on anti-Semitism, and Communist party literature on "the Negro question." There was the legacy of minstrelsy and Jewish Hollywood producers, complete with bottles of oil for blacking the face made by Jewish-owned companies.

But the exhibit seemed to me in some ways a fabrication. I didn't feel satisfied with the "Bridges and Boundaries" model: two histories laid side by side, exhibiting parallels of oppression and resistance, with a thread of partnership. To me, it seemed too facile, too superficial, as I watched the more suggestively complicated narratives of the people around me. The exhibit examined Blacks and Jews at the level of conflict and common ground, but there was very little in the way of the truly intimate history of family and friendship. I was hungry for something that would reveal these intimacies, fearless of any derision or political co-opting of those stories, in a way that said more than what the theologians, activists, and politicians had offered in the wake of the Crown Heights riots. I was seeking something of myself and the other Black and Jewish lives I saw glimpses of. I wanted something that could also help me to imagine my birth mother and her history with my birth father.

I had been trying to imagine my birth mother. I looked closely at myself for signs of her, but I could not call up the outlines of a person at all. I just saw a formless whiteness. If I tried very hard, I could sometimes conjure Anjelica Huston, talking smart like Grace Paley. My imagination just couldn't open any wider.

I began turning my sights to a more comfortable place: *A man who would be in his seventies, who worked in Boston as an interior decorator and "enjoyed art as a hobby," married and unwilling to care for another child.* I knew even a degree less about him, but these details dovetailed easily into fantasy: my Black father, manipulating space, making art out of structure in the 1950s and 1960s. This was romance. He might be forgiven for being married, unwilling. He was an artist, not a man to be wed to practical demands.

Since college, I had collected old photographs of Black people—a kind of ritualized search for suggestions of Black kin. I looked for my birth father now in those photographs. I looked for him in my friends' fathers and relatives. And when I found a doll in a shop—a wooden carving of a dapper man in a Western suit, made by the Baule people of the Ivory Coast to represent otherworld kin who were attended to like the living—I called it "Pop" and sat it up in my room and hoped that talking to it might reveal him. It was a little ridiculous, but it was also comforting.

I started pouring over art books and cultural history books, checking artists' photographs and their biographies for dates and signs of things that might connect to my birth father. I would get excited by an artist's work and imagine it was his until something discredited the tie. I read historiographies of the various schools of artists and Black arts movements. I imagined him like the self-exiled painter Beauford Delany or the cartoonist Oliver Harrington, making a life in Paris. I saw a catalog for an exhibit on Black male quilters and fastened on to the idea of him making quilts. Then I fixed on James Baldwin, and I imagined my birth father cut from the same cloth: a wonderful, if needy—even parasitic—friend whose work let you forgive him. I imagined him as one of Jimmy's Paris contemporaries—properly creative and visionary and bohemian. I imagined he was gay—a beautiful Black gay man who let my mother down only because he needed to discover something of himself. If his leaving her was about questions as big as exile or art or loving men, then he and I would be okay.

I had a frequent fantasy: I imagined him coming to New York City for the weekend as soon as I found him. We'd meet at his hotel on Central Park, and I'd go with him to the museums and galleries before we'd hang out with the old boys in the Village and at the gay spots in Harlem.

I made a pact with the Spirits of Search: if I could just find the man, I would love and forgive him. I would love him no matter what kind of man he was—even if he only painted women and wild cats of the jungle on velvet.

When I imagined him, I always saw him atop a ladder, lithely stretching upward, a gold wedding band on a hand clasped at the wrist by a bluebird-colored sleeve, resting on a kelly-green-clad hip. I always imagined these same clothes. I could not imagine his face. I only saw him acting, in motion, stretching for something above what I could see. If I really worked hard to call up his face, I would see a chameleon, with those wide-set, protruding eyes like Jimmy Baldwin or Yoruba *obiji* figures and that kind of slumber-filled grin lizards always seem to have on their mouths. Then his hands and arms would grow brilliant green scales, and my imagination would fold.

One day I called a friend who worked at the Studio Museum in Harlem to make a lunch date. We met a few days later, and I asked her if she could help me get into their archives to see if there was any information about Black interior decorators. She took me back to her office and introduced me to some of the staff, telling them that I was doing a research project that I needed help on. I left with a date to meet with one of the archivists and the phone number for a woman who had spent a lot of time in Boston's Black arts scene in the 1960s and 1970s and worked for the Schomburg Library. I stepped out onto 125th Street feeling excited. This kind of detective work was fun and more academic than emotional, and even if it didn't lead anywhere, I got something from it that I couldn't get from researching plain identity facts. When I got to 7th Avenue, I remembered that the National Association of Black Social Workers (NABSW) offices were in the grand old St. Theresa Hotel building at that corner. I decided to go and check them out.

NABSW had been the most prominent and certainly the only organized Black institutional voice in the public debate about transracial adoption. As an organization, they came down vehemently against intraracial placements—going so far as to suggest that it was a form of genocide—and they became a powerful force in the eventual review of policy and adoption practice. I'd visited NABSW in the late 1980s when I was doing my transracial adoption research in college. I'd first read their famous 1972 position paper on transracial adoption when I was in high school. Written in the wake of the Civil Rights Movement, in the new fire of Black Power protest, the position paper had done a lot to shut down the so-called golden era of transracial adoption—the window between 1967 (the year I was born) and 1971, when these adoptions received focused public attention and leapt to an eventual high of about 2,500 per year. (It is estimated that 12,000 transracial adoptions occurred between 1960 and 1976—a phenomenon that had begun only twelve years earlier with formal government-sponsored and private agency–sponsored adoptions of Black and "mixed-race" children.)

NABSW offered the only voice that answered my need for a clear, politicized analysis of transracial adoption. In college I was deep inside Black activist communities, embracing Afrocentrism and its universe of nationalist politics to the extent that I could stomach its sexual politics and "purist" Black rhetoric. My anger and struggles with my family, and some of my personal truths, attached strongly to NABSW's stance. During those years, I read their position paper again and eventually sought them out as if they were a shelter.

> The National Association of Black Social Workers has taken a vehement stand against the placement of Black children in white homes for any reason. We affirm the inviolable position of Black children in Black families where they belong physically and culturally in order that they receive the total sense of themselves and develop a sound projection of their future.
>
> ... The family is the basic unit of society; one's first, most pervasive and only consistent culturing life experience ... Black children in white homes are cut off from the healthy development of them-

selves as Black people, which development is the normal expectation
and only true humanistic goal . . . The bi-racial family cannot be anymore isolated from society than others.

Special programming in learning to handle Black children's hair,
learning Black culture, "trying to become Black," puts normal family
activities in the form of special family projects to accommodate the
odd member of the family . . . These actions highlight the unnatural
character of trans-racial adoption . . .

We denounce the assertions that Black families will not adopt;
we affirm the fact that Black people, in large number, cannot maneu-
ver the obstacle course of the traditional adoption process . . . The
emphasis on high income, educational achievement, residential status and other accoutrements of white middle-class lifestyle elimi-
nates Black applicants by the score.

The National Association of Black Social Workers asserts the
conviction that children should not remain in foster homes or institutions. We stand firm, though, on the conviction that a white home
is not a suitable placement for Black children and contend that it is
totally unnecessary.

I had some warm conversations on the telephone with the
NABSW's director of adoption services, who had been with the
organization during that era, before I went to meet with her. But our
meeting would reveal some philosophical contradictions that I hadn't
expected.

Our appointment turned into something more like a summit by the
time I arrived; the director asked if it would be all right if we were
joined by some of her staff and some of the staff at Harlem-Dowling
Children's Services, who shared their space. I sat with six other people
around a conference table. We were supposed to be meeting about my
research, but I could feel their curiosity about me and at least one
woman's bored skepticism. They started to ask me questions, and I

imagined the notes being penned at that table: *Middle-class kid. From a Seven Sisters college up the road. High yella. Could pass for white but she's wearing her hair in an afro and she has on an African print dress.* However, it felt kind of nice to have an audience, and I was eager to show them how versant I was at nineteen about the intricacies of adoption policy and how it related to issues of race. I imagined that after I was done, they would revise their notes and celebrate my bucking all the predicted dire outcomes for growing up Black with white parents. But I was still not good at talking about myself. The meeting quickly became uncomfortable as their questions seemed to angle for answers that they already thought they knew. One woman kept interrupting me to probe everything I said as if she were my caseworker. Others talked among themselves, and the skeptic sat quietly, her face twisted with suspicion. I struggled to speak, and as the words came out, I started to see a fault line in my thinking. I thought I was aligned with NABSW's political position, but I realized that I couldn't reconcile my upbringing with their absolute opposition to transracial adoption. I began to feel like I was betraying my family and myself, and some of my more interesting and attractive contradictions as I held onto that radical posture.

I left there with hurt feelings and a suggestion that we begin to look into "ways of working together," which had nothing to do with what any of us had intended for the meeting. As I walked to the train, I imagined that I'd get a letter from the director saying something like: *Thank you for meeting with us. We've reviewed your application. We are sorry we will not be able to use you. You are not the transracial adoptee we needed. (And we do admit that we are no longer very focused on that issue.) You held the line down pretty well, but you could not ultimately say that you were against transracial adoption. Yes, you did*

*not say it was just fine; you have your political objections. And you did
express Black pride. But your answers weren't quite what we were looking for.*

On the train ride home I looked over the literature they'd given to
me. There were no explicit services for adult adoptees, and transracial adoption wasn't mentioned at all. NABSW's focus on adoption in
the 1980s was with placement of the tens of thousands of Black children who were languishing in foster care and state institutions
because Black adoptive families couldn't absorb those numbers.
White adoptive parents had turned to Latin America and Asia. Nevertheless, included in the packet of literature was an old, slightly yel-
lowed copy of the 1972 position paper.

Now, several years later, I was standing on 125th Street, thinking
about dropping in to see what they were up to. I wandered across the
street and through the hallways of the beautiful old building, wanting
to get back the old feeling of being next to something that had been
powerful to me. I went upstairs to the NABSW office and collected
some literature at the reception desk. Now the fight was for "crack
babies" and HIV- and AIDS-infected children, alongside the same
crisis in child welfare and adoption.

I began to think about the limits of NABSW's support for transracial adoptees. Could they have intervened with more than just the
radical posturing that had altered adoption policy and public consciousness in the 1970s? It seemed to me now that they had looked at
transracial adoption as an emblem of the extremities of white racial
domination. It became a powerful locus for a set of concerns that
found other moorings as transracial placements halted and the less
than 12,000 adoptions disappeared from broad public view.

That evening, I called my mother and told her about my visit to

NABSW. I told her my feelings about going back there this time—that it made me, remember all of our angry arguments—the many times I used the NABSW position, to speak to my own hurt. Although I was grateful to have had that political voice when I needed it, I was glad that I was able to work past many of those feelings and develop my own consciousness living inside transracial adoption's contradictions.

"I wish they could help me now," I said. "But I guess a bunch of grown-up, mostly middle-class Black adoptees with white parents are not the NABSW's real constituency."

I was telling her that I was now really searching for my birth parents. We hadn't talked about it in a few years—not since I had shared the letter from the New England Home for Little Wanderers with her. Now I told her about the dead ends I had kept hitting and my visit to the agency. I didn't tell her about the record of my birth mother's mental illness or the new steps Mary Steed was taking. It felt too unformed to mention. I don't think my mother really said much in response. We were both being careful of each other. But I could tell that she was a little excited about my seeing the New England Home for Little Wanderers, so I told her what Mary Steed was like and how the place had looked.

She remembered the viewing room Mary Steed had shown me, and she said, "There were a lot social workers of her type around at the time." Then she started to talk about history—something we never really talked about. William had been adopted in 1965, when my parents were living in New Jersey. William was what adoption workers often referred to as a "blue ribbon baby"—the increasingly unavailable, white infant in good health whose physical traits and family background could be closely matched to the usually middle- or upper-middle-class prospective parents. My parents knew that they wanted to adopt again, and they knew the wait for a child could be long—it could easily take years—so right after he was settled in, they started consulting agencies again.

My parents had a close friend from college who had adopted a Peruvian child at the same time they had adopted William, and as they watched that family, they became interested in transracial adoption. They began to ask the agencies if they made different-race placements, and the social workers all responded with some amount of alarm. Each one said that they thought it was better to discourage that type of arrangement, or simply that they didn't sanction transracial adoptions. My mother is enough of a fighter that I imagine the social workers' responses might have made her think about the idea that much more seriously.

Then, in just the two years between William's adoption and 1967, when they would bring me home, there was a radical shift in adoption practices. The fruits of the feminist movement—including greater access to contraceptives and legalized abortion, changing social attitudes, and a rise in the number of unmarried mothers, had all conspired to seriously tip the balance of supply and demand. "Blue ribbon babies" became an even scarcer commodity, while there was a steadily increasing number of unadopted Black children. My parents were now in Massachusetts, and they found a much more liberal system when they went to the Boston agencies. My mother said that transracial adoption was actually an option on the intake forms, and they checked that box. She remembered that the social worker who went over their paperwork asked if she and my father were serious about it. "Are *you* serious?" my mother asked.

My adoption was set in motion.

My mother, ever the history teacher, reminded me that in 1967, the year they brought me home, the courts ruled in *Loving v. Virginia,* deciding that the laws barring interracial marriages—still upheld in sixteen states, including Massachusetts—were unconstitutional. I know that there were fewer than 300 interracial marriages recorded in the census that year, she said.

"I believe transracial adoptions were even illegal in quite a few places through the early 1970s—certainly in many of the southern states." She laughed, remembering one of the things the social worker who handled my adoption had made clear she and my father could not do: relocate to the South. "It didn't matter that Boston was having its own terrible racial conflicts," she remembered. "But it was funny how ordinary it felt to adopt you when it was kind of a great social experiment to other people."

I thought about Jimmy, my cousin. He was adopted in Kentucky in the early 1970s, and he'd been relinquished to the state a few years later. I stopped myself from pointing out to her that his adoption— and the way my aunt and her husband, perhaps our family, gave up on him—added a whole other dimension to what she was saying.

She remembered a caseworker coming for a "home visit" in my first months with them. A For Sale sign had gone up in front of a neighbor's house, and that had alarmed her. The caseworker was sure that all of the many home studies and interviews that the agency had conducted to ensure my placement in a safe, nonracist environment had failed in the end: the neighbors were selling out, and white flight had set in. "I had to laugh," my mother said. "It seemed so ridiculous to me. The people wanted to move. And for Christ's sake, it's only a baby!" It was this kind of flip toward naiveté that always led to our fights.

"You know, for the first six months that you were with us, the adoption was not official. At the end of that period they do a big review, and we all had to go and stand before a judge. The judge took you into her chambers and did whatever it is they do to assess whether you were happy and well-adjusted. As soon as she brought you back into the courtroom, you looked for your father and kind of reached toward him and smiled. The judge watched you and then signed the approval. She said that alone was enough."

I listened to her without speaking. It was funny that we'd never talked about this history. I was happy to be talking to her in a way that opened us up to each other a little more.

I went back to the Studio Museum in Harlem, and I went to places like the Schomburg Center for Research on Black Culture and the National Center of Afro-American Artists in Boston to find information about interior decorators. I talked to people who had orbited the Boston and New York Black arts scenes since the 1950s. I didn't have much information about my birth father to go on, so what I got were some interesting history lessons. A few people told me stories about men they used to know who "sound like that cat." But it was impossible to get any further than someone's promise that they would ask around for me.

Someone gave me a telephone number for a national organization of Black interior designers that was based in Washington, D.C. I talked with the director, but it was clear that it was a new organization, and they were concerned with contracting and network building. The project of history and archiving was on the agenda but it was to be taken up much later.

Then I met a woman I had been watching in SoHo for several years. She wore Fulani-style braids, a thick moustache, heavy kohl lines around her eyes, a neckful of amber and ivory teeth, and one-piece snowsuits all winter. I had gone to visit an old boss one day, and this woman walked into her office. Then I met Camille Billops, an artist who, with her husband, Jim Hatch, ran a well-known gallery and archive called the Hatch-Billops Collection. A few months later, I went to a screening of independent videos and films. One of them was "Finding Christa," Camille's documentary about her reunion with a daughter she had given up for adoption thirty-some years earlier. She had raised Christa for four years and then she made a decision to give her up so that she could pursue her art. The video disturbed me completely. On an intellectual level I felt sympathy for Camille and enjoyed her irreverence toward motherhood, but her insistence that there was nothing wrong with her choices, her daughter's enormous pain, and the uncomfortable, unexamined tensions that kept erupting between the two women were almost unbearable to watch. Still, the story was compelling. The way that she talked about art and her family's bitterness toward her for breaking mythic Black family covenants while they refused to help her after she escaped from her first marriage and was struggling to care for Christa, mixed with ego and complete self-focus to make her repellingly heroic.

In time, I met Camille again, and I talked to her quite a bit about my search. We listened to each other's stories, both respectfully holding back our comments. I really enjoyed her, even though she mostly appalled me. I called her quite a bit as I continued to search through arts communities, and she offered me the names of three of her friends in Boston—artists who had been a part of the scene there for as long as my birth father might have been around.

I called these men and told them that I was doing an article on the history of Black interior designers. Each one gave me an education on Boston artists of my father's generation, but they knew very little about the design scene. One of the men, Napoleon Rocket, and I talked for a long time and hit it off so well that I took a chance and told him that what I was really doing was searching for my father. "Oh, I know what that is about. I have adopted children of my own," he said. He told me that he had been keeping records for his daughters of anything he knew of their birth families. They were both in their early twenties and had never talked about searching, but he decided it would be good to have something when they did ask questions. He promised that he'd make some calls for me, and then he told me that I should try to talk to "old Man Blakely," at Blakely Interiors, a mom-and-pop interior design shop that had been around since at least the early 1960s. He offered to make the first call for me, saying, "You have to be careful with these bloods—they got their wives and families. No telling what you could stir up."

Anytime I found out about a man who might be in my birth father's universe, I would call Mary Steed and asked her if he could be Daddy X. We played a polite guessing game, one where she didn't undermine my vulnerable faith in the process and she was not asked to cross the line. After I spoke with Napoleon Rocket, I called her to ask if there were any Blakelys in my file.

"No, that name doesn't mean anything for you," she said.

A few weeks later, I read an article about Alfre Woodard, an actress I like. In the article, she talked about her seventy-something-year-old father being an interior decorator, and she mentioned her schooling in Boston. These details seemed remarkable; they were as much a lead as anything I had encountered. I called the FMN girls for a war council. Henri insisted that Alfre and I looked a bit alike, with the earnestness she had offered me back in the days of Mattie. I don't look at all like Alfre, but I guess it was not a completely absurd claim in an adoptee's small world of drama. She and Vanessa made projections of my new life in Hollywood, how the reunion would be okay because Alfre is married to a white guy and has adopted children. I was on my way! And please please bring the FMN girls along!

I called Oklahoma directory assistance and got the number for Alfre's daddy right away. When he answered the phone, I told him that I was doing research for an article on Black interior decorators of his generation. We talked for nearly an hour. He told me about the history of Black men in the profession and how many men had come to it through their training as draftsmen. We had a nice conversation, and I hung up convinced, with very little reason, that he was my father.

I called Mary Steed the next morning.

"I know I just came to you with a name," I said, "but can you please just confirm whether my birth father's name is Woodard?"

"Oh, no!" she laughed, not at all unkindly. And then as I listened to her recount my father's narrow particulars, I was able to squeeze out another drop: "You know that your birth father was approximately forty-four years old at the time of your birth, a high school graduate, and that he worked as an interior decorator for some time. He also owned an art gallery here in Boston. It says he had considerable talent in art. It looks like he and your mother were out of contact by the time you were born."

I was thinking about how much time I had wasted not being able to tell the people I had talked to that my father had been a gallery owner, when Mary Steed gave me a reason not to be so mad at her.

She said that she had looked into the question about my getting state assistance with my search. Through some loophole, she now had the authority to try to locate my birth mother and notify her that I wished to make contact. She wouldn't have the same access to my birth father. But we no longer had to wait for my birth mother to initiate a search of her own. She said that she had already gone as far as looking for her in the state records of vital statistics. "I have not been able to find her name in the motor vehicles registry or anywhere else, but I'm also confident that she is not listed in the deaths."

She said that she had found one of my birth mother's sisters, but her phone number was unlisted, and she was not sure she could bypass the restrictions on obtaining it. In the meantime, she would try to reach my birth mother by sending a letter through her sister. "The letter will simply state that you wish to have contact with her. Your birth mother will have the right to refuse contact. If she refuses, we will have to respect her wishes," she said. She explained that my only option then might be to petition the court to force her to respond based on specific questions about her mental health. "And if your birth mother is willing to have contact," Mary Steed said, "either I or another staff member would be willing to act as an intermediary for an exchange of letters or a meeting."

I was almost embarrassed by how my excitement sounded against Mary Steed's usual detached calm. I hung up the phone, forgetting to be mad at her about anything.

1995

In the spring of 1995, I decided to go back to my list of Massachusetts adoption support service organizations. I had waited for more than six months for a reply to Mary Steed's second letter to my birth mother, which had followed the first one by almost as many months. I kept going back to her to ask whether there wasn't another way to try to make contact, or whether she would at least resend the letter more "officially," maybe requiring confirmation that it had actually been received by someone, instead of just dropping it in the mail. But she was insistent: "Presumably, the first letter has gotten into the right hands. And the second letter is just an assurance." She cautioned me to wait and allow time for my birth mother to receive the letter from her sister and go through her own process of thinking about a possibility that she might not have anticipated or that she might, at least initially, reject.

I had tried not to think about what Mary Steed was doing, but after the second letter was sent and the months passed, I became worn out with the waiting and the disappointment. I felt an intense self-loathing creep in. Suddenly, I was aware of how *wrong* I felt. It had always been there—since I was a child—carried in my painful shyness and a bit of defensive arrogance, my difficulty being close to people no matter how easily I made friends, and the slow grinding anger that seemed to always be holding me. It should have been a time of happiness and contentment. *Afrekete,* my first book, had just been published, and I was finishing a book tour. I'd received a big writing grant. I was traveling a lot. I'd quit my job to freelance. I had a great apartment. I was in love. All of my hard work to make a free and comfortable life for myself in New York was beginning to pay off. But even as I tallied these accomplishments, I knew that I was slipping into a crisis of faith. Over the next months, I receded from the people and the activities that had been important to me. I spent a lot of time alone, hiding.

I took myself so deep into my bad feelings that year that I felt I was losing my way. I would be working, or grocery shopping, or riding on the train, and suddenly I would feel like I was boiling. It wasn't so much a sensation of heat, but of something nearing eruption, becoming uncontained. I would manage to stop myself before I took the sharp thing I held in my hands—a pen or keys or a fork—and thrust it into myself. A few times I was sitting at home, and I actually found myself about to push something into my thigh. The first time I felt my hand raise up, I was surprised. The force of the desire scared me. I do not know if I wanted to hurt myself so much as pierce the alternately invading numbness in my body and head. I had always managed to keep my anger at a low grade, simmering in my gut, but now I was struggling all the time with so much unfixed pain. It was exhausting trying to contain it. The anger became more and more abstracted—it became rage at my mother, my landlord, the weather, the subway token seller, or the slow woman in the line in front of me. Every day was a struggle to tame that anger and remind myself that it was misplaced.

TRACE was a support network and advocacy group for adoptees, adoptive families, and birth parents, based in western Massachusetts. It was the organization that everyone I consulted suggested as my next route—and possibly the last—if the letters to my birth mother did not succeed. I had written to TRACE many years before but was disappointed when I received their newsletters. They were steeped in the language of the recovery movement, filled with fluffy articles, sandwiching inspirational poems and adoption-language anagrams. I couldn't imagine TRACE being effective against The System. But I was truly at an end, so I wrote to the office again to request their materials. The message was the same, but better presented, and the formerly watery, purple mimeographed type had changed to xerox, so I put aside some of my resistance.

When I called the TRACE offices, the woman who answered the phone responded cagily to my questions about the process of registering to search. "We can only *assist* you in your efforts; we cannot promise results," she said. She encouraged me to attend their regular support groups, until I explained that I was calling from New York. I asked her just what kind of assistance they gave, and she insisted that I start with sending her a membership fee and even the most incidental details I had about my birth parents. "We'll go from there," she said.

I didn't want to do this. The money she was asking for was hardly anything, but I was gun-shy and skeptical. A year before, I had made payments to two other search organizations, which had disappointed me. One was a new agency, started by a man who had also been a New England Home for Little Wanderers baby. He had found his birth parents through the search engines at whatever firm in whatever profession he worked in, and he worked out an agreement with his boss that allowed him to conduct searches for other people. Mary Steed told me about him, and I thought that the way she was almost insisting that I contact him might be a signal that she was getting ready to finally sell out her social worker's integrity. I called him, and I invested just a little bit of money, but after many months he admitted to me that he no longer had his job.

Family Connect had been my next hope. They were an agency in Boston that had been recommended by someone I met at a conference. After I had a nice conversation with the director, I sent in several hundred dollars as a deposit on my search. I did it simply because of their promise: full results within three months or a full refund. I knew that was an ambitious claim, but it was also a huge assurance after many vaguer promises and so many disappointments. Long past the three month deadline, after my letters and the messages I left with their answering service were ignored, Mary Steed sent me a consumer complaint column from a Boston newspaper with a letter from a man who had invested hundreds of dollars for his daughter's search and who now believed that Family Connect had duped them. He was advised to go to the Boston Consumer Council. I also called the council, and I found out that they had collected a half dozen similar complaints. They traced Family Connect to a Mailboxes, Etc. location and then tracked down a man in his early twenties running the business from his parents' house. A television news reporter pursued the story and caught him on tape belligerently denying the claims.

A few weeks after I talked to the woman at TRACE, I received a check for an essay on adoption that I had written for an anthology. I decided to use the money as gambling funds and sent them my membership fee. I was certain now that if I wanted to find my people, I would have to keep putting my faith in the unregulated, and sometimes unscrupulous, underground.

Fall 1996

In September of 1996, more than four months after I registered with TRACE, Ann Kendry, the founder and director, called me. She said that she felt she had gone as far as she could with my search. She had tried every source, every possible ruse, and she had not been able to turn up anything.

I listened to her and felt the cool of melancholy sweep over my head.

It was fall, a time when inexplicable sadness seemed to take over my body and hold it for months on end. It was the time of year I associated with almost ritualized loss: unwanted departures; distance from home; my conflicts about schooling; the beginning of weather that deepened my isolation, while for my family it began a season of pleasurable outdooring. I was born in April, but I came home with the McKinleys in late September, and for some of my adoptive family, such as my mother's sister, September is the month she still associates with my birth. Fall had become the season when I would travel to Vermont, enticed by the changing leaves, and the pang—part longing, part obligation—that came from not having seen my parents for many months, sometimes since the previous Christmas. Those visits always reopened our disappointments and conflicts with each other. And although I wasn't really conscious of this emotional stringing of events, it seemed as though the impressions of many separations were awakened as the cool weather descended.

I was beginning to feel that I was losing myself to the process of searching. There was always the great rush of hope when I found something that might hold promise. Then over the months of waiting, my hope would dissolve into a dull, persistent ache that turned into melancholy as it became clear that another possibility was foreclosed. It seemed as though searching had become a way of extending that ritualized mourning. Now I was so consumed by the heartache of searching that I felt I was beginning to lose sight of what I was looking for.

Ann Kendry could not tell me what she had done to try to help me, and she could not answer any of my questions. Everything she did depended on anonymity and on a procession of undocumented acts. She told me just before she hung up that she was going to try one last possibility, but that she was not sure that it would turn up anything. She said that she might not be able to get to it for several months, because what she would attempt to do was very sensitive. It was the very last thing she knew to do.

I cannot remember what I did in the balance of those months before I heard from her again. I had given up on Mary Steed's letter writing, on the possibility that she could help me. I tried to push away my fear that my birth mother had decided to ignore us. But I was losing faith in the process, and the only thing that sustains a search is faith if not self-punishment.

The FMN girls seemed to be living in an alternate universe. Henri had found her birth mother the year before. A few days after Henri's first contact with her, she had her birth father's phone number. She was getting to know both of them and their families, including three half sisters and three grandparents. She had even had a few family gatherings with both her large adoptive family and her birth parents, who were seeing each other for the first time since high school. Her relationships with them were often difficult, but she was pleased to have people to struggle with.

Vanessa was beginning a happier reconnection with her birth mother, whom she had seen only once in the five years since they had met. Although they had had some terrible battles over the years, they were making plans to meet again. She had also made progress in reaching her birth father. An administrator at the high school her birth father attended had had some recent contact with him and agreed to help. And someone at her birth father's college alumni association assured her that he had a recent address. He seemed to be just a letter away.

I felt like I had been pinned down by sadness and disappointment. I was increasingly aware of how the years were stacking up while I remained stuck in the unresolved quandary of my past.

I didn't really expect to hear from Ann Kendry again. I'd paid her so little money. I knew people who had paid hundreds of dollars for much less or paid thousands of dollars in retainer fees. It would be very easy for her to slide out of her promise, and I'd have very little to protest.

A few days before Thanksgiving, there was a message from Ann Kendry on my answering machine.

"I am making some progress here and should have some news to share with you. I will be coming home from Boston later in the evening. It will be too late to talk, and then I have a busy morning. Can you call me tomorrow after 4:00 P.M.?"

When I heard her message, I just smiled. *Yes, news.* There was this funny calm creeping into my gut. The tone of her voice lifted my feelings to a certainty that I had not felt in a long time. But within a few hours, my stomach was screeching like a water pump with the pressure of release. I tried to talk myself through the pain and heaving, blaming it on the Korean soul food dinner I'd eaten earlier. When I was younger and I'd felt abandoned or rejected, I could spend the good part of a day doubled up, fighting waves of the same sickness. I knew that I was touching the edges of feelings that usually dwelled in me as a quiet ache, and I turned off the lights and retreated into sleep.

I woke up in that calm I'd felt just after her call, not anxious about waiting or what I would find out. It was the kind of peace that can unsettle one more than the torrent that usually comes in its wake.

Then it was late afternoon, and Ann Kendry was on the phone.

She said that we needed to talk about payment—I would have to send her $165 for what she was about to tell me. She was willing to wait for the money if I could promise to get it to her that week. (I remembered that Henri had to FedEx a certified payment to the man who found her birth mother before he would talk, so I felt especially lucky.)

"Her name is Esther Hope Khan, born February 22, 1943, in Boston, Massachusetts, at 2:55 A.M. Her father was twenty-eight years old and her mother was twenty-five years old—her parents started a little late. They lived in Sharon, Massachusetts, at the time. She had sisters born in 1945 and 1948. There was noise about her having real emotional problems. She was married—she may still be." She explained that she had done some checking to try to find out where Esther Khan was living. She had gone to all of the available records, but there was no record of her marriage, no credit record, no name in the nurses registry. But there also was no death record. She promised to keep checking and call me again.

Then as we said goodbye, she added, "I think that your birth mother's husband is Black, but I don't think that he is your birth father."

I called Mary Steed the second after we hung up and told her what I had learned. She asked me to wait while she went to get my file, and there was caution in her voice when she came back on the line. "The name does seem to match the one in your records."

Her name is Esther Hope Khan. She didn't ask me how I'd learned it. She seemed to be thumbing through the pages. Then the holy file spake: "She was depressed and suicidal and had been hospitalized because of it just before your birth. She had left home just before this and was living with a group of friends, but the living arrangement broke up. She wanted to keep you, but she and your birth father had parted some months before—they had quite a long history. She did not want to be back in her parents' home again. Her father was ill, perhaps manic-depressive. He was described as exhibiting abusive and infantile behavior. All of this preceded her breakdown. She was bright, highly motivated, and attractive, but she seemed to be giving in to what was happening around her." This was the third time my birth mother's mental illness had been underscored. But I was feeling overwhelmed by all of the information I suddenly had and more annoyed by Mary Steed's parceling of my story than worried about what she was saying.

Then, as we said goodbye, she said something that was like a funny congratulations and told me that I should take my time proceeding. She was willing to be an intermediary or a support any time I felt I needed one.

I called the FMN girls, screaming my news. They were cheering just as loud. Through the Thanksgiving weekend we celebrated and kept rehashing the information I had. Henri and I called directory assistance a thousand times, using the Boston and area listings with any possible abbreviation of her name, and even imagined nicknames, but nothing came up.

It didn't really matter. I felt content with what I had—her *name*. *Esther Hope Khan.*

All of a sudden, I realized how much finding my birth mother mattered—as much as finding my Black family. I was like the cartoon character getting whacked with a reality stick. I couldn't tell myself that she was just a route to my birth father anymore.

Now I was starting to imagine her face. I pictured her fat, brown-haired, freckled, someone like the intimidatingly competent Irish charge nurse who had been my supervisor at the nursing home where I'd worked all those years. She could lift a six-foot-tall man whose limbs were paralyzed from a stroke onto a bed pan while she flirted and cracked Irish jokes. And the first time a patient on my shift died and I had to be evaluated while I washed and prepared the body for the mortuary, she had sat next to the bed with her clipboard and sang a little song to take me past my nausea and fear. I didn't realize until then that I had white women in that warehouse of fantasies of Who My Mother Is.

Before I had finished absorbing all this change, the holiday was over, and Ann Kendry called me again. She said that she had been able to get my birth mother's sisters' names: Miriam and Joyce Khan. She also told me that Esther Khan had married a man named Dirk Laakso. "Not a very Black name," she said. "But then you're Catherine McKinley." There was no sign that they had divorced, so after she failed to find a listing for my birth mother, she decided to try him. "I found a Dirk Laakso in Eugene, Oregon, and called there over the Thanksgiving weekend. A young man answered the phone, and I asked for Esther Khan. There was no Esther Khan at that number, and Dirk Laakso was not at home. I tried to get him to give me some hint about a connection to Esther Khan. It was kind of odd—he called someone in the house and asked, 'What was your mother's name again?'" She did not get an answer; he got impatient and asked her why she was calling. But she felt she was getting closer to the end.

December 1996

"Forget waiting. You better just go on and call her. You've waited two weeks for the number." The FMN girls were waiting for me to get back to them.

It was 2:25 P.M. I know the exact time, because I let my class go fifteen minutes early after inflicting a distracted lecture on African women's literature on them, walked up the stairs to my office, and quickly called my girls. Then I followed their command and dialed.

I was sure that she answered. *Hello.* Not unfriendly. But there was something in her voice that I decided sounded noncommittal. I spent several hours after this trying to extrapolate some character, trying to attach a person to this single word. *Hello.* Maybe her phone rarely rang, or it rang but she was apprehensive about answering. It seemed as if she had reached for the receiver asking herself, Should I? but picked it up feeling a little expectant, and a little wary about courting whoever was on the other end. What I read in that hello turned out later to be part of the person I have come to know. Her hello's would instantly move to surprised happiness or tip into a drone of sorrow. You can read its turn in an instant, right in the breath after that same-sounding *Hello.*

I hung up as soon as I heard it, not sure whether I was ready. Then I dialed again and hung up on the second ring.

I called Mary Steed. I wasn't sure why she was the one I called, except that she had strangely become my witness. She stayed on the phone with me with the Boston phone directory on her lap, trying to figure out what part of Cambridge Ashton Terrace was in. "The house might be in North Cambridge—that's the back door of Harvard," Mary Steed said, as if she were revising all optimism. Then she cautioned me that if I caught Esther Khan at home in the middle of the day, it might be a sign of what everyone feared: she might be a mad woman. I thought about that *Hello.* I reminded her that she might still be working as a nurse and that she could work any shift. And how could catching someone at home tell you anything?

When we hung up, I decided to call William, who was newly married and living close to Cambridge at the time. I asked him if he knew where Ashton Terrace was, knowing that he loved a puzzle (his techie instincts had won out over music and theater, and he was designing computer software now), and being a McKinley, he would be loaded with maps.

"I've been looking for my birth mother for the past five years, and I just found her," I blurted out. "Can you try to find the street and maybe drive by and just look at the house? I want to know a little bit more about her before I try to make any moves."

We never asked each other for favors, and this one was really loaded. In fact, we rarely spoke apart from when we met on holidays. And then the differences between us had become so wide that we barely knew how to talk to each other. His surprise registered in his voice, but then he seemed kind of excited. He tried right away to run the address on the locators in his computer.

"You know, I've also done a little checking into my adoption history. Ana and I are thinking about having kids. I just want to make sure that we don't have any big health problems to worry about, but I'm not really interested in contacting anyone. I know that my birth parents were Polish and French, and my birth father was a scientist, I think." He was focused on the map now. I could hear his hands on the keyboard. "There's Ashland here, but I don't see Ashton. I could try something else." Then he paused. "Have you told Mom and Dad about this?" He was becoming uncomfortable. Then someone came into his office and interrupted our call. We said an uncomfortable goodbye. Later, I thought about why I had called him. I knew I was asking for too much from him. I guess I just wanted him to act like my big brother for awhile.

I had seen my parents just after Thanksgiving. We didn't gather for the holiday anymore because it was their biggest weekend for Christmas tree sales, and they stayed at the farm and worked around the clock. In one of the back bedrooms of my grandmother's house, I told them that I had just learned my birth mother's name and that I'd probably soon have information about where to find her. I could see for the first time that they were struggling with what I was doing. It was in their faces, but they didn't seem able to talk about it at all. They just listened. Before the weekend was over, we had some terrible argument about money matters, and we had left my grandmother's house angry at each other. With all the tension between us, I was wondering how I would introduce all that was now on the verge of happening.

That afternoon, I went to my favorite stationers and bought some oxblood-colored writing paper. Then I went home and wrote a letter to Esther Khan that was too precious, and in six or seven little lines as dramatic as the stationary. I thought that a letter was the gentlest approach. I told her that I had her phone number, but I'd let her call or write to me before I used it. I was thinking about her feelings; I couldn't feel any of my own.

What can you say to a birth mother? It's been twenty-eight years, but do you remember me? Are you well? Do you want to know me? Will you be good for me to know? If not, please let me down easy. Let me know Daddy X's name so maybe he can do better.

I wrote what I hoped would make it impossible for her to refuse me. I took the envelope to the mailbox at the top of my street, and then I took a long walk, feeling cold to what I'd just done. I called the FMN girls when I got home and responded stoically to their praise. "Girl, you are really strong." "You didn't talk to her? You're better than me!"

It seemed silly to be in my late twenties, wishing for a mommy, when there was a woman in Vermont who would tell me exactly who my mommy was. Sometimes I would watch the talk shows and envy those women who had stooped to TV therapy, saying to the family that has come looking for them, playing out the theatrics of my dreams: *I don't need you. I had a good childhood. It was better that you gave me up. You have no right to intrude on my life now. Yes, Jenny, adoption records should remain closed!* Sometimes I wished that I was that kind of daughter. The Caller of the Shots. Or someone like William, who would say that he got just what he wanted for a family. Someone who would never be stuck the way I was in a morass of longing.

I fell asleep early and easily, but by morning I was enveloped by an almost predictable pain, the kind that for a long time rose easily with the threat of someone's leave-taking, even when I wanted them to go. I lay in bed in a kind of paralysis between waves of diarrhea, feeling like I might really die this time.

I figured and refigured the days: it took no more than two days for mail to get from New York to Boston, add Sunday, add a day to digest it, a day to respond, two days in the return mail. The soonest I could hear from her would be a week. Or she might call—tomorrow even. I could hear from her that soon.

I moved through the days that followed inside some liminal, self-haunted space.

Ten days later, my letter came back. The address had been crossed out in heavy pen. The envelope was stamped RETURN TO SENDER—ADDRESSEE UNKNOWN.

The bitch sent it back. I was sure of it. She'd been tipped off by

Mary Steed's letters, saw my return address and the deep red envelope, and guessed who sent it. She'd evaded the mail again.

I was so angry and so worn out that I cried for hours.

It was almost Christmas. I called her house several times that evening. Each time a sweet child's voice spoke a perfectly dictated message on the answering machine. Had I dialed the same number as before? I couldn't match that *Hello,* what I imagined now was that woman's dulling loneliness, with the brightness of this child. Each time I heard it, the voice upset the fragile image I had of Esther Khan. I did the math over and over again—my birth mother would be fifty-three years old. What age could the child be? The voice was so androgynous—but maybe it was a little girl?

I remembered Mary Steed saying once, "Perhaps you'll be lucky and find some siblings. Those are usually easier relationships, and you can learn something about your birth parents as parents. Sometimes that is one of the best things you find when you search." I realized that I hadn't thought too much about this suggestion. Maybe she had meant it as a sign. I assumed that my birth father had children. *He was married and unwilling to provide support for your birth mother's baby.* Every fantasy I had of him, even the queer daddy scenarios, put me down in a passel of sisters and brothers and extended family who welcomed me, perhaps in some way expecting "outside" children from their father, an expansive, can't-help-himself-from-loving, family kind of man. This scenario of the "outside child" was so common. I imagined there could be some strong feelings about my showing up, but there would be enough familiarity with that scene that they would make room for me. I had always fantasized about finding Black brothers and sisters who would circle me with a ferocious protection of what was *theirs,* legitimizing my place in the tribe.

With my birth mother, my fantasies always held the two of us at the center. Anyone else who had claims to her stood in an area outside, too far in the distance for me to make out.

In my best imaginings—Anjelica Huston as Grace Paley—my birth mother was a wildly independent woman, a strong and intelligent woman, who had proven herself tougher than her troubles and who, in my estimation of enviable character, knew *just who she was.* She was going to be a Jewish approximation of a Black mother—but only to me. I imagined I'd find her not far from where she and I had broken off. She would have become that fierce woman, but a part of her would have stopped in time, and she would still be mourning her loss of me. I hoped I'd find her living in the endless and numbing longing for our reunion. The voice that answered my first phone call fit these fantasies.

I spoke with both Henri and Vanessa that evening, talking to each of them for stretches of time, then hanging up to call Esther Khan again. We talked about their own first calls to their birth mothers. They were stories I knew perfectly. I'd asked Vanessa to tell me her story again and again. I was trying to understand the failure that came before the end of that first year, after only one meeting, when the relationship was severed by their intense arguments. They seemed to have been battling each other's awesome, competing needs. I listened to Vanessa talk about her birth mother, hoping to discover some method to predict heartbreak, even while I held the possibility of it away.

Henri had sat on my living room floor and called the private investigator in Illinois who had promised her that he would deliver her birth mother's name and a phone number in just a few days if he could do it at all. She'd paid him a deposit, and then asked him to hold any news until after she'd taken her graduate exams. She had resisted calling him for several weeks, and that afternoon, when she had settled her bill and flown to New York to join her husband, she'd called to get the information. I sat with her, overwhelmed by my jealousy and voyeurism. When she called her birth mother, I sat scribbling as she repeated parts of what her birth mother was saying and passed her notes so she would not forget to ask any vital thing. Henri had the good luck of finding two extended families who embraced her. She and Vanessa represented two poles in what might happen with me and Esther Khan. I was glad to have those navigation points. At the same time, I was holding on to the idea that I was going to have an experience that would perfect on theirs.

As I talked with Henri and Vanessa, I went over and over the details I had on Esther Khan. We spun around new jokes and fantasies, feeling a druglike giddiness. As soon as those were laid out, we quickly came up with even more fearful, ironic possibilities. We went at Esther Khan the same way Vanessa and I would take her birth father from W.E.B. DuBois reborn as a 1990s Muppet Master and filmmaker—a spin on one set of facts—to Pimp Daddy Sly, the man held in the memory of her birth mother's family. In two minutes of conversation, we could make a full turn and settle resolutely on the Pimp Daddy. That kind of claim kept him more comfortably at a distance, even as Vanessa was catapulting toward him.

We carried on like this until after 10:00 P.M., when I was afraid it was getting too late to continue calling. The thought of having to wait another night was killing me, so I decided to dial one last time.

The same woman answered, this time in a laughter-filled voice that revised my idea of her again.

"Good evening. May I speak with Esther Khan?"

"This is Estie Khan." *Estie.* I liked this name and the deep warmth of her voice.

I was suddenly choking as I tried to speak just the way the adoption professionals advise—with clarity, immediate detail. "My name is Catherine McKinley. I was born April 25, 1967. I am calling—"

"When did you say you were born?"

We began just like that. I had dialed her number bolstered by my riffing with Vanessa, anticipating that I might find a woman mean enough to return my letters, that our conversation could become a battle. But we were both laughing a little bit now, and there was this ache in both of our voices. I had to cover the mouthpiece of my phone for a minute because this sound came out of my throat that I had never heard before, and I was afraid I was going to start sobbing. But then there was this strange control in my body again.

"I called earlier, and I wasn't sure I should call again this late," I said.

"Oh, we just came home from the Cape. We have this silly time-share, and I was sick last summer, so we tried to arrange a trade, and we got stuck going there in November—Go! Right now! Get in the tub!" There was no power in her voice. It was struggling for control. "That's Sarah. She's nine," she said.

Sarah. My stomach folded like it does when you clear a sharp, blind turn.

I felt a little breathless and I stammered, "I actually wrote you a letter—about ten days ago. I didn't want to call right away, but the letter was returned. The address I have is 4 Ashton Terrace. I thought a letter might be better—"

"Oh, we live on *Ashland*. Did you call before? My mother called me—I guess it was a couple of weeks ago—and said that a woman had called her and asked for my number. They said they were one of my former patients—I'm a psychiatric nurse." She was spinning my imaginings again. "I thought that it was odd that someone would call there. There are easier ways to find me—through the hospital. And then someone called here a day or two later and hung up when I answered. I had this funny feeling, you know, it's like you're always kind of waiting for this call—"

I imagined Ann Kendry had called her mother. I told her about working with Ann Kendry, about the letters Mary Steed had sent more than a year ago, how we had not been able to find her in any public records, and about chasing Dirk Laakso. Estie said that she had always been right there in Boston, and she drove and had more credit cards and memberships and licenses than anyone. "I was never married to anyone called Dirk Laakso," she said, laughing.

"The letters must have gone to Joyce—my other sister lives in North Carolina." She was quiet for a moment. "I'm not surprised that she didn't forward them to me. I don't think she even looks at her mail. She's kind of a compulsive shopper; she's always in some kind of financial or legal trouble. We aren't close—we barely talk. My sister is so damn self-centered that if she saw the letter, she would never imagine it could be anything important." She seemed to be adding things up. "And then I wonder if she would know about you at all. She was pretty young when I was pregnant, and my mother definitely tried to keep it a secret."

I was being relieved of my fears by the moment. And then I suddenly felt defensive of Estie—against my long-festering anger, my suspicions that she was ignoring the letters and that she was wicked enough to even return the one I sent her.

I thought about Ann Kendry and Mary Steed. They had both helped pull off my personal coup. And they had done it in spite of the way they seemed similarly inept—raising my hopes and then dashing them as they parceled out details and then backtracked, sometimes revising their claims, never keeping details together so that I had to constantly remind them of information they had previously revealed to me. I was always worried that they would miss the big breakthrough if it came. I had worried for such a long time about Mary Steed's unwillingness to pursue leads as hard as she could and then about Ann Kendry's clandestine approach to the search. I had ridden the loopholes for *five years,* and now I was finally free to let myself feel that finding Estie had come at some unnecessarily painful cost.

I was crying—tears were running out of me from exhaustion, while Estie told me that she worked as one of the directors of psychiatric nursing in a crisis unit at Massachusetts General Hospital. She'd landed in the brain aneurysm ward after years in the county hospital attending to suicidal patients and then earning a post-graduate degree.

I told her that I was a writer and that I taught creative writing. "Maybe we can send each other our work!" she said. "I'm also published—in a few medical journals."

She told me she was married. "Well, we're not really married, but we've been together for twenty-three years."

Malcolm McKinley McFarland. "That's Sarah's father. Isn't it funny that you are both McKinleys? Mac's mother was a McKinley—from West Virginia. Maybe you're related!" she said. "You're like

Sarah—Black with one of those damn Irish names! But she's got it worse—she's Sarah McKinley Khan-McFarland."

"Did you name me Sarah?" My heart was starting to ache.

"Yes, that was your name, too," she said quietly.

"Why Sarah?" I asked.

"Sarah was my therapist—Sarah Arnold. She helped me through the pregnancy and after the adoption. She died a few years ago."

She became silent, and then I thought I heard her crying. "I wish that she was here now so she could tell me what to do," she said. We both sat in choking silence for some time.

"I guess you're interested in your father. His name is Al Green. Not the singer! Not the singer!" she said.

"Really? Not the singer? Damn!"

"No, I wasn't the white girl with the band." She was laughing—a kind of hard, outlaw laughter. She is a funny woman, I thought.

"Your father is Cape Verdean. His real name is Alfredo Verdene. I guess that's Al Green in Portuguese! He's a crazy artist. Very good looking. He wears this little ponytail. Do you have dimples?"

I smiled just to feel where my dimples press in and stretched the phone cord to the bathroom mirror.

"Are you artistic? Well, you're a writer. Sarah likes to write, too, and she draws . . ."

"Your father has four kids—two sons, two daughters—maybe one was a stepdaughter. We were together for about six years, but he was married. I met him when I was in high school. He was a lot older—like twenty years? He was doing design work in a friend's parents' house, and I went to her house one day, and he was just standing there on his ladder looking down at me. He was so good-looking, very charming. It was hard for anyone not to like him. He knew everyone. He was very hip—he moved in hip circles.

Al Green was happily conforming to my fantasies.

"I guess dating him was sort of a rebellious thing to do, too. My father *hated* Black people."

She told me she was looking for an antidote and an escape from her family. "I ran straight toward everything that they couldn't stand."

"Are you still in touch with him?"

"He still calls me at least once a year—usually in the spring, around his birthday, or on holidays. He might even call soon with Christmas so close. He would be happy to know you," she said.

I felt so happy and so hopeful, and the feelings were etching a way through my body.

I told her about my family, about Attleboro and how I had grown up.

"I'm surprised! The social workers told me that you had gone to a Jewish family. A family with a son. I always imagined you as a Jew. Sarah's taking Hebrew lessons now. I think of you learning Hebrew. It's funny, I can never picture you more than seven or eight years old, but maybe that's because Sarah is just nine."

I started to feel resentful, as Sarah kept resonating in her thoughts. But I was also feeling this strange pleasure—the pleasure you can sometimes take in your small hatred of something. My rival was already kicking up a lot of feeling.

"I had a hysterectomy just two weeks ago, and I have been feeling awful. I wasn't really even ready to go to the Cape, but we had to take this time-share ... It's funny, I have been thinking a lot about you lately, especially after the surgery. It felt like the same kind of loss in a way."

The intimacy of what she was saying made me uncomfortable, but I needed to hear it; it was the affirmation that your birth parent *grieved* for you that adoptees who search always seek.

But before she could say anything more, Sarah tore into the room. Our conversation became awkward, and I knew that it was ending. I heard Sarah asking who was on the phone and whether she could stay home from school the next day. I realized that I was relieved by the interruption and the excuse to say goodnight. The conversation was finally overwhelming me.

"We're leaving to go to Jamaica the day after tomorrow. We'll be there until Sarah's school reopens. We have a house near Port Maria, and Mac stays there most of the year, so Sarah and I go down there whenever we can."

Estie was taking down my address and phone number and trying to handle Sarah, who was whining now with her mouth close to the phone. We didn't make any promises to talk again as we hung up. We just said goodnight in a kind of terrible, groping way.

I called Henri. It was close to midnight, and I felt exhausted, but I told her what I had learned, and then I listened as she riffed on all the ironies: the two Sarahs; Sarah and I both being McKinleys and Black and Jewish; Estie being a psychiatric nurse and not a patient; her having a house in Jamaica and my living there as a student at the University of the West Indies—that had been in the height of the Mattie years, when I had revised myself and made her my Jamaican mumma.

The next day I got a message from Estie. She called in the late morning, and it struck me right away that she had waited until I would have left home for work. I understood her need to avoid my picking up the phone, because I sat on my bed and listened to her voice run through the answering machine, wanting to hear from her but not wanting to respond.

"Actually, your father looks more like Chuck Berry. That big head, dimples. Pretty smile," she said, as I laughed with her.

1997

1997 was *extra*, as Jamaicans would say.

This was the beginning of days, too many to count, when I felt immense joy, a euphoria so heady, so boundless that it startled me. "*Let's stay together . . .*" The lyrics to every Al Green song I knew rang in my head. This new feeling was taking me so far from my crawl— the months when I traveled an arc of sorrow that gripped me every morning and seemed to intensify through the day, ending in numbed exhaustion. I felt all my fear, the crippling self-doubt retreat. I would wake up feeling so much hope and marvel at the feeling, testing its height, whether it would recede. Can I feel this good? Better even?

Then my feelings would just flip. For days I jumped when the phone rang, hoping it would be Estie.

She had left me her phone number in Jamaica when she called me that day after we first talked. She said that she thought it would be difficult to get an outgoing line from where they were in the countryside, but she would try, and so she hoped I wouldn't mind also trying her. I called her around New Year's, and we had a short, friendly conversation before the line was eaten up by static. I expected she would be home in Boston before the middle of the month. Now it was getting close to February, and it seemed that we were at some kind of standstill. Neither one of us was making a move to call. I felt like I had been pulled into the agony of something like teenage dating games: I kissed you; now you need to be the one to call and call and call again so that I know you are really mine. Now my stomach was grinding itself up with waiting and doubt.

One evening, walking home through the dark streets in my neighborhood in Brooklyn, I felt dropped inside some little girl's rage. I had this container—like a big lunchbox—that a Senegalese friend had made from recycled Nestlé baby formula cans. It was very fashionable, and I used to like to carry it. I caught myself scraping it across the length of brownstone fences, kicking violently at the patches of snow and ice on the sidewalk, at the tip of a terrible, destructive feeling.

My friend Camille Billops had warned me. She had seen that little girl rage in her own daughter, Christa, and tried to capture it in her film. When I told her I was near the end of my search for my birth mother, she had said, "Get ready. You are going to feel anger that you never thought you could touch." She said it would be a rage that could disfigure me and threaten every attachment I had if I did not take care of it. I was kind of attracted to what she said, but I thought it was a little melodramatic. Then I began to wonder if that anger had already disfigured me.

I felt myself beginning to court all of those feelings.

Can I be this angry? Angrier even?

One day in late January, I got a call from a woman named Luck, my neighbor in Park Slope, and Estie's cousin.

We talked for a while, and I enjoyed her somewhat quirky warmth, her excitement that would fold into a curious inscrutableness, as if she wanted to introduce some reasoned boundaries. She reminded me a little of Mary Steed. I was happy that another move had been made from Estie's side. But as Luck and I talked, I started to feel uncomfortable. Estie had asked her to call me. It felt like she had been sent to "check me out" and almost caution me.

Luck told me a careful story about Estie: As a young woman Estie Khan was "a toughie"—she smoked and cursed and was rebellious. She was raised in a middle-class family, but Leo Khan, Estie's father, squandered his money and felt that spending on three daughters was not a wise investment. The family was not particularly religious, but Estie and her sisters had been raised by parents who underscored that *other people* were not the same as Jews, and they should be kept at a distance. Estie's mother, Toby Khan, was "unable to give much of herself to her children." Her husband's needs always got in the way. "Leo Khan was fine to the naked eye, but he was actually a very ill, very violent man," she explained.

Luck told me that her mother had been like a mother to Estie, but she had probably never realized how much trouble Estie was in. Her mother had tried to help Estie when Toby wouldn't. She had stepped in when Estie was pregnant, and it had been a secret to most of the family. Luck's father was Leo's brother. He had been the one to recognize Estie's talents, and he had supported her nursing educa-tion, which had been Estie's way of keeping herself going. The rest of what Estie had she had given to herself. "She was always a big reader, and she fed her really great intelligence on her own. Then she kind of went out and had a lot of relationships outside her parents' world."

"Estie is my heroine of the modern world," Luck said. "She pulled her life together in her twenties after years and years of emotional ill-ness. We all thought she would not make it." She had gone back to school and done very well, and now she worked at the top of her profession. "She seems to pull her talents from everything she knew from her own history of depression. She is very warm and funny, high functioning. But she is vulnerable, too—she can be quite fragile actually. She is not really an easygoing person; she can feel overburdened very quickly."

"Estie waited for a long time to have a baby. She was already past forty, I think. Sarah's father is a nice man, and the two of them are very close. He's quite a bit older than Estie, and he is slowed down by heart trouble. I don't think he has Estie's education or her professional aspirations."

Then she seemed to hesitate. I wanted to ask her what she really meant to tell me.

"Estie has not told Sarah about you, and I think it will be difficult for her to do—it will take a bit of time."

I got out something about not having any intentions of intruding on their lives or doing anything to rush or hurt anyone. Especially a child.

I was beginning to feel that I was a dangerous thing. I was Estie Khan's given-up child. Someone to be slowly checked out. Luck was the little bird sent down into the mine.

I liked that feeling of being dangerous to her. I felt dangerous.

"My husband and I had brunch at a place in the Slope last Sunday. There was a bi-racial woman sitting near us, and I thought she looked a bit like Estie—a bit like I imagine you. You weren't in a restaurant last Sunday, were you?"

That woman wasn't me.

"Well, we'd like to meet you. And we're in the same neighborhood! Hard to imagine!" She invited me to come to brunch the following Saturday. And then she was rushing off the phone with this sudden officiousness, reminding me that she was at work, as if I had called her and was asking a lot of her on company time.

I knew that I would go to have brunch with her. In a way it felt like my ticket to Estie. I wondered what Estie was feeling that made her ask Luck to step in. I knew it couldn't be just Sarah. I was grateful for the little bit of history Luck had told me. I had wanted to ask a hundred questions. I was becoming more curious about Estie's emotional history. Before it had seemed too mysterious and abstract. But I also felt a bit offended by Luck's approach and silly for returning her strange message to me with so much warmth. In the moment, I had been afraid of estranging her, and so I had answered all of her questions about my schooling and my work and family like I was a beauty contestant. But why did she think she had the right to come to me like this and at the same time insist on some kind of protection for Estie and, in a way, for herself?

That weekend I had tea with Luck and her husband, Abe, in their apartment on Prospect Park. As Luck served us, I realized that part of what had offended me was more just who she was—a very thin, petite, rather nervous woman who seemed to overanalyze everything, even mundane questions like what to serve tea.

As soon as she and her husband saw me they got excited about how much I looked like Sarah. They stared at my face for a while, quite intensely, and I swallowed hard to keep my eyes from tearing. I wasn't sure whether it was the reference to Sarah, or the realization of the intimate connections we were making, or my old discomfort of being in someone's scrutinizing gaze. Luck eventually stood back from me and pronounced, "But, Abe, you really see Estie—her nose and that oval face."

I pulled out my best WASP manners, aware that I was trying to make them comfortable with me. They asked me a lot of questions about my family and my childhood and schooling as we had tea and kosher brunch, and they traded my answers with stories about their own daughter, who was five years younger than I was, and general stories about the Khans that floated over me. Then Luck pulled out her photo albums, and I sat with them looking at images I found hard to take in. Most were of distant relations. But I didn't really feel anything even when I saw photos of Toby and Leo Khan. When we got to Luck's one photograph of Sarah, I saw a tiny brown girl in a group of relatives who was too far from the camera to make out clearly. There was only one shot of Estie, on a lounge chair in someone's backyard wearing shorts, with one leg crossed over the other so that it looked like it hung oddly in the air. Her face was partly hidden by the angle of the camera, but I could see a sliver of her face and one side of a big, brown Jewfro. The photo looked like it was from the 1960s, and I guessed that she would have been in her early twenties. Her leg was definitely mine—the same calf, same ankle, which was kind of nice to see, but I couldn't discern anything more of her.

I flipped through more albums, listening to Luck and Abe's stories, smiling and nodding, but I still couldn't register the images. I was suddenly feeling exhausted. And I noticed Luck beginning to shift a little nervously.

"I'm going to have to retire now and work for awhile," she said, with that same regimented manner that had hurt my feelings on the telephone. But this time I was ready to leave. My posture of sweetness and compliance, the way I felt exposed while they sat in their comfortable distance from Estie and me, had worn me out.

A few days after our meeting, I came home from school and found a card from Estie. It was my first sign that she was real and that I had found her—the first thing I could hold in my hand. It was a quick, friendly note. She wrote in funny, elliptical phrases about feeling surprised still, and happy. She wrote in near calligraphy, using two different pens. I tried to see if there was any similarity in our handwriting, but it could only be in the same painful preciseness I've tried to lose since first grade. At the bottom of the card she had written her two work numbers and her hospital page.

I called her at one of the numbers the next morning. I called very early, around 7:00 A.M., just trying it out really, and not expecting her to be there. But she answered the phone and seemed happy to hear from me. She said that she liked to go to work early, as soon as she dropped Sarah off at school. Her office was her favorite hideout; the early morning was her favorite time of the day. She liked to sit there and read—there was lots of sunlight, and she didn't have to be a nurse or a mother for a little while. "I usually don't answer the phone this early. I get angry when someone interrupts me. I have at least an hour before the person I share the office with arrives—but I was kind of hoping it might be you," she said.

Then she invited me in. We began to talk in that slice of morning nearly every day.

For the first two months, we sent each other a flurry of mail, trying to express some closeness, some feeling. It was too difficult for me to talk outright—in a letter or in person—about what I was feeling then. Instead I sent her copies of stories I'd written, beautiful cards, images I liked, and photos—a tiny string of them, trying to patch together a mini-narrative of 1967, high school, college, up to the FMN girls "mulatta" cult shots.

She sent me her medical writings—articles on the care of brain aneurysm patients and "The Art of Setting Limits" for nursing professionals, a story of exile from Russia just published in a local leftie newspaper by "our" Aunt Rose, a ninety-five-year-old socialist (and a rabid racist, Estie added) who lived near her in Boston. Then there were books. Estie went to hear an author we both liked read one night in Cambridge and sent me her new book "to read first." We started a tradition in those two months, going to readings and bookstores in our two cities and passing books between us.

Estie sent me notes—for a while I got one nearly every day. I'd come home to envelopes addressed to me in her calligraphylike writing. They had deliberate-feeling messages, broken up and written in different corners of the page, the thoughts not always cohering. Her words would seem to offer admissions, but I never knew what she was telling me: *I dreamt that everything I own was up for sale in a giant stoop sale in Brooklyn.* Then bits of incidental news, about work, about Sarah. Then in another corner, before she signed off, she might add another suggestion of her feelings: *I saw the doctor that delivered you today in the corridor here at work. He is now a big shot M.G.H. Chief of Service and a Harvard professor. Frederick D. Firgoletti, M.D.* These messages were mysterious, sometimes a bit alarming, and precious, too, because she was knitting together tiny bits of my history. As Zora Neale Hurston complimented a friend in a letter I once read in a library archive, Estie's letters were "the best things in stamps" for me.

In those first months, the phone calls, the exchanges with Estie, felt like the acts of a love affair. I have heard other adoptees say this. I started to live for our morning calls. They set the quality of each day, replacing the anxious feelings, the melancholy. I was surprised by how this woman, who I'd long believed was secondary in my desires, took hold of my heart. Our relationship became so devoted, and the feeling of love I had was so natural and powerful. I was surprised by it; I wondered if it was proof of the terrible way we'd been cheated of each other, or if the expectation of love had defined the province of all that feeling.

But if my relationship with Estie was like a love affair, then I'd have to say it was like loving a married person in out-of-town hotel rooms. There was all of the pleasure and contentment of finding an idea of love, the heady absorption, but there were so many things kept hidden. We mostly talked when she was at work; it was understood that it would take some time to figure out how Sarah was going to fit into our relationship. I wasn't sure whether she'd told Mac. We never let our families enter; we stayed intensely focused on who we were to each other in that moment. This was easier for me than for Estie. I was not the one who was "married." I wasn't keeping secrets. (All of my family knew about Estie now and spared me the burden of their feelings.) And being the lover who began to want more, I started to feel angry and impatient.

Estie had my photos. She had picked one that she loved, a school picture from fourth grade, which she kept with her. She told me that she liked to take it out and look at it while we talked. And she kept remarking about how much I looked like Sarah. I used to like hearing that. It might have made someone else feel funny or angry or jealous. It made me feel so satisfied—to look like another human being, to look like my mother's child. I begged Estie to send me photos, but nothing came—for weeks, for more than a month. She was no longer being cautious or self-absorbed. She didn't just want to keep me sacred and *hers* in that hotel room. She was holding me off.

I wanted to send out birth announcements. I felt that I needed to re-announce myself. I imagined real cards, making everything very plain: the McKinleys, the Khans, the Greens/Verdenes. The WASPs, the Jews, the Black Jews, the Cape Verdeans. I wanted to share my good news and not exhaust myself with the retelling. Wasn't this a major life passage, as significant as a death or new baby, or any kind of con-ferring? It felt odd not to have any formal way to recognize it. I wanted to wave a bit of my new sense of self in the world, and I wanted to have everyone who was dear or not dear to me reorder their sense of who I was. I had hidden such huge parts of myself and told so many lies to so many people. I wanted to come clean and put everyone on the same page, with the full story. That way I could absolve myself with some humor (I would make it sweet and funny) and disarm those who might otherwise react sanctimoniously, or pre-tend that they'd never told lies about themselves.

I decided that as soon as I got to Al Green this was exactly what I would do.

March 1997

"I can't wait to see you. I want to touch your skin. Just smell you." She said it so quietly, in the pause after some casual thought passed between us. I wondered if she'd really spoken, but her words had shot under my skin. I nearly dropped the phone tearing at the back of my thigh, feeling a sudden stinging.

She was talking now about buying a size 22 black dress for Miss Birdie, her neighbor in Jamaica, to take with her on her next trip. "And a black bra; she said it has to have lace. Where in all of Boston am I going to find a bra to fit Miss Birdie? Lesroy wants a million CDs, and Everton wants sneakers, and Teeny wants all kinds of makeup and stuff like Crest toothpaste with peroxide and extra whitening—I don't even buy our family toothpaste with all that mess; I get whatever is on sale..."

My skin felt like it was blazing. I looked at my leg in the mirror, but there was no sign of anything. I am *too* stressed out, I thought. What is happening to me?

But there it was again: "You must have beautiful skin. I remember touching your little hands."

I was choking a little. "I am not that baby anymore," I tried to joke with her. "I am a funky, grown-ass woman. No amount of baby powder can change that."

We both laughed a little uncomfortably. I could feel her retreating, and I wanted to take back what I'd said, but I found myself making excuses, scrambling to hang up the line.

I went to run a bath, to try to relax. Those first few months, I found myself reaching for kind of punishing comforts each time Estie and I talked. When we ended our calls, I would put myself through these rituals that extended the mix of pleasure and the excruciating feelings of being close to her. I knelt in the tub enjoying the shock of the cold enamel on my skin. Then I opened the hot water tap and felt the cold come quickly off. The balls of my feet, my kneecaps, my hands and wrists—all bracing me—turned puffy and red from the scald of the water, but I kept myself from flinching. I began to feel dizzy against the punch of heat and the wall of steam that rose out of the tap.

I want to feel your skin. Her voice filled my head, and I felt myself getting angry. I thought about Camille's warning. Attachments. Disfiguring anger. But these are not words for Estie to say to me. They are so intimate, maternal. They are not words my mother, the one who mothered me, would have ever used. I was frightened by how her words ignored who we really were to one another. I was afraid that one of us would be pushed by them over some line protecting us from our selves.

I tried to imagine my mother, the one who raised me, talking to me like this. I couldn't remember our sharing the kind of intimacy I see between some mothers and their children—the physical ease and quick affection I sometimes feel envious of. I only remember my endless reaching and her irritation, her pushing me away, or my spiteful shrinking from her. But when I look at old photos of us together, or take myself way back in time, before so many difficult feelings erupted between us, I realize that of course we'd acted like those other mothers and their children. I remember when I do not make myself forget. For a long time, it was so hard for me to reach back into my memories of when we were *family,* back to the time before I felt that my *survival,* my ability to carve out a life on my own terms, was dependent on forgetting who we were to one another.

My mother and I had rituals that encompassed all the tenderness and all of the conflicts of our affections. I guess it is part of every Black girl's story: hair grooming.

My mother is a woman who has not been inside a beauty parlor or barber shop in more than thirty years. In the early years of marriage, she gave up cigarettes and red lipstick, her only fashion staple, and she gave up on her hair. She has hair that is very fine and was then very black, that she grew long enough to sit on. It seems like an odd vanity for someone like my mother to grow her hair that long, but in a way it was a release from vanity itself. Every morning she combs out her hair and tucks and folds it into a small envelope-like bun. It looks just like that—an envelope—and when you look at her for the first time, you think she wears it cut short and parted simply at the side of her head. It's economical; she doesn't spend on anything more than some hairpins. In the end, she looks androgynous, which she doesn't mind at all.

My head was not such an easy case, especially back in those days when it was only me and white people, and I was on the other side of "good hair" (my hair was nappy) than the one I am on now (my hair is curly). I wore my hair in afro-puffs for awhile, but afro-puffs had their demands; the least were daily combings. And afro-puffs did not go over well on camping trips or at Willet's Ballet School, where tiny, neat buns were required. Even with the help of one of our neighbors who knew a lot about hair styling, my hair could not be worked into a proper-enough bun, so my mother had to master braids. Braids were a boon. They stayed neat for at least a week, and they could be pinned up into a crown for dance. Into the second week, I could add some barrettes and hold them down for a few more days. Then every other Sunday we'd face the battle royale.

Until I was eleven and we finally opted for a short afro, I would sit shirtless in the purple Toughskin jeans that I always reserved for weekends and press my back against the cool of the toilet tank while I unbraided my hair and ran the bath. Then I would inch down in the tub, watching my hair slowly became engorged with water, restoring kink to each long, flattened section. I would lie there and dream until I heard my mother's feet on the landing at the top of the stairs. Then she would be kneeling at the edge of the tub with a plastic cup for rinsing and maybe a glass of sherry. She would roll up the sleeves of her shirt and sit back on her Adidas.

I loved the scratch of her nails on my scalp and the soothing stream of rinse water as it cut trails in my hair. When I got out of the tub, I was always amazed at the greenish Prell lather mixing into the dirt that had come off of my head. Afterward, we would go downstairs to my parents' bedroom, and I would sit between her knees. She'd rub in No More Tears conditioner, and then I'd submit myself to the pain of her fine-tooth comb ripping through the knottiness of my hair. I would give into it and bawl, adding a measure for any other injustices that I felt I'd been subjected to.

Finally, the gentle dressing would begin—the oiling, the pleasant tug of her hands as they braided it, slipped and unbraided it, and began weaving again. It seemed like all of my feelings lived in my hair. I imagined that this was a process of attending to and exorcising a fracas—taming down that life in my head into more manageable order before I went out for another two-week term. My mother became the orchestrator, taking me through a tour of emotions that I could not otherwise express. I had her undivided attention; I was under her care. She was helping me to find a grip somehow. At the end of it all, with my head aching from crying as much as from her comb, she would hold me in her arms with a love that made the whole affair worthwhile. Then I'd pick up the balls of hair that had come off of me, take them upstairs to my bed, and save them in a corner of my pillow case to make afro wigs for my dolls.

But before long, my rage grew so large that it could no longer be assuaged by my mother's attention. I started to draw baths that were as hot as my body could bear, and I would lie there waiting for her as the water cooled with a washcloth lying diamond-shaped across me so that its corners covered my chest and the wedge of my thighs. My body was changing; ten is too early, people were saying. When I compared myself with my mother, or the girls at ballet, or in the gym locker room, I was disturbed by the purple brownness of my nipples, unlike their pinkness, and the kinky darkness of my body hair. I don't remember not liking the color or the way those parts of myself looked, but our differences embarrassed me. And when I saw my mother getting dressed, or got close to her body or the clothes she had worn, or saw her hair in the bristles of her hairbrush, I started to feel that I hated her—her *skin* even, the smell of her, for being so different from my own. I felt humiliated by all of the trouble it took to take care of my appearance, by the way it made me feel indebted—like a special-needs case, and by having new breasts when I still wore two baby girl's braids. And then something about the pleasure I had felt before, alongside the struggle, embarrassed me.

My mother seemed to be more distracted from her work, more irritated at having to do it. It seemed like she was saying that bathing a pubescent child was more than she had signed on for.

The whole process started to hurt more than ever. I began to walk out on her hugs and go to bed early, crying until the tears and the dampness of my braids soaked my pillow and sleep took over. In the morning I would stay in bed and listen to her go out to walk the dog and then go to the chicken shed. I would wait for her to shower and pretend to sleep through her goodbyes, until I heard the squeal of the old Volvo turning into the street. Then I would go downstairs and look for the tiny speckled egg from her favorite little Rock Island hen, still stuck with droppings and spiked with clinging feathers, that she would leave for me next to the frying pan as a peace offering.

By the time we traveled to Scotland, we had agreed to have my hair cut into a short afro.

Before Estie's comment about my skin, she had told me that she thought she was ready to meet me. We had spent a lot of time talking, indulging in that long stretch of almost daily calls, but it couldn't quite bridge our distance from one another or the feeling that our connection was distorted, rather unreal.

"I think I'd like to meet you. I just cannot get myself ready somehow," she'd said a few weeks earlier, when I'd finally allowed myself some insistence about arranging a visit. Now I was realizing that even as I had been pushing for it, I was not really sure that I was ready to meet her. The time we'd spent on the phone now seemed like no time at all, though earlier it had felt like forever. In some way, I was counting on her to hold the line of hesitancy.

We had talked about logistics for several weeks; we debated whether I should come to Boston or whether she should come to New York. This journey across two states had suddenly become so complicated. We talked about Providence and New Haven as neutral places and a kind of compromise, but we could never settle on anything. Part of the indecisiveness was my fault: I was waiting for her to take the initiative, to take the risk and come to me. As the weeks went by, I started to realize that she wasn't going to do it. Even if it meant not meeting me for many, many months, she was going to wait for me to come. So when she said that she was going to make a reservation for me on the New York–Boston air shuttle, I told her to see what was available the following Wednesday.

I was angry with her for playing that kind of hand. But I was going to meet my birth mother.

I lay in the bathtub trying to imagine what it would be like to finally meet. I could not fix my thoughts, and I soaked and soaked in some blank space until the bathwater became cold.

I came out of the narrow passage that led into the terminal and turned into a phalanx of velvet ropes separating the passengers from the small crowd waiting in the vestibule. I was grateful for the time I would have to adjust my eyes to the blur of faces. But I felt caged, wending my way through the unnecessary maze. I felt uncomfortably on display—somehow at a disadvantage. I started to panic—maybe my unmistakableness would betray me. I was the only Black woman on the flight, one of the last to disembark. Estie could not confuse me with anyone else. She might see me and decide to abandon this meeting, look past me as if she were there for somebody else and then slip away. If she had come at all.

But as soon as I could see clearly, a woman's eyes caught and held mine. I walked toward her, knocking my hip into the rope so that the poles teetered, not letting go of her with my eyes.

She didn't look like the woman in the photograph she'd eventually sent me; she was now a little heavier, with somewhat straightened, longish gray hair. But I could not mistake her; there was my mouth quivering on her face in an awe-filled smile. In the photograph, her hair was light brown, in the same curly Jewfro as the photo I'd seen at Luck's house. She was freckled and tan, and some of my friends— maybe a little uncomfortable with the racial narrative my search was revealing—had joked that she was really a Black woman. (*She's just light-skinned!*) The photo had made me feel sad. In it, she was standing pressed girlishly against Mac, whose shirt opened on a smooth brown chest, puckered slightly with age. He was standing cocksure, hand on hip, his other arm not quite holding her. The Jamaican night sky was surrounding them, and she was pushing her cheek up toward his mouth. You could feel a teeth-kissing of impatience pressing through his lips. She had cut into the photo with scissors in a line that took most of her body out of the picture, while it left him intact. I remember doing that with photos in junior high school—cutting out my body. It was such an odd, teenage act of shame. Had she done it for me?

I remembered then that Luck had said that Estie's father had always made fun of how she looked. Estie was too fat. Estie, the dark child, the most Semitic-looking in the family, was not beautiful. Estie was saved only by some minor grace: she was smart. Light-haired, paper-thin Miriam was the pretty one. And thank God that Joyce was practical.

The picture was of someone so different from the woman I was meeting on the phone. She didn't seem like any fool for Mac, and she was smart and much more confident and able to laugh at herself. In the part of her left intact in the photo, I saw the arch of my jaw, the same oval face, the flat tip of my nose—as if someone had rested a fingertip there too long, and I felt the surge of something moving into place.

Estie had sent me photos of Sarah sooner than her own. It was as if she were offering her up to me as the only good thing she had. In the photos I saw a beautiful little girl, fat-bellied, darker than I am, with thick, reddish, nappier hair, always in some kind of rambunctious motion. She was chunkier and shorter than I had been at her age. But our chin and eyes and cheekbones and smile were almost identical. I fell in love with Sarah right away. It is really rather inexplicable. It's a rare experience—seeing yourself reflected in another person for the first time when you are twenty-something, thirty-something, sixty. Perhaps it's something akin to the clichés people use to describe the first sight of their newborns. There's a lot of ego and instant love and fear for something that new and fragile. I was ecstatic to finally have this first evidence of my connection with the Khans, and with my Black family—even if the "chocolate was on the other side" of Estie. I carried Sarah's photos with me all the time, and I couldn't stop looking at them. But mixed up in all of that pleasure was intense jealousy. In one of the photos, Sarah was playing with a big plastic bow and arrow in a funky sun dress out in front of a big white stucco house. A sign saying "Sarah's Villa" hung on the iron gate. Every time I looked at it, I felt a surge of envy toward her—pretty, brown-skinned, spoiled princess of Estie's world.

I felt a little silly when I realized I was hurrying to stand in front of Estie for what—a hug? Suddenly there was the press of her body against me, and it felt familiar to me, uninhibited and total in a way I didn't think it would be. I thought later that it was the nicest hug I'd ever had. But perhaps this is not true.

We sat down somewhere in the Delta Airlines terminal, and for a while, we couldn't speak. We just sat there looking nervously at each other and then quickly looking away. A wave of grief welled up in my chest when I let myself think about what I was doing, who I was with, but then her hand touched the skin at my wrist, and the swell of pain in my chest was pushed down in my surprise at her easy intimacy.

"You have Al's skin. It's so soft. It makes me think—oh, he used to smell like olive oil or something," she almost whispered, and she reached for my hand and kind of leaned into me. Her sense of an intimate right to me—what she'd revealed in many of her letters and in our phone calls—suddenly wasn't frightening.

Soon we were comparing eyes and teeth, fingers, taking off our boots and stockings to show each other our feet, rolling up our pants to compare our legs. We stripped down to our last skin of clothing to show each other our arms, the outline of our breasts beneath our t-shirts. I took stock of myself: I had her exact hips and feet; my breasts were thankfully smaller. I was glad to inherit those legs, but I'd have to watch my belly. Soon we were bawling and laughing. When we realized people were watching us, we retreated to another bench and shifted shyly to the photos we'd both brought.

We pulled them from our bags and spread them over our laps. Estie now had plenty. I noticed right away that as we looked at them, we both quickly passed over certain ones and returned to others, betraying our feelings about those we were eager to know more about and those we would be resistant or slow to claim. I was most interested in Sarah and in the photos of Estie from the 1960s. Estie couldn't hide her curiosity in William or her attachment to my grade school photos, the ones where I am closest to Sarah's age. Her sisters, my parents, Mac, and more recent shots got shuttled to the side.

After looking at the photos, Estie handed me a package. In it was a beautiful, hand-bound album. She had picked some photos to add to it—ones of Sarah and her cat Kenneth and others of her parents in the early 1970s—Leo with his bulbous nose and a wicked light in his eye that made him look like a demented Mr. Magoo, and big titty, cool-eyed grandma Toby, in a tight green ribbed turtleneck sweater with what I later learned from Estie's stories about how Leo battered her was more a look of fear, of sliding away. In all of the old photos I've seen of her, she looks like a starlet, like a pin-up from old 1950s movies, always with those same eyes.

I was waiting for her to pull out photos of my father. I don't know why I expected her to have some. I had asked about it before, and she had said that she didn't think she would have kept any that long. But I had started to think this was part of her way of holding off.

"Do you think I look like Al Green?" I asked. She made a triangle with her two hands and framed my eyes and nose. "That's Al Green, right there. Especially those beady little eyes. And add the dimples." I felt a little miserable.

Later, as we walked to get a bus into town, Estie started to tell me something like a confession, as if she had been withholding terrible news. I felt like she was about to take me to the ruins of something devastating. She was kind of choked up as she told me a story about Al Green. When he was a child, he had been hit and dragged beneath a city bus in Brooklyn. The accident was so bad that he had spent a whole year in the hospital and went home with a leg that is still terribly mangled. A big part of the muscle was missing. It was inches shorter than the other one, so he walked with a pronounced limp. Then, as if she wanted to turn my eyes from the wreck, she told me about his long, beautiful hair that was wavy and silver before his thirties, which he wore tied back in a ponytail, and how that hair looked in contrast to his dark, red-cast skin. "He's a pretty man," she said. "A styler."

It was an odd moment. I started to think that she was somehow preparing me, that she might be taking me to him. But she asked me if I'd rather go to Cambridge or downtown—maybe somewhere near the commons—pushing Al Green out of sight.

As I looked at the city from the bus, I could not recognize any part of it. The place was suddenly new to me. It was Estie's Boston. My father's city. It was no longer the place I ran off to with Penda to play out fantasies of ourselves as hard-rock urban teens. When the bus reached Massachusetts General Hospital, Estie asked me if I minded walking and then motioned to get down. We walked from there to Harvard Square, tracing Estie's regular lunch-time route. She seemed a little nervous as she pointed out people from the hospital as they passed us, telling me stories about each one that were funny in the way she is about people. We shared a fascination with the funny side of human suffering. I loved her stories about her patients—the ones about the celebrity madpeople whom she worked with at McLean, and a woman who just a few weeks earlier had jumped off the roof of Filene's, Boston's famous department store, with a suicide note pinned to a dress she'd just taken off the rack. She started to tell me about a patient she had once who had come in looking for counseling for the "bi-racial" daughter she'd adopted who was the same age as me. The child was about to be brought in for a consultation, and she said that she had been terrified. She had to ask someone to go to check the child's birthdate. "This is the only time I ever talked to anyone about 'the baby,'" she said. Then someone passing held her attention. It was a young, blond-haired man in perfect executive get-up. "He's one of the big hospital directors—I met him in the loony bin," she said laughing. We had never discussed her being sick. I had never asked her about the references to her illness I'd heard from Mary Steed and Ann Kendry and Luck. And I never felt comfortable pressing her to say more than what she wanted to about anything she brought up. Now she was talking like she wanted to share more of it with me, but I also had a feeling that she thought I knew much more than I did, and so maybe she felt like she had to.

When we'd gotten off the bus, she had said, laughing at herself, that she hoped that she didn't run into anyone she knew. But as we walked, I felt a little like I was being shown off. Like she was proud of me. Like it might finally be all right for her to risk exposing the secret she'd been carrying for so many years. It might just be a relief. This was how I began to experience Estie; she would put all the difficult, unweildy things she had carried down in front of you, happy for you to unpack it all for her, but if you didn't, she would just pick the familiar weight back up and carry it along.

I was wondering the whole time what we looked like together. I wanted to ask people what they saw as they looked at us. Young Black woman with her older white friend? Co-workers out for lunch? Mother and daughter? Strangers helping each other along? I felt myself attach to her and detach, shifting my posture with each wave of emotion, like I would with the McKinleys, driven by my anxiety about people's perceptions and their grating interest in me. I liked having the power to play on those perceptions. In one instant, I could reveal that we were family, and in another, we could appear as strangers, passing unremarked.

That fear that we would discover for ourselves that we were truly unconnected tore at me as Estie and I said a too-early goodbye. Within three hours, we met, compared teeth, looked in some of the bookstores, ate lunch, and said fare-thee-well. Somewhere between Mass General and our goodbye, I felt that I had lost her.

She was all there with me in the bookstore in Harvard Square as we pulled things off the shelves. I wanted to scream *This is my mother!* every time she went for a book. Angela Carter, Eudora Welty, Wole Soyinka, James Baldwin, Jamaica Kincaid. It seemed we had been reading together for years. I handed her all kinds of books, testing her, and she didn't flinch. I thought with a little guilt—what if I had grown up in her house? My mother, the one who raised me, had given me a reading heritage, and most of her old library had become my own. But my developing tastes seemed a world apart from that former intellectual life. Now Estie and I were looking at the Caribbean titles. She told me that she had bought many of these books at the campus store at the University of the West Indies. Mac would leave her there on their trips to Kingston to buy cement blocks or get any of the endless permits they needed to build their house. Had we been in that bookstore at the same time in 1989, when I was a student there, passing over those same shelves? I thought about the occasional American women I had encountered. Would I have been able to recognize myself in her then? I'm sure I would not have. I was focused too intently on my fantasies of Mattie.

I must have been reading something, just before I looked up at Estie, about to ask her a question. She was standing there, leaning against a shelf. I saw amazement and affection quivering on her face. She said, "Oh my god, I can't believe we're doing this. I just can't believe it." She kept repeating this as we walked across the street to a Mexican place and squeezed into a table in the middle of the Harvard lunch crowd.

She was hurrying as we ate and seemed anxious to leave, and I didn't know if being with me was becoming too much for her, if she was seeking release from the intensity of our meeting. I asked her if she was worried about the time, and she told me that she had to be home by 2:45 P.M. to meet Sarah, but that she might be able to squeeze in a little more time because Mac would be there to meet her bus. I don't know why I thought we might spend the whole day together. Had I flown to Boston to spend just those few hours?

"I wish I could come home with you," I said. "I can't wait to meet Sarah. I wish that telling her wasn't such a difficult thing to do."

"Oh, you should! That would make it so much easier. Oh, you could, you know—just be at the house when she comes home." Then she was insisting that I go home with her. There was such a terrible desperation in her voice. I realized that she might really let me just show up, let me be the one to break the news.

The check was already on the table, and Estie put down money as she talked. Then we were out on the street, and I didn't realize how soon her goodbye was coming. We got a few yards from the restaurant, and she was suddenly sobbing. "Please don't hate me. I did not want to do it. I had to do it. I did not want to," she pleaded. My heart started to burn. I needed to hear her say this. But hearing it was so *terrible*. I was watching a stranger—the woman who was my birth mother—come apart in the street. I didn't know how to comfort or hold her—we hardly knew how to talk at times.

"I don't hate you, Estie. I don't hate you," I said again and again standing stiff next to her. But what was this feeling then? Suddenly I wanted to knock her in the mouth. I hated her for doing this to me, especially when I had tried so hard to temper all of my feelings.

She seemed to pull herself together as quickly as she let go, which was just as frightening to watch. In a minute she was wiping her face and hugging me goodbye kind of cheerily.

"Here, you better take a cab home," I offered, stepping into the street to flag one, reaching for money to pay the fare.

"Somehow I always feel like you're the mother," she said, closing my hand back around the bills.

The ground rolled under me as the taxi drove off. I could not move. Everything seemed to be spinning. I was confused about where I was going. I wanted to fold myself down on the sidewalk until I could get together the sense and the will to get up and make my way home. Instead, I started walking, away from Harvard Square. As I walked, the rain that had been holding off all morning started to come down. The coat I was wearing was not enough protection, and I didn't have an umbrella, but I kept on walking, out toward the Charles River, letting the cold rain rake my head. When it felt like too much, I found a phone booth and stood under its puny shelter, sobbing. I thought: *I will die here. She has left me.* The feelings felt so old, as if I'd always been carrying them. Was that what it felt like the first time she left me? Or was this what some other experience or my imagination had scripted for me?

I stood there and called Vanessa. I could barely talk when she picked up. I cried and cried into the phone, and she kept saying, "Come home, yellow girl. Come home. Get a cab from JFK and come to my house." After we hung up, I started to walk again. I walked across the Charles, my jacket and clothing soaked with rain. Then I found a taxi and made my way back toward the airport. In less than two hours I was home, dreaming in Technicolor in Vanessa's bed.

Spring 1997

My Brooklyn neighborhood was slowly remaking itself. New shops were coming in, breaking up the unending pattern of bodega, liquor store, church, house of curls, Korean grocer, and check-cashing parlor. I watched for weeks as an abandoned storefront a few blocks from my apartment promised resurrection. A big steel container was moved onto the sidewalk and filled up with building scrap. Then one day, on the glass behind the store's metal gate, I saw the word *Creola* beautifully hand-lettered in gold paint. I passed by in the evening a few weeks later and saw that the gate was pulled up and antique lace curtains were in the windows. The door to the shop was open, and I stepped into orange and blue light, and voices breaking the mourn of fado music. Three women were inside, bent over boxes. One of them turned when she heard me. She had small, sharp eyes, and her thin face and strong neck, and the plaits sticking out on her head, were bird-like. Her nose curved so sharply that it looked like it was a pointer to her expansive pregnant belly. We both smiled, and she asked me something I couldn't hear because it mixed in with the music, and then the three of them started laughing—long enough to make me worried.

"Oh, she thought you were Creole!" a woman with citrine-colored dreadlocks said, coming closer.

They were Cape Verdeans!

Before I knew it, I was buying a little oak kitchen table, and Tuzy, the bird woman, was making tea to celebrate their first sale. Tuzy, and Maria, who had a softer-edged version of her sister's face, owned the shop. Tilly, the third woman, was their cousin. They told me that they had grown up in Cape Verde and in Paris and had come to the United States five years earlier to join a brother. They had been good immigrant daughters, caring for people in their large family and the community of Cape Verdean exiles and expatriates—helping people to move or return home, burying the dead, raising money for emergencies. "There was always furniture and old-old things being left with us. And we love antiques, so we decided to open this shop," Tuzy told me.

Cape Verdeans are not a people everyone is familiar with. Perhaps you remember *Moby Dick,* or are a southern coastal New Englander, or have become a Cesaria Evora fan. But for most Americans, Cape Verdeans are unknown, undifferentiated amongst other Black immigrants and Portuguese-speaking Creoles. The same was true of my father: Alfredo Verdene had become Al Green. And what must have mattered in the New England Home for Little Wanderers essentializing record-keeping was the fact that he was Black. Maybe they'd written down that he was "Negro" or "colored"—whatever the parlance of social services was in the late 1960s. And by the late 1990s, of course, he had become African American. Where would I be looking if I hadn't found Estie?

I didn't know anything about Cape Verdean communities in New York—not in the way that I had come to know them in Providence and Massachusetts.

I remember Penda and her sister and some of the other kids from church doing battle with the Cape Verdean kids in Norton. There was a growing community there because of the pull of farm labor. At that time, we had simple ideas about who was Black. On the one hand, we were wary of a Black person who spoke Portuguese, or any other language for that matter. On the other hand, the Creole their parents spoke sounded a lot like Penda's Geechie mother. But the Cape Verdean kid's crime was that they would insist that they were Portuguese, *not Black*. And most of them were obviously "mixed" kids, with their blondish afros or long wavy hair, or the hundred other ways they looked "different" and suspect. It was an argument that never died, and one day Penda got caught up in it and almost fought someone in school. Afterward, she rode all of the way to my house to tell me about it and went home with our big heavy Britannica world atlas on the handlebars of her bike. She took the atlas to show "those hincty Porch-u-niggers": "Ya'll are Africans! Ya'll are Black! See Cape Verde! Cape Verde is an African nation!"

Estie had told me that Al Green, aka Alfredo Verdene, had lived in Norton for some of the time they were together. He moved his family there and spent a few years working on an old Victorian house that had been damaged by fire. I had my mother wrack her memory—had she ever known the Green/Verdene kids? It would have been an extraordinary coincidence and a little eerie. Estie said the kids were high school-age at the time. Norton had a tiny school system all in one compound, and everyone there knew every Black face. But in the end, we did the math and decided that Al Green had probably left by the time my mother started teaching there in 1975.

When I began to want long hair again in junior high school, and my mother and I had given up after a failed $170 hair relaxer from

Saks Fifth Avenue in Boston—the only place we knew to go—a neighbor who owned a shop in Providence recommended that we try a place down the road from her. The salon turned out to be owned by Cape Verdeans. The hairdressers' hands worked over my head with ease—the texture and inconsistencies in my hair were familiar to them. No one commented on me, or what kind of mix I was, or got curious about my mother, the way they always had in other salons. They just did hair and talked in Creole and left me to my grateful half-breed self. So every month, my mother drove me to Providence and sat and graded papers while I got my hair done.

I wondered how different my life would have been if I had known that my birth father was Cape Verdean when I was growing up. Certainly this knowledge would have given me a sense of connection to a specific site, if nothing else. Being Jewish and Cape Verdean gave you a lot more to hang your hat on than being just Black and white in life. And with the huge communities of Cape people in Providence and New Bedford right at our back door, I liked to imagine I could have had the experience of living in the perpetual ease of that salon. I suppose that I would have built some fierce fantasies about having an African father. But the further I went with this, the more I knew it would have just been the same load of problems and yearnings I had been dealing with, but cast in somewhat different terms.

Now, along with my newfound Jewish family, I had a whole new facet of Blackness to discover. I hung out with Tuzy and Maria and Tilly for a while that night, and it wasn't long before I was telling them about Al Green/Alfredo Verdene—that he was a Cape man and that I wanted to find him.

"Of course, we see it all over you!" they said. "Our brother Eddie—you'll meet him—had a baby with this Jewish woman, and she put the baby up for adoption. The family did not let him have any say in it. They sent her away for a while, and when she came back, the papers were signed. He's fighting it now..."

I could feel anger working between them. "We're not Americans— we could have raised this baby," Tilly said.

We signed a funny kind of pact after that. I had a place there with them. I started to hang out at Creola in the evenings, soaking up the community that passed through there. As each family member and friend came into the shop, Tuzy and Maria introduced me with a story in French or Creole. The person would nod and smile at me, and I would be pulled in a little closer. They enjoyed feeding me, and I started to tutor Maria in English and read her school papers. When Tuzy found old Portuguese primers, or Cape Verde history books, almost always written in Portuguese, on her rounds of antiques traders, she would give them to me.

Once again I was the stranger, sitting inside of someone else's Black world that I was supposed to be a part of, hoping that in time I'd learn the vernacular of their lives and bring it to what I was beginning to think of as my own expanding trans-bi Creolité.

One day I remembered something that made me call my friend Rita. A few years before, she had sent me an invitation for a show at her father's gallery that I hadn't been able to go to. The artist had orbited the famous Spiral era, and I was sure that his name had been Al Green. Rita said that Al Green sounded familiar to her, too. She was going to call her father.

That night my phone rang. "That man, girl, his name was James Brown."

Suddenly it was spring and in less than a month, Estie and I had gone from hesitancy to trying to be family. She had settled things with Mac, who she said had always known about me and had responded with his usual nonchalance. "What can he say? He has about thirteen children," she said. He was just worried about how she would break it to Sarah. She never shared with me how she eventually told her. I don't know how Sarah reacted before her excitement about meeting me was pressing on Estie, and Estie suggested that we all meet in Jamaica during Sarah's school holidays.

Sarah wrote me a few excited letters in the weeks before the trip, and I replied to the details of things she hoped we'd do together—go horseback riding, stone the mango trees because it was mango season, eat french fries in the swimming pool. Another letter was about her new goldfish, Catherine and Sarah. Talking to Estie had become easier; we were losing our feeling of separation. And so I left for Jamaica certain that we were over the hardest part of our reunion.

My flight arrived in Montego Bay three hours before theirs, and I was grateful to have time to take Jamaica back into my lungs before we met for the long drive across the coast to their house near Port Maria. I thought about going into town to see if the jerk spot I loved had survived the ten years since I had last been there. But I enjoy being a spectator at airports. I sat on a bench in the courtyard outside the arrivals gate waiting for the taxi men to lose interest in me:

Shhhk skkkh. Yes, daughtah! Which way yuh going?
Yes, sistren! Me want to carry yuh go ah resort.
Cho! Resort! I-man want to carry yuh go a wedding ceremony!"

I watched the women in variations of batty-rider shorts with platform heel sneakers and fishnet stockings, the "higglers" selling biscuits and candy and curl activator for the journey. I took in the parade of Tupac and O.J. t-shirts, the soldierlike, swing-arm, turned-out-feet cock walk of the men, the rich Jamaicans walking with their drivers and fancy guard dogs. I looked over at a Dred saying a long, emotion-filled grace over lunch at the open-air cafeteria, his hands joined with those of a white tourist couple. The smell of fried chicken lunches and the dry-looking beef patties at the counter made my stomach churn. Ten years was not enough time to erase the memories of meals in the Mary Seacole Hall cafeteria at the University of the West Indies. I thought about how the time I had spent in Jamaica was so much a part of my consciousness. In just a few minutes at the airport, I had touched a thousand familiar sensations—the excitements, the pleasures, discomforts, and near revulsions of that place. It was so stunningly ironic to be coming back to Jamaica now to spend time with my birth mother and new family.

It is difficult for me to pin down when Jamaica became so entwined in my fantasies. It may have been as simple as listening to Ron Brown sing "Jamaican Funk" on the civil rights dial in Attleboro, or a visit to my grandmother's elevator company in Long Island City where I heard Jamaican patois for the first time. The men's talk in that workshop felt powerful and protesting when my own voice felt so tentative. And maybe it all really blossomed when I was thirteen, away at summer school. I had a terrible crush on a Jamaican girl in my dorm whose father was rumored to be Jewish. He and her mother ran a chain of the best Jamaican bakeries in New York. We all agreed that she and her sister were the prettiest girls we'd ever seen. She made "half" girls like me feel especially left behind. I know that by the time I went away to boarding school and put Mattie's photograph on my dresser, Jamaica was the compass point for all of my yearnings. And by the end of my sophomore year in college, I had arranged to go to the University of the West Indies, intent on escaping my uncomfortably elite education and who I was at home.

I was thinking of all of this history as I sat waiting. After a while, the crowd began to thin, and the remaining taxi drivers gave up on me and settled into naps, sprawled across the backseats of their cars with their feet sticking out of the open door. I also slept for a while—until I felt a man slide around the circle of bench I was on.

"Mi don't usually talk to brownings, but mi like yuh. Yuh need some sun, man, but mi can see di Black a run inna yuh vein. And true mi like yuh hair," he said, admiring my uncombed head.

Jamaica was coming down on me with a vengeance. The intense sorting by color, which happened in most every social exchange, and being called "browning" (a light-skinned woman armed with color privilege, hated and glorified) had made me leave Jamaica after that year in school and not look back. Every time someone would call out my color, I would feel that I had been cast outside. It hurt that much.

But now I had to laugh. The man was reminding me of a friend's son when he was in the throes of potty training. Once I had picked him up to swing him onto my shoulders and felt that his jeans were soaked. I handed him to his mother.

"Did you pee on yourself?" she said.

"No, he peed on me," he answered, pointing at an imaginary man.

It was the same kind of foolish thing—denying that you had anything to do with something you probably enjoyed quite a bit.

The man didn't miss a beat. He launched into a Bible-thumper routine that was really a pick-up, turning churchifying into sexual play. I started getting my things together so I could find another seat, when Estie came out of the gate. She looked great—every bit a "Jamaica white" woman actually, with her already olive skin, full mouth, her now short Jewfro, and uniform of a neat designer dress and low pumps and gold jewelry.

She waved and called out to me. My bench companion said, "A who dat? Yuh muddah? Ah, so yuh muddah is a coolie."

"Actually, she's an Israelite. A true daughter of Zion," I quipped as I walked away. Estie and I hugged nervously, and then we went back into the terminal and out another door where Sarah and a school friend stood waiting for us as Mac loaded shipping barrels and wilting cardboard boxes, a television, and huge suitcases into a waiting minivan.

We all paused as soon as Sarah's and my eyes met. I don't remember anything about that moment but her excitement-sprung eyes and the powerful happiness I felt. Then we were loaded in the van, and the reggae music that boomed from the speakers saved us from talking. I was feeling nervous now, and suddenly exhausted. I watched Mac in the side mirror, trying to figure out what kind of man he was and what he might be feeling that I couldn't detect in his warm hug. Estie slept instantly. And Sarah seemed to quickly forget the moment. She played car games and bossed her friend Juliette, who was twice Sarah's size. In no time, the two of them erupted into tears in a fight over candy, reminding me that they were only nine years old and soothing my slightly hurt feelings.

We drove for two hours, until the driver turned off the main road into a cove of half-built villas nestled between a hill and a long bluff that dropped down to the sea. We drove through the neighborhood slowly, checking to see who had made progress building in the months that Estie and Mac had been away. Then the van drove up to the gate of a pretty white house with a sign saying SARAH'S VILLA hanging from the grillwork.

Estie showed me around the place. It was actually two houses, with a verandah built between them. One house was used as a rental; she took me to my room there. The house they lived in was simply furnished, littered with half-unpacked shipping barrels. She took me to Sarah's bedroom—it was the most finished room in the house, with a complete furniture set and good linen, and photos on the walls. I was interested in how they lived—in the otherwise spare house with the dozen locked doors and cabinets she and Mac were now opening. Estie said they had to put everything away over the long periods they were gone. Now things were appearing: the kitchen utensils, her collection of books, a few knick-knacks, Sarah's toys, and Mac's video collection and many electronics—all in various states of repair or dismantled to protect them from being used by the house help.

Teeny, the housekeeper, had prepared dinner for us, and we sat down to eat on the verandah, while Sarah's two straggly cats and several stray dogs circled us. Soon the "bout-yah" children (the yardboys and children of the area squatters and watchmen who live "'bout yah place") showed up, appearing along the edges of the yard until Estie called them to come and join us. I was grateful for the distraction, amazed at the swirl of bodies as people from the neighborhood stopped by to say hello. Miss Birdie, who lived across the street, came to the yard, and as soon as she saw me, she said, "Ah yuh dat, Sarah? Jesus Peace! What a way yuh grow!" Everyone laughed, but no one said a word.

I sat and watched Sarah caught up in the excitement over who was in the yard, and who had grown or come or left since Christmas, and who had tamarind and mangoes to share. Estie and Mac kept disappearing, seeing to things in the house. Then by nightfall it began to storm, and soon the power went off. I used the darkness as an excuse to retreat to my room, grateful to be released into sleep.

I slept hard and long, and I was embarrassed when Estie knocked on the door and woke me around 9:30 the next morning to call me to go to town. I sat between Sarah and Juliette in the backseat of Mac's car, feeling a bit like a third, overgrown kid. Estie and Mac were silent in the front seat. I felt Juliette and Sarah inspecting my hair and the dark brown lipstick I was wearing, and then Sarah broke the quiet between us, fingering the tattoo on my arm and saying in a little voice, "Did that hurt? It's pretty cool."

When we got to the market, Sarah and Juliette each took one of my hands, and we went off to explore. It was easy like that. And soon Sarah and I were moving like we were one body with Juliette close at the hip, and she confessed to me that at first she was a little afraid: *I saw you at the airport and I thought I was looking at a big me!*

People on the street in Port Maria, and in the Ocho Rios markets, all knew Estie. That morning as we were leaving the house, the fishermen came to the gate and called Estie to come and see her favorite fish. In the market, they called out to her in a way that was familiar and easy. And when they saw me and Sarah together, they would look back and forth between us and talk about how much we looked alike. So, where had they been hiding me? "She lives in New York," Sarah said with a little shrug. That was enough for all of us. Almost everyone in Jamaica has a husband or a child or a mother in New York or some other American city who might not get home regularly.

I had expected that Estie, and maybe all of us, would encounter tension in a society spoiling with tourism, but as I watched Estie move about, I slowly relaxed my defenses. When I was in school there, my parents and my grandmother came to visit me. They hated the city and were apprehensive about coming to infamous Kingston and intruding on my life on campus, so we decided to meet on the north coast and drive to Port Antonio in the east, which was a naturalist's heaven. We drove most of one day to our destination and then spent three days roaming the countryside with binoculars, watching birds and inspecting every growing thing. We had painful interactions with people, mostly because my family was feeling a little timid and because of the two different Englishes being spoken. In the same way that some smell fear in others and go after it, many people around us returned my family's squint-eyed vulnerability and discomfort with not always kind humor and sometimes plain hostility. But here was Estie, moving casually about.

After the market, we went back to the house, and Estie excused herself to take a nap. For the rest of the day, I entered Sarah and Juliette's world of pool games and adventures, with one eye watching the movements in the house. Mac, seeming indifferent to all of us, moved in slow circles inspecting the car and the house and his things in it. Estie shuttled rather restlessly between her bedroom and the pool, always with a book in her hand. Sometimes I would feel her looking at me. Enjoying it and not wanting to scare her off, I would stay longer at whatever I was doing. We hardly interacted. She almost seemed to offer Sarah up in her place, just as she had with the first photographs she sent, letting her take care of the bonding.

Then Sarah bumped her head on the side of the pool, and I took her inside the house to find Estie to put something on the scrape. We walked into her bedroom and found her smoking a joint, and I realized that this explained some of why she kept disappearing and coming back to doze in the sun. She handed me the blunt while she took care of Sarah. A little later, while I sat on the wall that ran along the side of the house, she came and sat beside me and lit up another joint. Sarah joined us and sweetly put my hand in Estie's, and we sat a bit uncomfortably while Estie had a funny, zooted conversation with us about the sea and the area people passing. It was the first time we'd really talked since we'd arrived.

On the third day of my visit, Nisha, a friend from New York, came down to join us. She had supported me as I made contact with Estie, and she decided to make her first real vacation in a long time a trip into my psycho-drama. The morning after she arrived, we got up at dawn to travel to Kingston so we could escape the quiet intensity and the swallow of that house. We took a "quarter-million" bus, a lumbering old Russian giant that made the hundred fifteen miles across the hills a nearly five-hour trip. I was full of nostalgia—so overwhelmed by it that even the broken-seated bus seemed like a wonderful thing to me. I felt the phantom of a goat moving between my feet and a chicken pecking at me through a hole in an imagined crocus bag. I didn't mind when the two women who squeezed into the bus near us dropped toddlers on each of our laps and between us on the seat. I didn't mind the crush of bodies or the foul odors of sweat or the gamble that the bus, with its overloaded roof, would make the corners and not tip over into the precipice at our side. We spent a whirlwind day in Kingston, retracing my old paths through the city, and then found a minibus going back to Ocho Rios that evening.

We rode in exhausted silence over the pot-holed, mostly one-lane mountain road. The road seemed to double back on itself, snaking along the base of hills so steep you couldn't believe that someone could climb up there to plant bananas or that the trees wouldn't lose their toehold. Deep ravines dropped down on the other side of the road.

Suddenly the minibus driver turned off the headlights, and everyone on the bus gasped. The driver yelled out, "What kind of pussy is yuh? Cho! God is I-man light. Mi know dis yah road like de back ah mi hand!"

I felt so much fear that my organs shuddered. I thought of how I had ridden these roads on the back of a friend's motorcycle, with only an old helmet he'd given me that felt as protective as a metal pan. Back at home, I moved in and out of danger all the time. But now, since I'd met Estie, I had a terrible new fear of dying. I saw death on every corner. I became so aware of my mortality—it's funny, and a little over-dramatic, but I had never felt this before. When I told the FMN girls, they said they understood; they remembered feeling overwhelmingly vulnerable and *human* when they met their biological families. I became almost obsessed with the idea of my parents' mortality and my own. I would imagine Estie dying before I could really know her and make up for so many lost years. I would think about my birth father dying before I could meet him—wasn't he now nearing eighty? I would worry about not having time to sort out all of these changes with the McKinleys and about having to lose two sets of parents. I panic at times even now, thinking they could all die one after another and leave me devastated and locked in loss once again. I was almost sick with fear for the rest of the ride home, with the driver flicking the lights back off at times to terrorize us all over again.

When we arrived at Sarah's Villa, I found Estie sitting on the wall, looking down a corridor of palm trees that ended at the ocean cliff.

She had tears in her eyes and I asked her what was wrong. "I've been worrying about you all day." She told me that every time I hung up the phone, or left her, even just to take a walk, she was afraid that she would be hearing my voice or seeing me for the last time. We sat there together for a long time, not talking, just listening to the ocean and night noises—Lesroy, the caretaker, playing old ska on his radio, religious hymns from a church meeting down the road, dogs barking, the neighbor's old ox snorting, Miss Birdie's harsh talk at her nephew.

When we started to talk, we were matching dates again. 1987. I was in school in Kingston. She and Mac had finally closed on the land and were beginning to build their house. "I remember I was pregnant, and Mac and Lesroy had gone off to Kingston to buy roofing and some other kind of damn screw they needed. They were gone for a long time, and it was starting to get dark, and I remember that I sat down on the foundation—I must have been in my fifth month—I was thinking of you, and I cried and cried," she told me quietly.

Sometimes it's better to have a child on your soul than on your lap. As she talked, this line that I'd read somewhere, maybe in a book on folk culture, ran through my head. I started to think about my own life in Kingston that year.

I spent that period feeling like the mistaken post-Black Power, trans-bi mulatta heroine, dropped down in my African print mini ("White rasta!" men would call on the street) in a feverish late 1980s version of Jean Rhys's *Wide Sargasso Sea*. An intense depression was pulling me down underneath my excitement about my course of African and Caribbean studies and the intoxication with *just being there*. I had my accent and patois so perfected that when my African American literature professor asked me to recite the lyrics to a Negro spiritual for the benefit of the lecture hall, some of my classmates, who thought of me as a "Jamerican" argued over whether I sounded like a Jamaican trying to be Jamerican, or a Yankee poser, or maybe a little bit like a Trinidadian. But I could not escape being a spectacle on the buses and on the streets or being constantly called "browning," as if it were my name. It wasn't that Jamaica didn't have plenty of its own citizens just like me, but not many of them wore Black feminist or anti-apartheid t-shirts or lived so close to the ground.

And in Mary Seacole Hall, the prize girl's dormitory where I lived, I got a taste of vicious hazing, in concert with our hall brothers' sexual play, which underscored the alienation I was feeling. My roommate— who was a pre-med student from the Cayman Islands and had a Black Jamaican mother and white British father—had "tall hair" that reached the top of a beautiful backside, and she spent Yankee dollars. We both resisted the hazing that went on behind the rituals of "Hall Induction." So we and the few others who also protested were sub-ject to the spite passed across the courtyard and around the four walls and three stories of balcony-lined dorm rooms. Something like an early morning trip to the lobby of our brother hall to use the only phone with an international line would elicit so much punishment: "You, Miss, you really must be more discreet coming home in the mornings." Or, "Dat bwoy, him doan love yuh a-tall!" My roommate and I became the last of the sluts—me, coming in at dawn from par-ties where I danced all night with a girl I liked named Zalia, and my roommate with her too short shorts that she wore all the time, even under her lab coat.

I spent a lot of time wandering about the campus, staring at the achingly beautiful Blue Mountains that you could see from nearly every point. I would look at them and think of home on the other side and of my parents' wilderness, and they would take me back inside my almost narcotic-like unhappiness. The mountains are the great barrier between Kingston and the north coast. They also were dividing Estie and me, but we didn't know it then. I remember feeling that whole year like I was stuck at some uncomfortable midpoint—waiting to tip over into a life that felt as if it were mine.

That year I was beginning to find the confidence to approach my sexual feelings, but before the end of my first semester, Zalia's father died, and she was forced to leave school and go home to St. Vincent. In summer school, and later, when I went to board in high school, I had had feverish crushes on my friends. We would lie in our beds during study hall, evading the hall monitors, and listen to music on our Walkmans and dream. We would give each other massages and perform these elaborate rituals of grooming before late recess, when we would go and meet our friends who lived in other dorms. We'd compete for boys, hiding so that we could watch each other kiss the same one on different nights. When Darnell, a boy I kissed sometimes, told me that he did not know any Black girls my age in Trenton, his hometown, who were virgins, I thought, Well, wasn't I a Black girl? And wasn't I feeling lonely inside my questions about who I was and reckless in my needs? I only had to think about it for one night before I made plans to sneak out of the Friday night dance with him. We went to the woods behind our dorm with a sleeping bag and a "box" so we could do it to Stacy Latisaw and New Edition. The next morning I told my friends; all of them were Trenton girls. "Eeeew! You're nasty! I can't believe you did it, girl! You better watch your fast ass! You're like one of these nasty white girls," they squealed. I was devastated by that. But sleeping with Darnell offered me a bit of protection against the treacheries of our posse. It made me "his" in a sense and cut out some of the crueler competition. I must have remembered this, because after a few months in Mary Seacole Hall, I took on a short string of boyfriends. (The other offer of protection came from my hall sisters who were recruiting for the university branch of the Church of Christ and demonstrating for Jesus on campus.) Dating roughneck boys from our brother hall kept the Seacole sisters off of me in any serious way. And I lost myself and my loneliness in sex.

At the end of the Christmas holidays, instead of going home to Attleboro, I went to visit Henri in Atlanta. She was spending her year at Spelman College. As soon as she saw me she said, "Girl, you look like you're pregnant! Your nose is getting that heifer spread." I laughed at what she was saying. And by the time I got back to Kingston and made my way to a doctor, I was ten weeks into trouble. After ducking around to ask questions and have covert examinations, I arranged to have an abortion, with the help of a professor I had confided in. I called my mother, and we agreed that it would be too disruptive and not really necessary to come all of the way back home, although part of me was begging for her to insist that I do that. She sent me $300, a hefty sum in Jamaican dollars. My doctor explained that abortion was not illegal, but it was legal only if a woman had her husband's consent, or if the contraceptives I'd been prescribed had failed. So I was checked into a hospital for a "D&C."

Even through the haze of anesthesia, I remember that it felt like flagellation—a calculated, punishing tearing apart of my insides. I remember sleeping in the recovery room and waking up to the sound of roosters and city traffic while something I'd read about the African diaspora and "natal alienation" tore through my brain. I didn't know whether I was in New York or at my parents' house, until I heard the nurse ask again what kind of medicine Dr. Woodruff, my professor, practiced.

How could one explain the coincidence of Estie's pregnancy with mine? Or the related grief we felt? Or the fact that we both chose Jamaica? Even ordinary things, like the books we chose to read, or the exact same blue and white bedspread we each had, or our love of the color indigo—the blue so deep a sedative. And then there were a thousand other small passions that we shared.

For the last two days of my visit, we stayed between the house and the local beach. My friend and Estie got left behind on a lot of my adventures with Sarah, who remained tireless, alternately bossing Juliette and playing democrat, trying to take care of everyone. Sarah and Estie and I inhabited an ease with each other, and at times it felt like we had a seamless connection in a world apart from Mac and our friends. At times I'd look up from where we were—like the three of us sitting on the verandah together eating bammy and fried fish with three pairs of the same legs swinging under our seats—aware of the lushness between us, an ease to how we communicated with little so talking. I'd look at them and think, What's the big deal?

And then something would happen that would cleave our intimacy.

Someone would come to the house, a casual friend. Estie would introduce me as "Catherine McKinley." Simple. And my heart would burn from wanting her to recognize me as *hers*.

"When I got out of the nuthouse in 1969 and was getting my life together—" Estie might say, prefacing an otherwise ordinary thought, and I'd be pulled back into our drama. I would think, was she in the nuthouse for *two years?* Was she institutionalized again later? *Psychotic depression?* I wanted to ask her more, but I couldn't bring myself to do it. It felt too curiously demanding, too invasive, and I didn't know how to ask about those things. I was also a little scared of the answers. And then Sarah and our friends were always nearby; Estie always seemed a little too near to tears. I knew that the details about her illness was something that I eventually needed to know. More than anything she could say to me about how much I was wanted, I needed to know how much she was incapable of giving and how much she could not have offered me.

Sometimes I could imagine the future, when all of this might grind down to "normal." Would I be left feeling this same terrible loneliness that persisted even with my good feelings? Was I on the way to mending it? Closing the gap between me and my two mammas, between me and my many selves? I thought of a quote by Toni Morrison, about women in their twenties not yet being fully formed. I was just shy of thirty. Was this my final push out the door toward womanhood?

Summer 1997

Estie had told me about Verdene's, the gallery on Newbury Street in South Boston that Al Green/Al Verdene had owned. Verdene's was in the heart of an Irish and Italian community. It seemed like an odd place for a Black-owned art gallery to be—there on the other side of two warring communities, in the high heat of the city's racial violence of the late 1960s. But Estie said that Al Green was a man who seemed to know everyone, and he was always putting himself in unusual places, so it hadn't surprised her.

"He was such a beautiful artist," Estie said. "I can't really describe his paintings—very abstract, very modern. He also did a lot of murals—they might still be up in some of the old clubs and restaurants he worked on. Well, I know Hudson's has been remodeled. Mac and I went to a wedding there a few months ago. I guess a lot of them would have gone out of business. When you come up to Boston, we'll go and look around."

I asked her again if she had any photographs of him, any traces of his work, or even any letters or cards. She had started to cry. "That man never gave me *anything*." I was surprised, and a little embarrassed for her as she said, "I swear when we hear from him I'm going to go and buy him some stuff and make him paint something for both of us. He was not exactly someone who could keep himself in paint," she said, kind of laughing now.

I called Napoleon Rocket again and other artist friends to tell them what I knew, but no one had any memory of Al Green/Alfredo Verdene. "Now, I knew *of* Verdene's, but I was still doing my thing in California during those days," Napoleon told me. "You might want to call this sister I know who works at the Schomburg library—she was a photographer and would have a closer tie to that world." I called her, and she seemed excited. "Yeah, a Cape Verdean brother—the man had a gallery on Newbury Street, right? He used to wear a ponytail? It was a great spot. I think it ran on mob ties—the Italians—numbers running." But she couldn't go any further than a few loose memories of shows she had gone to. The rest of the people I talked to kept turning me back to archives and city records.

I had lost patience with that kind of searching.

I started to write to various people in Boston who had been recommended to me by others. For a while I wrote to a woman who was a professor at Wellesley, who had returned to her hometown in Cape Verde, but I never heard back from her. I sent letters off to others without a lot of faith, but feeling that I was doing *something* at least. Because for the first time, Al Green wasn't calling.

I must have sent about twelve letters, and I received one response: A brochure from a Creole-American genealogical society in New York dedicated to "the social, psychological, historical, and genealogical needs of the bi-racial and miscegenated person." The founder described herself as "a mother of bi-racial children with a particular interest in Cape Verdean communities" and explained a mission to preserve Creole languages and culture, included fighting exclusions and omissions in genealogical records. They claimed to keep extensive databases. All of that seemed perfectly consistent with my situation.

I called the number on the brochure, and the woman I talked to said she would send me more materials and a registration form. She explained that there was a small membership fee and that I would need to submit a four-generation genealogical chart showing Creole ancestry, attested to by a board-certified genealogist. I explained to her that I was an adoptee, and I had no papers. She was adamant that I would at least need to have some proof of my father's identity. When I tried to explain that problem to her, she just became more insistent. I was so frustrated and offended, I gave up on the whole thing.

Around this time, I began planning a trip to West Africa. When I went to get my immunizations updated, the nurse who gave me my shots and went over the dizzying CDC alerts for cholera and typhoid fever and malaria and river blindness said at the end that she didn't want to make me uncomfortable, but she was interested in "mixed-faith" marriages, and she wanted to ask me about my background.

Her question was so odd; I didn't really know what she was getting at. People assume I'm all kinds of things. What they assume usually says a lot about their own desires and fascinations. But it is very rare that someone, like this nurse, thinks that I'm Jewish.

I gave her the short version of my story. I explained that I had not grown up with any connection to Judaism, but I was interested in having one some day. I thought about Sarah, who had just given up Hebrew school. When I asked her why she wanted to stop, she seemed a little ashamed of something and wouldn't talk about the reasons. Did she feel she didn't belong there, or was she feeling some kind of pressure? I was surprised by Estie's lack of protest. "She used to enjoy it a lot. But anyway, what is she really going to do with Hebrew?" she said.

I thought about Leo and Toby Khan. After our trip to Jamaica, Estie had told her mother that we had met. It was the first time they had ever spoken directly about *what had happened.*

"The baby is back," she told her.

"Oh, yes, I think about the baby sometimes and wonder what happened to her," her mother admitted. Estie said that Toby had been really surprised by the news, and the conversation had made her nervous.

I asked Estie how her mother felt about having Black grandchildren. "I never told anyone that Al Green was Black." I knew enough about Leo Khan's hatreds and his and Toby's rather dull interest in Sarah. Estie insisted that it was the same reception they gave to everyone. But later she did admit that her parents had taken some time to accept their Black granddaughter, and maybe they had never completely warmed to Sarah.

I had not met any other Khans. The connections I had to my Jewish family and to Judaism were very tenuous.

"We have a wonderful, very progressive woman rabbi and quite a few Black worshipers at the synagogue I go to," the nurse offered. I told her that I might like to come sometime, and she got excited and asked me if I would mind if she called her rabbi to tell her about me. She made the call right there in the exam room. Her rabbi asked her questions, and I found myself spilling out more details, not sure why I had allowed myself to go this far with her. Sometimes I just get curious about what people will reveal about themselves when they're looking into me. I sat and listened to one side of a conversation about whether I would be recognized as a Jew or not. My birth mother is a Jew, so I am a Jew, they agreed. But could I provide some document that I was once Sarah Khan and that my mother was Estie Khan, a Jew? I knew I couldn't prove any of that if I tried—not without going to court. She and the rabbi went back and forth on this. Then I got a temporary verdict: my religion was most likely withheld at the time of my adoption—this was common in the case of adoptions through non-Jewish agencies. Perhaps I could settle this matter without a lot of hassle—at least for now I should come to service.

I was dizzy from all of this. I didn't care about confirming my bloodlines on paper. I was going to go after the flesh and find my birth father. The synagogue and the Creole societies would have to wait.

For my birthday, Estie pulled out all the stops. It was going to be as good as my very first party. She and Mac and Sarah arrived in Brooklyn with a bottle of fish sauce and a Thai recipe she'd clipped from the *Boston Globe*. She'd baked a chocolate mousse cake that arrived lopsided from the journey. Vanessa joined us, and we sat at the little table in my kitchen and ate colorless and curious smelling but not wholly unappetizing pad thai. We spent most of the meal trying to guess how fish sauce might be made. Mac was kind of turned sideways in his chair, muttering through it all. His muttering—usually prompted by someone's stupidity or bad service or bad food—can stretch on forever and the low jumble of complaint will start to dull all other conversation until whatever problem he has is remedied.

"The man will not eat anything he can't immediately recognize," Estie scoffed. "Mac will sleep with you before he eats your cooking. It must be a West Virginia thing. When his family gets together for the holidays, they won't even let me bring the salad. *Don't trust that white girl with none of the cooking!*" She got up and lit up the joint she'd half-smoked and stashed in the stove.

Mac's feelings about me, about our new relationship with each other, were beginning to show. A few weeks before, Vanessa and I had gone to Boston for a conference. We spent the night with them in Cambridge in the tiny two-floor apartment in the row house they owned. I was surprised at how run-down and uncomfortable the house was. "*Squalor*, girl," Vanessa said. But Estie explained that they had put everything they had into buying it and keeping up Sarah's Villa. Mac had seemed grouchy and distant then, but he had barely spent any time in the house. He borrowed the rental car Vanessa and I had driven up in and disappeared until dawn. The next morning, as we were preparing to leave, waiting for Estie to shower, Mac's sister, who lived in the apartment next door, came in and sat down with Mac on the living room couch. She looked back and forth between Sarah and me and said, "You two could pass for sisters!"

"We *are* sisters," Sarah said. It just hung there in the air while Mac sat muttering, turning the pages of his newspaper.

Just a short while before this, I had been standing in Estie's kitchen washing the breakfast dishes. Dishwashing is one of those domestic acts I love; it was the housework I always did growing up. Being in Estie's kitchen felt very comfortable, and I was relaxed and kind of lost in the bliss of the warm water on my hands and the sound of Ella singing "You're My Thrill" on the living room stereo. Just then Estie called out *Sarah!* from another room, and it went right through me.

I was and I am Sarah Khan. I wanted to be one of the Khan girls then, to somehow be grown-up and who I was in the world but also to move in—as if it were just a matter of finally coming home from college.

Mac was killing my good feelings.

He had quieted down by the time we got to the cake. Estie put a candle in its center, held in a pink plastic ballerina's outstretched hand. "I saved it from Sarah's last cake," she said. Then as she started to sing "Happy Birthday," Estie broke down. Her singing started to sputter, and it was not clear where her tears left off and became embarrassed laughter. Then Sarah also started to cry.

Vanessa jumped up to get the cookies she had baked from off the stove. "Sarah, don't cry! Have a cookie," she said, just as the plate got in the way of Sarah's now full tantrum. Mac was muttering again and headed toward the door. Vanessa was also looking for an exit. It was a five-ring circus of desire.

I felt like I'd been kicked in the stomach, losing my place in the center of all of them.

Somehow everyone got themselves together—almost as fast as they had broken down. The cake was quickly eaten, and Mac started packing up the car. "Oh, leave the dishes," Vanessa insisted. Then they were getting themselves back on the road. Sarah was halfway out of the car window, clinging to me, screaming that she wanted to stay and go rollerblading. "Leave me, Daddy! I want to stay!" she cried. She wanted to set up her sideshow there with me.

As they set off, Estie handed me a birthday card and said that she had almost forgotten to tell me that she'd remembered the name of Al Green's friend who might help me find him; his name was Barrus Blackshear.

One day a few months before, Estie and I were talking about Al Green/Alfredo Verdene, and she said that she was trying to remember the name of one of his friends he had probably remained close to. "I remembered he was the very first Black judge in Boston," she said. "He was your father's age or a little older. He was Jamaican. He was a pretty man just like Al, and he had a bunch of children with white women."

Estie promised she would try to get her mind around what this man's name was. "It's ridiculous," she said. "How could I forget it like this?" I decided that she had told me enough. I got the numbers for Boston City Hall, for the Boston chapter of the NAACP, the Black Bar Association.

With Boston being so legendary for its racial exclusion, and my father's generation so crowded with Black "firsts," was I being naïve to think that during the 1950s or 1960s, my father's closest friend had been the first Black judge in a Massachusetts court? It only took one call to learn that the first Black judge in Boston predated my father's generation by many years. Enough others had followed.

Now I had a name: Barrus Blackshear.

I sat down on my stoop with Vanessa and opened Estie's card. It had the same kind of elliptical message I'd come to expect from her. On one side she wrote that she hoped that I'd come back to Jamaica with them later that summer. Across from this she wrote:

> Happy Birthday! Place: Boston Lying-In Hospital. I remember a few hours after your birth my psychiatrist, Dr. Sharpley, a Black, thin, tall, elegant man (who had happy/sad dichotomy clown drawings in his office) came into the hospital room and sat down on my bed while I gave you a little bottle of sugar and water. We talked about separation and saying goodbye and letting go, I remember. While he held you he cried.

> I miss you,

> Your Madre Naturale.

Along the fold of the card, in a different blue pen, she said, *For a long time —it seems like I feel it sometimes even now —my arm would ache from holding you that day.*

"I can't take this shit, Vanessa," I said. And we both started to cry.

I told the judge's secretary that I was calling regarding Al Green/Alfredo Verdene, and within a few seconds Judge Blackshear picked up the phone. I told him my name and started to choke out who I was, but he stopped me.

"Of course I know who you are! How is your mother? Yes, yes, I know Estie Khan, of course I do. And you have a sister, right?" He spoke with only the trace of a Jamaican accent in his voice. I was surprised by how much he knew and how comfortable he was.

He said that he had been thinking of Al Green just that morning, wondering about his silence for so many months. "I just told my secretary to put any call from him through no matter what I was doing. The last time I heard from him, he was in town for a few days—he was living in Pennsylvania—should still be. I was presiding in a case in another county. My secretary gave him directions and told him that he would have to arrive there between certain hours or he wouldn't be able to see me." He said that Al Green drove all the way there, arrived two hours late and cursed out the clerk because he couldn't see him. The judge hadn't heard from him since.

"Your father is something else," he laughed. "Do you want to know your Daddy?" He told me a story about a time he hired Al Green to do some work on his house. "I would see him every morning when I left for court, but by evening, the work wouldn't have advanced much beyond where he'd started. After a few days, I figured out that Al would leave as soon as he saw my back. After a week and a lot more bucks, I decided to run him. I took the battery out of his car. He already owed money to the mechanic we used—the man refused to even look at him. So he was stuck at my house, and of course, Al is a man who knows which side his bread is buttered on, so the brother got to work!"

Barrus said that part of their deal was that Al Green was going to make him a set of white leather sofas. (It was the 1970s.) "Al is a serious furniture maker, you know. He's about as talented as he is untrustworthy. For a while, I was planning to invest and set him up in a custom business—we could have outdone all of the small import shops. Anyway, I gave him the money to buy materials and months passed and the couches still weren't made. When I finally got angry and stood on him, you know, Al told me that there had been a fire in his workshop, and everything had burned. He said he had been too ashamed to tell me; he was trying to raise the cash to buy everything back. This is Al: 'My money is funny, Barrus. And look now, I've disappointed you and got you upset—the two things I didn't want to do.'" Barrus said a few weeks later he went to a party at a friend's house, one of the old boys from the Bar Association, and he saw some couches that made him worry.

"That looks like Al Green's work," Barrus told his friend.

"Well, you know it is! Fine work, isn't it! He made them up for me a few months ago."

"You could never get mad at Al!" Barrus said, laughing, echoing Estie. "That Al Green, I don't know—you just never could stay mad at him or something," she'd said several times. She'd tell me stories of Al Green's outrages: how he would invite her to dinner, but she'd get there and there'd be nothing cooked, and he'd tell her he was broke and would beg her to go shopping. Then halfway through dinner, some woman would show up at his door with groceries or maybe carrying his dry cleaning. Or she'd tell me stories that began to change my reel of fantasies about him into Blaxploitation stories. Al Green, King of Love on a Warped Leg. Al Green, God of Cadillacs. ("But they always ended up looking like kidnapper cars, and he always had the trunk filled with crates of LPs.") Al Green, the man who ruled the streets of Boston on his gimp leg with his arsonist son. Al Green, who worked for the mob and the FBI. I was getting confused by the ambivalence of her memory. In one breath she'd tell me how sensitive he was, how kind he could be, and in the next she'd be crying, telling me that he would put a gun to her head when she tried to leave him.

That same ability my birth father had to almost delight people with his abuses and still keep them burning for him on very little faith had Estie dreaming of sleeping with him again. "Just give me one more night with that Al," she said to me once in Jamaica. I didn't know why she was saying it. Maybe she thought it would reassure me. I couldn't imagine she could still hold on to that feeling. As soon as she said it, I imagined his leg—twisted, with whole chunks of flesh missing, smoothed over with skin that was so unblemished that it looked like a child's, even though it was tough as weathered cowhide. Estie told me that he wore an elevated shoe on that foot, with about six inches of heel that he built himself. I pictured a shoe as graceful as I imagined his hand. I wondered how they made love. Were they sensual together? Did he undress? Take his pants all the way off and remove his shoe? What did he give to Estie to keep them together for almost six years?

Who was Al Green to Barrus besides his designer? The judge and the bad man, the hustler. I wondered what the other history was between them and what kept Barrus's affection for him as sharp as Estie's.

The judge wrote down how to reach me and promised he would look over his old phone bills. "I could have only made so many calls to Pennsylvania. We're bound to turn him up. You'll hear from me in a couple of days."

"The Pennsylvania phone number that appears on my bill has been disconnected," Barrus said when we talked again. "Now did he spell his name with an 'e' on the end? I should know because I did his name change for him." I asked him about Alfredo Verdene, and Barrus said, "He let go of that one long ago."

He promised to see what else he could find out, but from that day on I didn't hear back from him. I waited a few weeks, but then each time I called, his secretary told me that he wasn't available. So, I sent Barrus a note and some photographs to try to encourage him. A few more weeks passed, and my faith was folding. It was the same terrible feeling I'd had with Ann Kendry and Mary Steed. But then an envelope arrived from him one day. Inside were sheets of stationary with a list of telephone numbers with Pennsylvania exchanges scrawled on them. The lists were headed "A." and "Alfred Green" and "Greene." No other message was attached. I wouldn't have been sure they were from Barrus except that on the back of one sheet, he had started a letter to an attorney.

I wondered what had changed in those few weeks.

Dialing for Al Green was a dogged game. I had already been through Massachusetts, so I knew. You say you are looking for a man who is Cape Verdean to the Al Greens/Al Greenes who don't sound like they are Black. The Caucasian-sounding women and children you might feel out a bit more. You run through the "Al Greenes" and "Al Greens" quickly. The "A. Greenes" and "A. Greens" might take you for a crank call. There were too many disconnects, too many fax lines and suspicious women on Barrus's list. But there was one nice man who, when I decided to just go for broke and tell him exactly what I was doing, told me that he was an adopted person too and was beginning his own sleuthing. He wished me luck and, before I hung up, suggested that we pray together.

Then, one time, when I had just finished a call and was crossing off another name, my phone rang. A very nice Jamaican woman asked me if I was a McKinley from Sav-la-Mar. We were all dialing for family fortunes. There was something exciting in this kind of mystery work.

When I got to the end of the list, I decided to call Barrus and let him know that I hadn't had any luck. This time he took my call. He promised that he would keep working on it, but there was something in his voice that stopped me from calling him again. Instead I chose another photograph—one of me and Estie in Jamaica—and wrote a short note to Al Green with information on how he could contact me. I sent it to Barrus, with a note to thank him, and I asked him if he could send me a photograph of Al Green, or of the paintings Al had done that he had boasted about having.

I never heard from Barrus Blackshear again. I imagined there was something sinister in how he seemed to have changed his mind. When I told Estie about the trouble I was having, she said, "I'm not surprised. I mean, I'm sure Al would be very happy to know you, but Barrus always looked out for his friend. He was very protective of him." I wondered what protection he could possibly need in my case. I liked the idea of my birth father as a pulp fiction–styled anti-hero, and I thought of all kinds of possible scenarios that might be holding him and Barrus up. But, in truth, it seemed like the scenario I feared most was playing itself out: Al Green really didn't want to know me. He seemed to have given up on his yearly calls to Estie, and Barrus certainly had to be the end of the line of help.

I started to feel my familiar melancholy set in. I was feeling manipulated again by people's promises and what felt like their withholding. Even when I knew this was not their intent, Mary Steed, and Ann Kendry, and now Barrus had each left me with this terrible feeling.

I couldn't bear the idea of Al Green running away from me. I tired to prepare myself for it, but I just didn't know how to manage that possibility. By now, my relationship with Estie was becoming overwhelmed by a thousand unnamable tensions and our increasingly sad, kind of wacky meetings. And my parents, the ones I was truly attached to, seemed at a remote distance. We checked in regularly, but we had no idea, really, about what each other was feeling.

I was becoming worried about how I was going to handle all of these entanglements.

I came home one evening and found Vanessa on my stoop. She was holding a tiny pewter picture frame that had her birth father's photograph inside. At a glance, it looked like an old grainy black and white shot. It didn't look at all like a xerox of a page from her father's high school yearbook. Someone at the school had finally sent it to her after months of coaxing, when the administrator's promise to pass on a letter to her birth father hadn't gone anywhere. The young man in the photo was DuBoisesque, in the way she fantasized, with a longish afro and delicate wire glasses. He had Vanessa's elegant, broad cheekbones and delicate jaw. She had cut out the caption with his roll of credits: honor student, track team, debate team, film club. This was nobody's pusher man, no Pimp Daddy. He was not at all the man her birth mother's witnesses recalled—people whose memories had seemed the most reliable.

I felt a deep gut-wrench of envy that she had this much of him. Estie had once said that she was pretty sure that one of her friends from the old days would have some photos of Al Green. I had been periodically reminding her to ask them but nothing had materialized. One time when I visited her in Boston, she came downstairs with a discovery. It was the closest thing to him: a photo he had taken of some people at a rally on the Boston Commons holding a sign saying TODAY'S PIG IS TOMORROW'S BACON.

Every time I would express my ache for some piece of him, she would grope for something to offer me. "There he is—right there!" she would say, framing my eyes and nose in the triangle of her fingers like she did that day we met. "Be patient, he will call." Then she'd tell me about his call a little over a year ago, or two years before this, when she had run into him in front of a pizza shop near the hospital—"the kind that sold a slice and a nickel bag." She remembered that he had on a dark green suit and a blue collar, blue hat, blue tie. It was almost the way I'd seen him in my chameleon fantasies. She said that he was still wearing his hair in a ponytail. "He's pushing eighty now, and he hasn't changed a bit!" He told her that he had a diamond to give her. "It was funny, but I kind of believed him," she said. "This time we'll get a diamond from him—really! You wait."

I kept wondering if I was asking too much of her, pushing these crazy kinds of promises. My friends tried to help me reason: maybe she was done with him; she'd earned the right to want to put him behind her. But she wasn't done with him—she was still talking about wanting to sleep with him again. It seemed as if there was something willful about what she couldn't turn up in her memory and among her things. But then Henri reminded me that maybe she had been in very bad shape during those years—who knows what she had let go of if she couldn't keep herself together then? I realized that I was having trouble integrating all of the pieces I knew of her past with who she was now. I was trying to understand her behavior, understand "psychotic depression" as some category of mental illness, and understand the facets of that history that were evident even now in her moods and her drugging, which I was beginning to suspect was more than pot smoking.

Estie had me feeling *wrung out*. But I was pushing as hard as I could to find Al Green, nevertheless.

Sometimes, even now, I wonder whether a photograph, something like what Vanessa had of her birth father, would have been all that I needed of him. In a photo he could live on with a power that could also be satisfying. A photo could be my papers. My proof of my very own Black folk. The photo might be more precious, I was starting to think, than the breathing man who, with his growing record of imperfections, might come to disappoint me. I started to think that it might be better to make due with the fantasy of Al Green, to hold that fine little thread of him, as Estie and I began to hit a wall.

September 1997

One weekend Estie sent Sarah down to visit me. I stood waiting in the Delta terminal until I saw her wild reddish head of hair bobbing beside a stewardess. I was so happy to see her. I loved the feeling of being the big sister waiting with an ID to claim her. The stewardess laughed when she saw me and said we looked like mis-sized twins. We were both wearing our hair tied into afro-puffs with bright scarves. It was a style Sarah started to copy from me in Jamaica. "I'm Tia and she's Tamara," Sarah announced. She liked to play at being the twins on her favorite TV show. "Well, I don't want to keep you two apart," the stewardess said, and turned Sarah over to me.

All summer long, afro-puffs had been raging in New York. *I'm rough and tough with my afro puffs/Rage!/Rock on wit yo' bad self!* blared from car radios and store fronts all over town—a '90s revolution in sound, a synthetic revolution, like the weaved-in naps shaking on a lot of heads. Even Lani Guinier was wearing afro-puffs in her fight on Capitol Hill. I was watching her, trying to let myself really like her looks—the ivory skin, long, high-bridged nose, and the Semitic-Black contours of her long face. My hairstyle was really a fallback on my limited hair-styling skills, a McKinley legacy. But the afro-puffs also satisfied a piece of my little girl self that was hungry, resurrected by my courtship with Estie. I would wake up in the morning and check to see whether I was my three-year-old self or my near thirty-year-old self. Most days I felt like an angry little girl, hiding behind a sweet face, stuffing my rage until it distilled into melancholy. I realized that I liked this image of myself.

As we stood waiting for a taxi, I looked at Sarah and told her that she better just wait until we got back to my place, because I knew that head of hers—she could stand in front of you for inspection with her hair slicked down with water and grease, but underneath she would be growing a rasta's trunk-like dreadlocks. She started laughing, pulling the neck of her shirt over her head to hide. I realized that she was not dressed for the early cool weather. She had on her favorite nylon running pants and a light cotton top, but it was sweater weather. I looked in her bag for warmer clothes, but all she had was a t-shirt, her toothbrush, Vaseline, and some books. I saw a kind of frightened look in Sarah's eyes. "Mama let me pack everything myself."

I felt kind of panicked. What was wrong with Estie? I had never been alone with Sarah, much less responsible for her care, and she seemed so vulnerable just then. Suddenly I felt like I didn't know how to talk to her or how to be the grown-up. I felt like we were two destinationless girls, waiting to be picked up. Sarah must have sensed my crisis. She looked at me, and I saw the frightened look go out of her eyes.

"Catherine, do you know I wasn't scared at all on the flight?"

I found my grown-up self again as soon as she spoke. I realized then that I identified too many of my feelings with what I imagined were her own. It was a difficult complication of our new bond and the strange triad with Estie.

We were next in line for a cab; we were headed for Manhattan. We had a circus date a few hours later with a friend of mine. As we were riding and chatting about Sarah's football team, I saw a brown speck move down on her forehead and then disappear back into her hairline. My stomach sank. I untied one side of her hair and parted it and there they were—countless gray-brown lice. Sarah had had lice before. When we were in Jamaica she had them. I was sure they were coming when I watched Sarah and Juliette and the area girls pass a comb between themselves and even share it with the cats. But how could Estie have missed an infestation like this?

I had begun to notice something about Estie in Jamaica—she certainly showed Sarah affection—with hugs and words and play—but there was this kind of odd lack of territoriality that should have been there. Estie's hands were never on her—making sure she had properly bathed and brushed her teeth, in her hair to make sure it was clean and combed, seeing to her clothes. I remember watching her dress a cut Sarah had, and I would have never been able to guess that she was a nurse. She acted too tentative, too unsure of what to do. I didn't know whether it was motivated by some kind of fear or a conflict she felt about her responsibilities, or whether she was overwhelmed by my entry and was struggling just to take care of herself. But this seemed extreme. Was Estie in some kind of crisis? Was it drugs? And where was Mac?

We changed paths and went to my house. I bought RID at the drugstore on the corner and tried not to give away my anger or let Sarah feel bad, as I attended to her hair. We got her head together, and I gave her one of my short-sleeved mini-sweaters, which somehow fit and made her happy, and we made it to the circus.

The rest of the weekend went well. It was a holiday weekend, so we had almost three days together. But by Monday afternoon, Estie and Mac had not showed up to get Sarah like they had planned. It seemed strange for them to drive such a long way and not just have me put Sarah back on the shuttle, but when I spoke to Estie the night before she had said that the drive didn't bother them and that Mac liked stopping off at the big casinos in Connecticut. When I told her about Sarah's lice she said, "Oh, there's so much of that going around at school. You can't get rid of them." Then she paused and said, "I like to think about you two there together. Maybe I'll just leave her with you." It was a joke, but by Tuesday night she and Mac still hadn't arrived to collect her.

She had called on Monday night and said that they'd had car trouble and would come the next day. She said that I shouldn't worry about sending Sarah, and Sarah shouldn't worry about school. And she called again on Tuesday morning. By that evening I was tired of entertaining a child, and my anger at Estie, and Sarah's worry about where her parents were, collapsed our fun. On Wednesday morning I called in sick; I couldn't bring her to school with me again. And Sarah was disintegrating from abandonment. I didn't know how to help her; I was so close to those feelings myself.

I was beginning to wonder if Estie might have really just sent Sarah to live with me. I kept thinking about what a crazy scene this was—Estie might be trying to pass on her child to the first one she checked out on. I tried to figure out what to do if Estie and Mac didn't show up soon. Luck was out of town, from what Estie had told me, and perhaps calling her might just raise more alarm with Sarah. It seemed better to stay put than to take her to Boston and not find anyone there. I realized that I didn't know how to reach any of Estie's family, and I didn't know her friends. I had this child who was supposed to be my sister, but we were really just a little more than strangers. And if I had to, I wouldn't be able to prove we were actual kin to anyone.

But before we had to go as far as any of that, Mac arrived. It was close to midnight on Wednesday evening.

All of the feelings of my past nine months with Estie had finally caught up to me. The powerful sadness I'd felt at times in the past, which I thought had been put behind me, was beginning to creep back in. I felt tired and lonely all of the time. The isolation inside of these feelings was there once again. In the past, Vanessa and Henri had been part of the antidote, but our relationships were beginning to come apart. I guess it was inevitable. We were each caught up in the most difficult phases of own reunions and in other changes, and there were limits to who we could be to each other. Henri was living just around the corner, but we were seeing less and less of each other. Vanessa had decided earlier in the summer that she would go back to living at school to finish the last stages of her Ph.D. work. She was only in New Jersey, but we needed so much support from each other and were having so much trouble communicating that she felt as good as gone. Each of our experiences and identities and needs were changing, and suddenly the limits of FMN—the idea of some immutable sameness based on a trans-bi childhood—were being exposed. My loneliness felt even more intense without that closeness we'd had. I realized that I didn't know how to talk much about my experience with anyone else.

A natural place for support might have been my family, but there just didn't seem to be any *language* for us to communicate what was going on. They knew I had traveled to Jamaica with Estie—twice now—and they knew the outlines of our relationship, but how could we talk about the more difficult parts when we all had so much trouble with just the surface?

I was watching my body expand at an alarming rate. I had thickened in the past few years, but over those months I started to gain a remarkable amount of weight. I knew it was a strange way of making myself more a part of Estie and Sarah. Estie was fat. Sarah was a chunky kid. I had always been lean and muscular, a McKinley, brought up outdooring and athletic, always eating a careful diet, under the tyranny of WASPy ideals of a no-fat, angular body. I was, without a doubt, a Black woman—what I didn't have in a behind I made up for in my hips and thighs. Those parts of me transcended the Khans. My mother has always joked that I am like the old jingle for the cigars her father had smoked: "Firmly rolled and tightly packed." I had always wanted more of that. I wanted to be more of a Black woman's ideal and mourned not having something like a coffee table backside. When people were assessing whether I was white or Black, that was always the deciding point.

As my body began to fill out, I felt a powerful kind of intimacy with Estie and Sarah that I felt desperate for and that maybe there was no other way to achieve. And the new thickness and softness of my body felt oddly protective in the middle of so much painful reconfiguration.

All the comfort of that flesh now began to feel sarcophagus-like. I would look at myself in the mirror and see Estie, and I'd feel angry at my image.

After I saw Estie in the flesh, I never saw myself the same way again. During the months that followed, my face became like the broken matter in a kaleidoscope's lens. The lines of my face were shattered, and the lens was shifting again and again. My face opened up into a succession of new patterning. It was not a violent interruption; it was pleasurable. I would stand in front of the mirror and see an angle in my face that was not there before it was revealed to me in photos of Estie and Sarah. I would hold my face in a way that Sarah holds hers in a picture of her that I love. I would see the same arch of eyebrow, the same cut of our chin. My neck and arms and legs, the way I used my hands and the way my feet turned out when I walked—they were all Estie's. I enjoyed those parts of myself in a way I hadn't before. It made me think of how subtly *privileged* people are to come into the world so definitely attached to a people—if not a tribe, then at least persons whose image they reflect.

In those first few months, I felt good and anchored in myself in a way that felt new to me. But I was also getting a glimpse of how *free* I had been before—in my imagination, in my ability to see myself outside of everyone I was attached to.

Now I would be standing in the shower and I would feel an urge to hurt myself—I wanted to dash my head against the edge of the tub and kill that part of me that was her—the now-pudgy, depressed Jewish woman who had become so immobilized by the past. I wanted to escape back to a time when I saw myself outside of everyone I was attached to. I could look at my mother, the one who raised me, and see something of my mannerisms but feel liberated from her oddities, the troubles her genes had handed her, the predictions my grandmother and aunt made for her as they all aged. Sometimes I caught a glimpse of Estie in myself, and I knew it must be torture to grow up never feeling free of other people's legacy—however proud or horrifying.

| At Thirty |

Fall 1997

I was letting go of Al Green. It was October 1997 and after nearly a year of coaxing Estie's memory, after putting hope in Barrus Blackshear, writing to anyone from Boston to Harlem to Cape Verde, trying again with Ann Kendry, and watching my failures reverberate against the FMN girls' own disappointments, I was beginning to really let go.

Then I came home one night and heard the phone ringing through the door. I reached it by the fifth ring, and a man spoke to me in a low, warm voice, with a familiarity I couldn't place.

"Hello, O' great and famous one. Hee heeee he!"

I didn't say anything back.

"I'm looking for the great and famous Catherine McKinley!"

"Okay."

"Catherine, this is your father! Al Green. I got ahold of my friend Barrus today, and he gave me your number. Is it you? Because, my God, I'm so glad I found you!"

I found you —
Since we found you —
So glad we found you —oh, or you found us!

No one had been looking, I thought, but the words came so easily out of Estie and him.

It was my Daddy, live and direct from Las Vegas. But my head was feeling suddenly cold.

"We just moved here last winter. That's why you all couldn't get to me. It's me and Linda and your brothers, Barrus and Daryl—they're the youngest—fourteen and sixteen."

"Do they know about me?" I asked. I might have said a million things to him, but my protective reflex had just moved.

"Girl, you weren't no military secret! Everybody knows about you. Just nobody knew where to find you!" This was so different from Estie. "When Estie wasn't coming home from the hospital and there was no sign of you, I went to the po-lice, the state po-lice—but I had to stop with the FBI. I knew those muthafuckahs—pardon my language—hell, I used to work for them so I knew they weren't going to help me do a thing, even though I walked right in there with my badge! I could see the stop signs in their eyes. I was a sheriff, too, you know—did Barrus tell you? I shot about seven or eight people. Some of 'em Guineas, too!

"Barrus says you live in Brooklyn? Your sister Sen lives there in Queens. She is going to be eighteen soon. She and her boyfriend moved in with his mother when we came to Vegas. I had to get out of Pennsylvania. I have terrible asthma, and I've had two aneurysms—I need the dry heat. I had this accident as a child—it tore up my leg, and gave me an awful inferiority complex. Made me do all kinds of things I didn't need to do. But Vegas is a good town if you don't gamble or drink. Do you? None of this family can drink—it's a problem with the blood. There's a fortune to be made here. You just got to have some cash—gotta have two cents to rub together, then you can make things happen. The problem is you need money to get the million licenses to do the work that will make you money. And each of these licenses costs about $300. And I'm dead cold broke. Can't do a thing. What work do you do?"

"I'm a teacher and I write," I said, surprised to be talking.

"Oh, that must pay you good money—me, I never liked liquor unless I was selling liquor—we're too much-a Indians. As I said, it's the blood. I had a baby carriage when I was a boy—used to sell newspapers and little pints of gin. Made some fine money!"

"Indian?" I said, breaking in. "Estie told me you're Cape Verdean." And he sure sounded like a Black American man.

"She told you that? I ain't no Cape Verdean. I was born in Richmond, Virginia. Grew up mostly in Bed-Stuy. 671 Putnam Avenue! I got a brother still lives in that house. He was an NBA Hall of Famer. Lena Horne used to be his woman. But I just know him as a liar and a hypocrite—he's an alcoholic and a homo-sex-u-al."

Cancel the Portuguese lessons. Give up on the grant writing for research in Cape Verde. Hide yourself from your father.

"We have a wonderful heritage, a rich heritage—Choctaw Indian on both sides of my family. My mother's mother was pure-D African from Guinea. Then there's Negro slaves, of course. Your great-great-grandfather was an abolitionist—he helped to free about 103 slaves. Of course we have some white folks in there somewhere—something for a writer to write about! I've been trying to get this story written—you're a writer you say? Well!"

He didn't know that I was sitting with my pen, taking every line down.

"You were never known as Alfredo Verdene? That is how Estie

said she knew you. And Barrus. I was told you had a gallery called Verdene's..."

"I had a gallery. Sure. 'Verde' is 'green,' you know. Shit, I don't know where I got it from. I think it's an I-talian name."

He kept right on talking.

"You need some money in this town, and me, I'm dead cold *broke*. When are you moving to Vegas? We have a book to write!"

He told me about my older sister Song, and my brother Michael who lives near him in Vegas, and Ascencion and Manny, whom he hasn't heard from in years (but weren't those Portuguese names?), and a sister who would have been my age who died, my brother Irving, who works for Nike and is about a millionaire by now, and who also never calls him, and my nieces Kai and Jasmine. The names went on and on—more than I could absorb. I interrupted him as he went back to money and deal making.

"How many kids do you have?"

He started to name them again, sometimes repeating himself as I wrote out a count. I went over the list—thirteen?—and he told me, oh, well, yes, and there are a few others, too, but he doesn't count them. They were, as a friend's father once described his children, "stray shots." "Some of the ones I raised aren't actually mine, and I love them just the same. So let's not talk about that. If you can say anything about me, you can say that I'm a family gangster! Heee heee heee!"

I didn't ask him to explain. It was getting to be too funny. It was hard to connect the conversation to the event that it was. I was thinking that I couldn't wait to tell Sarah. One day, someone we were talking to had remarked at the almost twenty-year difference in our ages and asked how many siblings we had. She counted me and my brother William, herself, and Mac's kids: fifteen. I was mortified. I wasn't willing to claim more than her and William. I was glad not to be caught in that kind of parental mess.

Then Al Green was back to money and how he needed some and how Estie had money coming to her. "Between her father and that white boy she was married to. I don't remember his name, but he was a doctor. Died in a ski accident. Estie is probably still spending that money.

"Is her father still alive? That Leo Khan is a prejudiced bastard. Hates Black people! And he had a Black girlfriend, kept her in a fine pad across town! I blame him for everything that happened with you, for letting—no, for forcing Estie to do what she should not have had to. But Estie was always off in the wide blue yonder. Not always telling you everything. Anyway, she is a good person," he said, some kind of love evident again and again in his voice when he spoke of her. "No, we have to blame her family, not her."

My head was spinning. The conversation was becoming more and more bizarre and I was becoming hysterical with laughter I was trying to hide, and heartache. He started to tell me about his oil investments in Mexico—how he began the first minority-owned U.S. import-export business.

"What did we call it, Linda?" he yelled. "Citizens' Oil!"

He started in about the gold and diamond trade he was into in West Africa. "I always keep two diamonds in my pocket, Babygirl!" Was one of them Estie's?

"Which part of West Africa were you in? I've spent some time in Ghana and Mali and the Ivory Coast," I said, my voice squeaking, tears running down my face.

"Oh, then you know President General Jerry J. Rawlings! Anytime you go to Ghana, you tell him that you're Al Green's daughter. I have a village in Ghana, you know. I was thinking in 1989 of moving all of the family there and starting something like a commune." He told me that he would build good housing in some "sweet designs—make sure there is electricity and plumbing, let anyone who wants to live there. Everyone would have their own bedroom." All they had to do was adopt a child. Take in and raise one child who did not have parents to care for them. He started to sound a little choked up as he talked.

"When are you going to change your name? Catherine Green. Sounds real nice!"

He didn't linger too long in any sentiments, but between talk of cash and business plans, he took strolls through his life with Estie.

"It was an impossible situation, and we couldn't help you girls." His voice was catching with feeling again. *You girls. You girls.* He had said this before, but I kept getting lost in the pace of his talk, lost in questions I wanted to ask, the flurry of names, the stories, his gotta-get-me-some-money refrain. And I realized that I really had been feeling pretty anxious—not as numb as I first thought.

"You girls?"

"Your sister. You had a twin sister. Don't you know? I came to see you in the hospital—you two were so cute. Heee heee heee! And when I came back again, you were gone! Estie wasn't saying a thing!"

I was having trouble breathing now. "A *twin?* No, I never knew," I choked. I really felt like I was choking.

"Now, you ask your mother. She would have the last word on that."

I hung up and called Estie without pause. It was after midnight, and she was sleeping. My voice was shaking as I told her that Al Green had called. She sounded surprised, pleased, and I was surprised by that. She asked me where he was, how he got my number. Her response was so wide open with pleasure, and for a moment, the sureness of what he had told me slipped.

That crazy father of mine. Maker of so many children. Thirteen? And this Cape Verde of his? I hadn't told him anything about myself. Just that I don't have any real money. Did he know anything at all about anything?

"You know what that crazy bastard told me?" I said. But her silence shred the laughter in my voice. "Do I really have a twin sister?"

"Oh!" And then she didn't speak for awhile. "I didn't tell you?"

I hung up the phone. The connection was dead to me.

That night played histrionic. I kneeled on the bare wood floor, my hands thrown over my head, wailing for myself in the dark.

In an airport in New York, I had seen a woman once who showed me what mourning is. She came through the glass doors of the terminal in a burst of a gold-colored boubou and fell down to her knees. She started to moan, and then her cries pierced the hall and rose to awesome ululations. Her large, gold-ringed hands and wrists were crossed and flung over her head, which was covered with a sky blue damask cloth. Her cries would cease, and she would struggle to stand, and then find ten feet worth of steps and fall on her knees again. Behind her were two closed-faced men in dark tailored suits carrying her great suitcases. They spoke quietly to her, words that I imagined were meant to calm her, but instead they whipped the froth of another cry. She stopped all motion around her as she rose and fell and grieved her way to the ticket counter.

I remember watching her, feeling that her sorrow was going to tip me over. I wanted to be right there on my knees with her not because I was feeling any sadness of my own that day but because I was awed with all that pageantry and such a complete letting go. It rivaled anything I'd seen, even in church. It seemed at any moment, every one of us in the terminal might fall in with her, and we'd have this great mass wailing and then go on to board our planes.

I tried to match the woman's pitch there on my bedroom floor, trying to get out of me the cold, rubbery mass that felt lodged in my belly—like eating fufu the first time. The thick pounded cassava and plantain you're meant to swallow in fingerfuls without chewing soothed my mouth against the burn of pepper in the soup, and later twisted up my bowels. It made me think again of the danger of unexpelled griefs. In some way, I had thought of my search as a way to take myself out of melancholy's hands, to finally release myself from my perennial sadness, but it seemed that with each revelation I was walking into a deeper territory of pain. I tried to work my shock up into cries, but the sound and tears wouldn't really come, though the hurt of Estie's deception was certainly there. I got bored with my performing, and I lay down. I kept my sadness droning while I stared at a soundless TV screen until sunrise.

I spent an anxious morning wondering what to do with what I'd just learned. I decided finally to call Mary Steed. She had the Master File. To say that I trusted her would be dishonest, but somehow I did trust her. She was the one I had relied on to authenticate what I learned. But why hadn't she told me that I had a *twin?* It would be hard to miss that detail. Was it another item she could not list for me:

one twin sister? Was I supposed to guess this and bring it to her for confirmation before she could speak on it, the way I had done early on, trying out my birth parents' names?

Mary Steed's assistant answered her phone and told me that she was in Colombia for a meeting. It would be nearly a week before I could talk to her. I hung up the phone, raging at Mary Steed in an imaginary conversation, cursing her for being away, making dirty money on international adoptions. My anger felt so unfixed. I couldn't bear the feeling of it. And I couldn't bear to wait a week without knowing something.

I called Ann Kendry, and she listened to me with amazement. She said that she hadn't heard even a hint of my having a full sibling, much less a twin. "I'll go back to my sources and see what I can find out." I hung up the phone, sick with impatience and anger at still being captive to her and Mary Steed and the shaky reign of the underground.

There was no one else to call. I refused to call Estie again. I was afraid of my rage toward her, and I didn't trust her to tell me anything I could depend on. And I felt too tired to go back to explaining to my friends all of what had happened in just that night.

But then, in the late morning, a friend swung by my place and asked if I wanted to come for a drive to take some things up to her house in the country. It took a long time getting out of the city, and I sat beside her, feeling my body responding with the tension and angry pull of the traffic we were in. I started to tell her all the new revelations, and I found myself talking until I became breathless. Then we were driving on the narrow stretch of highway alongside the Hudson River, the road making quick curves, turning sharply on itself, slick with rain and fallen leaves. The blast of the car's heater against the wet that was hard to shake, the smell of her old Volvo, the desolate roads, were pulling me back to my parent's old gray 244 steaming up a northern highway. I felt those childhood aches again—heading for an isolated house, feeling lost to people, and caught in the fist of some unspecified, looming anger.

My friend, who is a wonderful children's author and who always seems to know the *inside* of families and feelings, told me stories as she drove—about her father, who had left when she was a child and who she hardly spoke of, telling her he was sending her and her sisters and brothers money and things for school when they talked again twenty-five years later. We talked about people and *damage.* And she joked about my being a twin: "That should fix your narcissistic ass. You thought having Sarah around was cute! But I wonder what the hell they called this other child?" She kept talking, telling me stories and gossip, making me laugh at the pitch I had wanted to wail at, and I felt the caste of sadness lifting. I let myself forget the whole problem. But when I returned to my apartment that evening, that rubbery mass in my gut felt like it was expanding, and I lay in bed unable to sleep, on an anxious edge of sorrow.

A twin. A twin, kept running in my head. I just couldn't get my mind around it. And I couldn't believe Estie had pulled off that much deception over so many months. If I had a twin sister, where would she have gone? These thoughts looped around in my brain for hours.

My phone rang around 2:00 A.M., startling me. I listened to Al Green talk into my answering machine. "I know it's late in New York, but it's early in Vegas! I'm just checking on my Peanuthead," he said, almost giggling. He didn't sound like comfort, but I reached for the phone, and we talked for awhile. He told me that he had been driving around town all day, thinking about me. "I was looking for a piece of property for you. We got to get you out here."

I tried to get him to talk further about Estie, about this twin sister, but he couldn't tell me anything more. He seemed embarrassed by this, and he turned back to his soon-to-be-won fortunes and his plans for all of his children and the lives we were going to have. I tried to talk over him, to tell him what this revelation about my twin sister meant to me—about how big a deception it was on Estie's part, about how involved she and I had become and how long she'd hid it, about how much I was hurting.

"Well, that's her way, you see. Estie doesn't tell the truth. And I guess in this case she couldn't because that Leo Khan—I think he *sold* you two... but, ah—now, Peanuthead, what is your favorite color? I'm going to put some new carpet down—we got a bedroom for you here at the house. You and Sen can share until we come up with something better. Maybe she'll come out here with you. But mind you, it's not like the rooms I'm going to build once we get this piece of land in Tahoe—man's got thirty-five acres for me on the lake, and we're just waiting for this diamond deal to close. I'm going to talk to the Board of Ed about getting you a teaching job—what grade is it you say you teach? I know a man there owes me a favor..."

I listened to him talk, feeling angry at his nonchalance and dreaming, his assumptions and wild ideas, but I was having a hard time holding him off. I needed this warmth, this expansiveness then. I gave in to him, settling into my bed, and laughing with him while tears squeezed out of my eyes. I let his talking carry me until I was on the edge of sleep.

The days until Mary Steed returned from Colombia felt like a slow grind. I would spend each day trying to center my rage at Estie and my disappointment at the two people I had worked so hard to find. But the feelings seemed to rule my head, and I spent those days useless and despairing.

When I got Mary Steed on the phone, she listened to me with concern, but even more, surprise, as she wrote down everything I told her. I realized as I talked how the story had become bigger and more complicated in ten months, and how each person that entered introduced another mammoth test of reliability—their own and that of everyone who came before them. Mary Steed promised to look again at my file, which had gone back to the archives, the normal practice when her relationship with a client ended. She promised that she would have it retrieved, and she would call me as soon as she could.

Then I called my parents and told them what I had learned. My father listened and said something quiet like, "No, we did not hear anything about this. It's strange—I mean, we certainly would have considered twins." Then he passed the phone to my mother as he does when something seems to require the caliber of her reply.

My mother became concerned in her very cautious way about what it would mean if I had indeed been separated from my twin. "Twins have a special relationship," she said. "That would be important to know."

I told her all about Al Green's call. And more about Estie—about watching her unravel. My mother just listened quietly. It was the first time that I had exposed the deep fault lines in that relationship. Before this, I had talked around them, feeling a little defensive about my choice to stay in the middle of the struggle. A Senegalese friend had told me once, "We have a proverb: All cats dig in the garbage; only the fools among them fall in. Anyway, it's your mother, your father. You can't trade that for anything." I was grateful for my mother's reserve as I spoke now, feeling so vulnerable, standing somewhere between that friend's two insights.

Two days later Mary Steed called. "I have checked your file, Catherine, and there is no record of a twin birth. There is an indication, however, that your mother gave birth to a girl on May 29, 1963. This is four years before you were born. It appears that the father of this child is also the man who is your birth father. The adoption was administered here in Boston by Jewish Family Services, but it appears that it was finalized in New York State."

A sister four years older? A sister at all? It was finally becoming too much to digest. My sense of betrayal suddenly shifted onto Mary Steed. *Why didn't you just tell me that to begin with? You have sat there for years with this goddamn file* — I wanted to shout at her. But the part of me that begs for fellowship and reason, the part that had accepted the rules we'd been given — that knowing is not an adoptee's right, it can never be an entitlement — had me thanking her as I hung up the phone.

Curiously, I shut off from all my feelings then. I tried not to feel a thing. I restricted my thoughts to one question: What's worse? A twin, or doing it twice? It was a question with no answer; it was simply an existential exercise, a diversion from a confounding reality.

I let my friends do the feeling for me, and I was grateful for their outrage and sadness and sense of disbelief. But many of them were excited about this revelation. They made it clear that they were holding out for a twin. It didn't matter to them that "the people" had said my sister was four years older. A twin was just the right ending for the story we were writing. It explained perfectly all that lifelong pain.

When I told my mother that I was not a twin but that there was a sister four years older, a sister who had the same two birth parents, her concern faded: "Twins have a special connection. That would have been something to look into—a twin sister. This seems like something that you can leave alone."

I decided to call Al Green to tell him that he had a daughter who was born on May 29, 1963. That day at the hospital, what twins had he seen? Had he even gone to see Estie? Was he rolling the two of us together in the huge gang of his children? Or did some woman have twins for him?

As I told him what I had learned, I felt a little bad about doubting him, and I thought about Estie's words again. *Didn't I tell you?* I wondered if Mary Steed could still have things a bit mixed up. But what he said showed that he was perhaps the most unreliable one: "I told you that your mother would have the last word on that!" He sounded a little uncomfortable now. "Well, if that's the case, we just have to find her. Peanuthead, you're good at that work!"

I had not heard from Estie in all those days since I talked to her on the tail of Al Green's call. I still felt too dangerously angry to call her, and she also had not made any move toward me. But I thought about how quickly we had spoken and how I had not allowed myself to ask her any real questions. I was thinking about calling her, trying to rehearse my lines, when a postcard came in the mail. On its face was Frieda Kahlo's "The Wounded Deer," a painting of Frieda's delicate head growing hide and antlers, her body a deer's body, stuck full of arrows and bleeding. On the back she'd written "HI" in that too neat calligraphy. It was the only thing on the card.

I looked at it again and again, trying to see whether this was a stab at reconciliation, an apology. But I knew that this had nothing to do with my feeling of betrayal. I was sure that the doe was her.

It felt like such a puny gesture, and such a powerful sign.

Repetitive disorder. This is how she explained it. Clinically. Like it is something outside of herself, pulled from the DES manual, or a technical blip on somebody's screen. *It's that damn repetitive disorder again.*

But I knew that she was struggling with what years of hiding had made into enormous horrors, and what these kinds of revelations demand when there are so many layers and so many attending people. I knew the cost of telling lies about yourself.

"She was four years older, not a twin. I only heard you ask me about a *sister* when you called that night. I was sleeping. I smoked a little just before I lay down. What was Al Green talking about? I do not know. I do not know," Estie said. "He told you that he came to see you, but he never came. He did not come the first time. He did not come when you were born. Just a few months before or after I delivered you, he had another daughter. Maybe this is what he is confusing. The baby died a few years later. She got into the street and was hit by a truck. I was so mad at him. He came to me crying about this child he had lost, and he had two others . . ."

I asked her what my sister's name was, and I felt the answer in my own mouth. *Sarah Khan.*

She talked to me with a voice so broken off from herself, and then with a funny pouting blame as if I might have made her do all of this. Any compassion I was working up from underneath my anger —

compassion for how much she must have struggled with this secret and for her need to put some boundaries on her pain—was lost with her strange disintegration into a childlike grief.

I replayed our first conversation over and over in my mind. Her first words to me, *When did you say your birthday was?* seemed like such an innocent question then—a small confirmation that I was hers, because you wouldn't want to be making the wrong reunion.

I tried to remember every conversation, each time we'd spent time together, to trace the warp in her story. There is no other way to say it: I felt so damn stupid and so betrayed. I had gone to her with too much faith. I had allowed her in too quickly, opening myself to her so completely, with unearned trust. I had expected the kind of parent my adopted parents had been, bonded by the assumption that she would feel the need for carefully attended reconciliation and by the covenant of a bloodline. Estie was a stranger, and it hadn't taken long to realize that she was a person who was in denial about so many things. My desire for a fantasy-driven sweet story was an old reflex that was tripping me up again and again.

In those first months, when I was beginning to get to know Estie, I had felt eager to put all of who I was—what often felt like secrets—on the table. I felt compelled to do it so that I wouldn't betray my new pledge of truth-telling and lose her affection. I wanted desperately to share myself with her, to present all the pieces of my story, so that she and I would have a strong framework to build on.

I knew that Estie's closest and oldest friend was gay, and so with some hope that she wouldn't reject me, I told her about my relationships with women. She was surprised—not so much about the revelation but my need to tell her. She was easy about it. "Oh, Tommy will be so happy!" she said. "He was guessing it all along." I laughed.

It was a sweet acknowledgment. But I kept wondering, Are you happy, too?

Then, as if she wanted to be sure that I knew she was comfortable and wanted to reinforce that honesty and intimacy, she told me that she also had a secret. "This one is kind of silly—it's not as big as what you're sharing." She told me about a man, a Gangster Lean, who came into the emergency room at Mass General with a fatal gunshot wound. Just before the mortuary attendant came, she had tried on his fur coat, which someone had laid at the foot of the hospital cooling-board. We laughed at the story and at our need for confession.

"Good, we have no more secrets," she said. And then she was silent for awhile. "Well, I do have to tell Sarah that she has a sister." I remember hanging up the phone feeling like a big weight had come off. Telling Sarah would only take time.

When I asked Estie why she had not told me about the other Sarah, she said that she had finally felt ready that summer. And when I'd gone to Jamaica again in August, she had worked up the nerve to do it by the time I was getting ready to leave. In the end, however, she had been too afraid. She imagined that she would have told me, and I would have been on a plane, lifting away from her. I would go home and cut off from her, and we'd be left to our separate worlds. "I wouldn't have been able to stand that."

But I remember feeling then that my leaving is what Estie wanted. She wanted me to go.

We had all spent a tense ten days together. Estie had been laid off from work just a few weeks earlier. She was feeling depressed and had decided to stay in Jamaica past the end of summer and find a school for Sarah and some kind of job for herself. She spent most of our time together getting high, lying by the pool, diagnosing all the kids who flowed through the yard—their mental problems, their digestive and social problems, who needed a good medical workup. I was watching Estie turn from modern-day heroine into unemployed slummer in just a few short months. Sarah had grown up almost overnight. She had turned ten, started her period, relaxed her hair, and was trying to keep up with her old pursuits in teen heels. Mac, I was sure, was having an affair with Teeny, the cook, who had made herself a madame in the house. The power was off. The water was off. No one would go any further than Ocho Rios and the Jamaica Grande casino. A woman from Brooklyn had rented the guest quarters. She let her six-year-old son, whose problems even Estie couldn't pin down, wander the yard, talking for days on end about wanting to have a birthday party, while she lay in her bedroom in lace-frilled lingerie waiting for a man to arrive who never did, spoiling her vacation. I sat in the middle of that knowing I had set myself up for just this kind of trouble.

The whole situation had me feeling suddenly mercenary. I ate from Mac's barrels like I had tapeworm, and when Teeny cooked, I would take my share and push aside the line of bout-yah children and take another. I watched my belly swell and tried to look for comfort in that little part of Estie and Sarah that I had to myself.

I remember the day I left Jamaica so well. I remember the ride, how we drove the two hours to Montego Bay through the banana and cane fields on the coast with sudden flashes of fierce rainstorm pelting out of a sunny sky. Nina Simone was singing "Mississippi Goddam" back to back on the tape deck, drowning out the car's motor and killing conversation. No one made a move to change the tape or turn the music off. The song evoked all my emotion—my sorrow for the failure of this last visit and the realization that the relationship between Estie and me had finally broken. It also felt like an anthem. Nina's strident voice, the lyrics, were a reminder of my own U.S. Colored Life and a plea to leave Jamaica behind—as if Jamaica had again become the symbol of all the things I'd attached too many childish yearnings to.

Estie had left everyone else at home for the trip to the airport, ignoring Sarah's tantrum as we loaded my things in the car. It was just the two of us traveling, with Lesroy driving. I was glad to finally be away from everyone in that house, happy for a few hours alone with her. And when we stopped at a gallery, and she bought me a painting on cut-out metal, a scene from an Anancy tale that I'd admired a few days before, and patties and tamarind balls for the road, things felt warm and easy between us for the first time in some days. But then we heard a storm warning, and we rushed to get to Montego Bay, afraid the rains could close the road. I watched Estie while she rode in the front seat, smoking a blunt and tearing at a thinning place in her hair. Every once in a while I would catch her eye in the side mirror, but we would both pretend to be looking out at the rolling coastline.

When we arrived at the airport, the line at the check-in counter stretched out the door. I hurried to join it, and Estie made an awkward excuse about not being able to safely park the car and still being worried about the storm. We said a quick, rather relieved goodbye, and I remember thinking, she must be happy to finally be left alone.

Jamaica is Estie's retreat. It's a place where she can live almost like a child, where she has no responsibilities that a cook and a housekeeper, a driver, and a yard boy can't attend to. She lives mostly inside the walls of Sarah's Villa, moving between the warm pool water and the drug haze she finds in her bedroom. Sarah has her playmates, other adults to watch her. Estie can let Mac play Poppa, let him handle everything right down to the cash. He spends his time orbiting but never really touching her—in town, checking out business opportunities, or puttering between the helpers' quarters and the house, taking inventory, muttering about how hard life is there, how backward "Jamaica niggers" are, how you can't trust the help, how you can't get all the channels on the thieving satellite TV. I realized now that Estie went to Sarah's Villa to retreat from all the things that tormented her. Even the choice to have me meet Sarah and Mac there, instead of Boston, seemed part of this logic of escape.

As I checked in for my flight, I was thinking that I was glad to be free of her as well. I could go home and get back my old life—my life Before Family. Boston, Jamaica could just be places I had my eyes set on for a time. Estie just a woman I knew. This relationship just a short-lived, bittersweet affair.

This many months later, as we talked on the telephone, she told me that on the way home from the airport, when she could not stop crying, Lesroy pulled up at a roadside bar and bought her another blunt and a beer. As they rode on, he said quietly, "Estie, wha mek yuh nevah seh Catherine a yuh daughtah? We nah friends for eleven years now?"

She said she could not answer, and he thought she did not hear him. "I couldn't even reply. I just sat making a list of all the words for what we are in my head and going over it again and again:

birth mother

alleged father

adopted child

mental patient," Estie told me, crying softly.

One night during that last visit, the power was out and it was storming again, and I took my lantern to the room I was sharing with Sarah to read. I fell asleep after a while and woke up later feverish from the heat, feeling the bite of mosquitoes and Sarah's flea-host kitten, which had taken a machete chop to its back, stretched across my pillow. The lamp had nearly expired, but in the dim light I saw Estie standing over me. "Oh, I was just getting the newspaper," she said. And then she almost whispered something about just wanting to stand there and watch me.

I thought of how I would stay up when I was young and read until late into the night using the light from the hallway so my mother wouldn't catch me. There was a painting on one wall of my bedroom, and the light played on the glass at a certain angle, so that when my mother started to come up the stairs, I would catch her reflection. I could hide my book and feign sleep before she reached the landing. Sometimes she would come into my room and press her cheek against mine and listen to my breathing. It was the kind of tenderness she didn't seem to want to risk and that I wouldn't allow her when I was awake.

Estie was wearing a nightgown with a cotton robe pulled around her. I could see the soft folds of her belly straining against the cloth. She seemed self-conscious—did she notice how I watched her? She sat down awkwardly on the edge of my bed, drawing her knees up to her chest, and I recognized my own instincts immediately—that need for nearness that is also a retreat from someone's gaze. We talked a little, about nothing really, our eyes never meeting. I was aware of myself tearing at the worn edge of the sheet, running the loose threads under my thumbnail, a little nervous about her being there. After a long silence, Estie unfolded her legs and leaned forward, as if she were about to get up, but then she started to talk again—small talk—while she shifted her body from one position at the bedside to another in this funny, automated way. She shifted and shifted, talking about taking a day trip up Nine Mile Mountain. *Why don't we do it? We can't stay home like this all the time.* Her shifting became agitated. She got up suddenly and made a tiny circle on the floor. She was circling, circling, the movement itself driving her more than the impulse that took her there. We were still talking—about Bob Marley lyrics now. Then suddenly she stopped. She smoothed down her nightgown, pulled the edges of her robe together, and looked intensely at the corner of the bed where she had been sitting. She stood there, tearing at her hair. She seemed to be on the verge of some action. But I was kind of scared—and mesmerized by her motion, the violence she was doing to her head. She was watching her place on the side of the bed, but she seemed ready for flight. In that pause, both of us watching, Sarah came in the room, breathless, chased home by Miss Birdie for some "damn pickney foolishness" she'd been into, giving Estie a reason to stay. She sat down again, and Sarah told us about the stick Miss Birdie had and her exploits with the donkey tied down the street.

Suddenly Estie stood up and started circling, circling that same patch of floor. She started shaking, tears running from her eyes. "I can't believe I'm here with my two daughters," she said, standing still now, watching Sarah and me, laughing a bit self-consciously. Then she just walked out of the room.

"Your mother is *weird*," Sarah said. She pulled her pajamas from the dresser and went into the bathroom. The smell of ganja drifted from the hall.

That night, Estie let me imagine *psychotic*—that place that I just couldn't quite attach to her. It felt like someone was waving their hands to flag me, peeling back a layer, asking me to look.

There was so much that I had been too timid to talk to Estie about—the loony bin, the territory she traveled giving up a child. I had been afraid of the answers, and I kept asking myself, asking other people, *Do I have a right?* It was the same problem that loomed during those years of searching: I felt that I had a right to all, and to none. Back then, the question rested on too many abstracts—a birth mother, a birth father, people who made me who were somewhere in the world. It was about simple entitlement—my own terrible, very personal struggle—and not another person's feelings.

After I learned the story of the first Sarah, Estie began to open up about a lot of things. One day she talked about her father's mistress, the Black woman Al Green had known. She told the story to me as if it were a primer to her suffering, as if to say, You didn't believe how well this path was laid out for me. "I went to my father's office one day when I was in high school—my father never brought any of us there, but my mother sent me for some reason. His secretary—she was West Indian, very young, beautiful—told me she was so glad to meet me, so sorry to hear that my mother had died. She let me know in so many words that she and my father were lovers; she wanted to let me know that she was ready to take up where my mother left off. My mother was at home probably nursing some slap my father had given her. That was when I started to really hate the man."

A few times I asked Estie questions that assaulted more of her shelter of secrecy. I wouldn't always know when I had done this. I might ask her something simple about nursing school, or one of her lighter memories, or one of Al Green's funny outrages, and her memories would become foggy. She would shut down. Or break down—

and any question, any claim I had on knowing, would dissolve in her tears.

Other times, things poured out of Estie as if she were begging for my understanding. "When I was pregnant the first time, I had a psychotic episode, and by the time the baby was born, I knew I couldn't take care of her. No one knew that I was pregnant the second time. I was back in the hospital again—I tried to commit suicide. After you were born, I stayed there for almost two years. No one came to see me, not ever. Not Toby, not Leo, not Al Green. I was all alone. Toby would come to see the social worker sometimes on Wednesdays, but she would leave without seeing me. I stayed cut off from my family for many years—until I was back on my feet and had finished nursing school."

Once she told me: "After I had you I didn't want sex or want to have a baby for a long time. When Sarah was born I didn't take a single thing with me to the hospital—not even a diaper or a change of clothes. I left the house like I was going to exercise class. I didn't think I was going to be taking a baby home with me. I didn't even have a baby shower until weeks after Sarah came home. And that was only because my friends kept insisting. I wanted her so much, but I couldn't believe that she was really coming and that I would be able to keep her with me."

I tried to put all of these stories together. I was desperate to understand her. I wanted to understand the line between her deceits and where she might have rewoven my story because she really did not have separate memories of our births.

Estie had been talking to me all along about the Crittendon Home for unwed mothers, the place where she said she stayed before she gave birth to me. She had remained close with a woman, Genie, whom she met there. Genie was my heroine of birth mothers. Estie told me that Genie smuggled a camera in with her, and when she came back from the labor room and her son was brought to her, the only time she was allowed to hold him, she had been able to sneak a photo. Genie still carried the photo with her. I remember hearing this and feeling a kind of envy that turned to contempt for Estie. Why hadn't she been capable of one of those little heroic acts?

How many times had Estie talked about making plans for us to visit Genie? I had taken this story of the Crittendon Home alongside all of the elliptical memories Estie shared and accepted it as truth. What Mary Steed had said about Estie being hospitalized didn't seem to contradict this. I had nothing to counter it; it still fit with all I'd learned before. I kept winding the pieces into some kind of master narrative, not realizing all of the improbabilities. Maybe Estie assumed that I had more information than I did; maybe she was counting on me to blow her cover.

I remembered how, when she first visited me in Brooklyn, she had left her diary at my house. I found it on my bedside table, and I had sat for a long time holding it, resisting opening it. When Estie got back to Cambridge, she called and told me she realized that she had left it there and she asked me to look for a phone number she'd written inside. "Don't worry, there aren't any secrets in there," she said. So I had looked at the pages, at the little notes she'd written in the spaces under certain dates, including the day I had first called her, my birthday, each visit. I couldn't understand any of what was written; I cannot remember it now. There was this *weight* attached to that book that hadn't made real sense to me. I believed that she had left the diary intentionally, as if she were leaving me a sign. But what sign? How was I supposed to read it?

Sarah had told me how she had learned about me. Estie had left a childhood photograph of me on a table one day, and Sarah said she thought it was an old picture of her babysitter, Carmen. Then a few days later, Estie asked Sarah to retrieve something she had in her brief-case, and Sarah had found another photo. "I asked my mom why she had so many pictures of Carmen, and she said, 'That's not Carmen, that's Catherine.' The next morning she asked me if I wanted to know who Catherine was." Was the diary meant to be like those photos?

Or maybe there was never any intent to pull back this third layer. She might have simply told me stories as she remembered them. *Estie Khan had a daughter named Sarah, with a man named Al Green. She gave Sarah up for adoption.*

This story of Sarah Khan was enough.

I started to realize that except for possibly Estie's aunt and Luck, no one knew about a second birth at all. When Estie talked to her mother, and Mac and Sarah and her sisters and a few friends, about "the baby" coming back, she was counting on it not mattering which one. I asked Estie about this, and she told me that Luck and her aunt, who was no longer living, had known. (Now I understood Luck's part in our not keeping up with each other.) She wasn't sure if her mother had been told on her visits to the social worker, but in all these years she had not told anyone about a second pregnancy—not even Tommy, her best friend. "And you know that was the time he and I were in trouble together in the loony bin," she said.

My story, which was so precious to me, was not my story. All of those little pieces of history that she'd given me in her string of letters and notes, when we talked, no longer belonged to me. They belonged to Sarah Khan. Now it felt as though the whole of my fragile new identity, my sense of self within this newly understood history, had been snatched from my hands.

I started struggling with the kind of anger that is beyond expression, that just folds you in its hand and holds you. Much later, when I could find my way out of anger's grip, I started to see the part of Estie that was me—the woman who was struggling to contain so much shame and the terrible weight of lying.

Estie Khan and Al Green were raising me unwittingly. They had come to make me the grown-up woman I needed to become. It was a cruel set of lessons, but slowly I was being forced to let go of my little girl postures, of my hopes of finding a new guard of parents with an awesome debt who would take care of what my family, the social welfare system had not done. It was a hard-knock school of parenting I'd enrolled in.

I set about finding my sister with an almost manic need. I wanted to see Estie Khan and Al Green's whole hand. I wanted to force the truth, to be in some control of how it would be doled out to me. And some part of me wanted to retreat into a more comfortable, simpler identity of someone searching for a past and a family. I wanted to go back and live inside the rituals of searching, inside the pleasures of longing, the elaborate fantasies. I knew on some level that I should wait and take care of myself, wait and think about what it was that I needed and whether I could handle another new relationship. But I ran fiercely over the beginnings of those questions.

It took Ann Kendry just a few days to determine that she couldn't do anything to help me. She said it appeared that my sister had been born in New York City, and she gave me a number for a woman in Brooklyn who knew her way around the New York search underground. New York City? Estie had never talked of living in New York, but Ann Kendry was echoing Mary Steed. *The adoption was administered in Boston but was finalized in New York.* It took me back to that other part of Estie's life that was still mysterious—the question of this man she had once married, whom Al Green had spoken of, and Dirk Laakso, the name Ann Kendry insisted was still turning up.

I had asked Estie about it, and she insisted that she was never married. "Don't you know Al Green by now?"

I called the woman Ann Kendry recommended, and she talked me through the steps, offering careful options to every move: "First, you should go to the 42nd Street branch of the New York Public Library and consult the birth records to see the female births listed on your sister's birth date. You can go to the library yourself, or I can do it for $25. Once you have those records, you can call me."

"For $15 . . . or you can do it yourself for about $8"—she outlined a process that, like Ann Kendry's, required such little money. She explained New York state adoption laws and the particular traps and loopholes involved in getting what I wanted. Even with New York's absurdities, I was glad that I was not going up against the Massachusetts system again.

That week, I went to the New York Public Library and sat at one of the long wooden tables in the reference room leafing through the heavy volume recording 1963 births. But there were no girl children listed on the date I had. I sat in one of the old phone booths in a back corridor of the library, looking at the Addams Family prints lining the wall across from me as I called Mary Steed. She confirmed the date for me again. "I don't know how I can really help you, but it seems

Jewish Family Services in Boston facilitated the adoption. I think the next step might be for you to call them." There were contradictions again in what I was being told.

I telephoned them right then. I called up all the drama of my situation and told the social worker on the other end of the line that I was searching for my twin sister, Sarah Khan, and I wanted to be sure that she had been placed through their agency. We spent a long time talking, and then she put me on hold for some time. When she came back on the line, she told me that she would try to confirm the record of adoption, but only Estie Khan or Al Green could make a search request; siblings could not search for one another without a court order. It was not a surprise.

I gave the woman Estie's birth date and my sister's, and she spent a few more minutes away from the phone, but when she returned she told me that she could not confirm anything until we proceeded with the required forms. I told her that Estie had mental health problems, and I was not sure I could get her to sign anything, and she started walking me through the legalities for assigning proxy. I started to plead with her a little, until she said, no doubt to shut me up:

"I just cannot help you. As it is, there are several births listed next to Estie Khan's name."

"*Several?* More than two?"

"There are several births listed next to Estie Khan's name."

Sometime in the early weeks of this search, I met Sen, my seventeen-year-old sister, Al Green's fourth youngest child. I found her waiting for me outside my office, standing in the whip of cold on lower Broadway. She was tall and slender, with pretty high cheekbones, smooth, ivory white skin, and small, dark eyes like mine. Her hair was relaxed and wrapped around her head in a cone fastened with hair-pins. She was dressed like an urban legend, in the latest hip-hop gear, but when she spoke, her voice was sweet and kind of country, barely more than a whisper. I tried to imagine her as the "something else," the hell-raiser that Al Green described.

As soon as I saw her, I remembered Mary Steed's words: siblings were the fun part. The best possibilities were with them. I wished that she had better advised me—told me what I would be up against with Estie and Al Green, begged me to drop the parents and go on to that sweet thing.

Sen and I went to a nearby café. As soon as we sat down and faced each other, all of our excitement and the ambivalence we felt about each other opened up. We sat there tongue-tied for a while, neither one of us able to say very much until she took out a stack of photos to show me. There were shots of my father's first two children, Al and Owen; my youngest brothers, Daryl and Barrus; Sen; and Linda, their mother. There were photos of Al Green with that last set of kids at Disney World in matching outfits, Al Green in church, at home in a Jesus sweatshirt (though he didn't seem to be religious), all dressed up at a banquet table, and lying on a couch playing with Sen and the boys on the floor before him when they were tiny kids. I was surprised at how innocuous he looked with his big, kind-looking smile, doing regular Dad things—very much the family man and not the family gangster. If you met a man with that face, you would have to like him.

He was dark red ochre-colored with dimples and small flashing eyes. And there I was in his nose and brow, in the wave of his silver hair, still in a ponytail. In the spread of his knuckles on the hand curled over the arm of a chair I saw my own hand. One photograph caught his profile, the braid down his back, the cut of his high cheek-bones—just like Sen's—the hook of his nose. He looked like a Choctaw, a Cape Verdean, a Black American man. His clothes were a bit outdated, but in each picture he was dressed to the nines. I thought of one of our first phone calls, how he stood in front of his closet talking to me: "I have a suede coat in every color. Red, black, green—a couple shades. Couple shades of blue, even some kind of pink, I guess siditty people like you would call it salmon, heee heee heee. I've got shoes in every color to match. I have more suits! And hats—I love hats! You know that, Peanuthead! When I used to have the gallery, those white kids would come by—didn't wash, half-dressed in some kind of rags—they thought that made them artists! I would drive my red convertible with whitewalls and white leather interior and two white Afghan hounds. I let them know Black people *are* culture, and we're *clean* while we're at it, too."

In one picture I could see the green and blue glass and corru-gated brass corner of one of his legendary tables. In another photo there was a canvas with beautiful shaded geometry propped against a radiator. "That's some of Dad's artwork," Sen said, in her funny kind of whisper, "but he doesn't really do that anymore."

When I saw Sen in front of me and Al Green and all the faces in those photos, it settled something for me. There we all were with dif-ferent traces of each other. My Black family. It was such an extraordi-narily good feeling. It took me straight back to my first days with Estie. It took an edge off all of the heartache that had followed. Sen let me go home with those photographs, and for days I couldn't stop looking at them, imagining the shadow of my own figure somewhere in each scene. I held the handle of the basket swinging into the frame in front of Sen, standing in her third-grade Easter dress. I was the person Barrus was making faces at across the room. I was helping Al Green in his "office" in the living room while he handled business on the phone. I had just pressed Song's pretty head of curls. I was a happy face, standing in the middle of Al Green's gang of family.

When I asked Sen questions about Al, about growing up with him, her voice grew even quieter as she talked.

"Is Al Green Cape Verdean?"

"I wouldn't even know," she said. "Our Dad has so many stories. I do know from our Auntie Em and Grandpa—you would have liked them, but they're both dead now—that we're definitely part Choctaw."

As I asked her more, her tongue seemed almost paralyzed, her voice got quieter and quieter. Was she feeling shy? She certainly wasn't being protective, because in one sudden burst of clear words, she told me that we had a ten-year-old sister—a child Al had with a woman whom he had brought home after he'd lived in Ghana for a time. He introduced the woman to the family as his business partner and moved her into the house. I realized then that the man was nearing eighty and had children between the ages of ten and fifty-six!

We sat together without talking for a while, sifting back through the photographs until the bill arrived. Then, as we left the café Sen said, in another burst, "I don't want to make you feel bad. I mean, we did miss you, but you probably grew up better off." I looked at her face, and she seemed so lonely to me then.

We left each other with promises to spend more time together. I invited her to go to a party with me the next weekend, and she seemed a little excited. "I'm going to call Song. She lives in Boston, and she wants to meet you. Maybe she'll come down." We walked for a while on Broadway in happy silence. As we neared the subway entrance, she pulled a camera out of her coat pocket and kind of shocked me, calling out to a man who was passing, "Hey, this is my sister! We just met! Take a picture for us, a'ight?" She was laughing, flirting with the man a little, hugging me. But when we said goodbye and I hugged her again before she retreated underground, I could feel her ambivalence. I could feel her pulling away, and I was trying to imagine what was underneath the strange changes I'd watched her go through.

I was not sure how I was really feeling at that moment either, but I knew that had I liked Sen right away.

Sen did not come to the party. She didn't return my calls. We did not talk again for several weeks. One afternoon she called and asked me, "Do you think you could give me $60? I have to pay for an attorney. I have a court date next week." She told me how she had gone with Song and her nieces to Great Adventure in August. "A woman was pushing us on the line. We got into an argument, and I don't know what happened, but I hit her," she said. "I got arrested. And maybe it would have been alright, but I had a previous summons for selling electronics without a license." She had told me that she worked with those bands of mostly young men you see in the city in shirts and ties pushing luggage carts of radios and teddy bears through the subway cars. Afterwards, I found myself looking for her as I moved around Manhattan, feeling a little protective when I watched those young people get hustled by the cops.

I told her that I didn't have money to give her, but that I would talk to a friend who practiced law about how she could get a free attorney. Then I told her about a friend of mine who owned a pet store in my neighborhood who was looking for help and said that he would be willing to check her out.

Later that day, I got a call from Al Green. He called to tell me what he "would have me to do." "Take your sister in for a few weeks. Things are not right there with her boyfriend, and I don't like it. I don't want her in that boy's mother's house, and I sure don't want her out on the streets. She can stay with you until she can sort out her court troubles, and I can get together some money, and then I'm going to send for you both. Your sister isn't into that rough stuff; she knows better. But she loves her nieces. And she's manic depressive, you know."

He was coughing, kind of breathing heavy as he talked. "I'm sick, Peanuthead. My heart is weak. I've had two bypasses. I have a prostate problem, and I have kidney stones." My father, maker and shepherd of his children, family gangster, has been hit in the most prophetic places.

"Can you send me a little money until the gold deal I'm working on is made? I'm just waiting for a call from this woman who is coming out of the bush in Ghana. Then I'm going to fly to JFK to meet her. I'm going to be in your city, girl!" We are about to be so rich, he tells me, he will be able to take care of me for all my days.

A digital voice interrupted him. "You have one minute remaining." His time was up. I did not offer to return the call.

My searching had begun again, and just that soon, the uneasy anticipation, a haze of sadness, settled over me with a comfortable familiarity.

The looking had become reflexive. Even for a time after I found Estie and Al, I would find myself still looking, returning to the anxiety and the pleasure of imagining that had been so much a part of my life. I began to look for the first Sarah everywhere now, in every Black woman's face. I would get up close to women and study their hands and mouths, the contours of their bodies, listening carefully to their conversations. As I moved about the city, I would feel pulled back to college, to the days Henri and I rode the subways and Metro-North trains at dawn, coming from parties in Manhattan, or in the afternoon after classes, on schedule with the domestic workers and other laborers traveling between Westchester County and the Bronx and Harlem. I would watch every Black person, their faces and gestures, their ticks and expressions, for some resemblance to my own. I would look for someone who was appealing in some way, because of their beauty, or some ordinary pleasure in them, or their repulsiveness — anyone who offered a suggestion of a story that my imagination could mount upon. I would go deep in my fantasies of what their lives were like, and how and where I would enter.

Now I moved through my days watching for her with the same intensity. Any woman who held my glance at any moment could become Sarah Khan. All of the caution that my reunions with Estie Khan and Al Green and Sen should have taught me slipped out of me. I wanted to find a sister who perfected me, who was all the FMN girls rolled into one person. Who would be mine. I realized then that even with small Sarah, I wanted to find something beyond what sometimes felt like the impermanence, the fragility of friendships, and bank on a lifetime of intimacy.

As the weather turned colder and the holidays approached, my days felt punctuated by the blues that came each year at this time. I was spiraling into a deeper and deeper sadness as all of the feeling I had been holding off began to crack through the hard shell I had cultivated in the previous months. Estie and I were about to mark our first anniversary. We talked to one another less and less now. Her constant flow of letters had slowed to postcard writing, and now that too had nearly stopped.

Sometimes when she called, I would sit listening to her speak into my answering machine, and I would talk back. *Damn, why are you calling me?* Sometimes I wanted to pick up the telephone, but even the idea of it exhausted me. And I realized I was terrified, too, of the intimacy that it would require for me to share my anger with her—letting myself *feel* it, exposing myself, the work of talking things through. When Estie caught me on the phone, we would have these tight but kind of breezy conversations. Instead of leading myself into any danger, I would ask her questions about complicated medical problems. Instead of telling her how much I was hurting, I would talk to her about the tour of anti-depressants I'd begun taking, and we'd fix on questions about the brain's thresholds. She would talk to me as if she'd packed away her professional wisdom with her uniforms, and I'd hang up feeling like I had crack advice and nothing more.

One day, a supply of anti-depressants arrived in the mail. The expiration date on one bottle was dated three years earlier.

Sometimes she would call me, and I would be surprised to hear sharp, guided anger in her voice. In one conversation she told me: "You explained it to me one time when we first began talking, but I want you to tell me again—why did you come looking for me? Because I wish you had never bothered to look. This year has been a worse hell than what I lived with before. It's like you brought back all of the feelings and memories of my illness—like you're pushing me back to *that place*."

She called again a few days later and left a message on my machine. "I hate it when you don't call me. You make me feel like Al

Green always did—like I'm always waiting, while people I love keep me on hold."

Al Green would call me at all hours of the night. He would leave a friendly message, then call again in the morning, again in the afternoon. Each message would get more heated until he would finally shout into my answering machine: "Catherine, where are you? You have got some pretty lousy communication skills! I have never been subjected to this in my life! I've done business with all kinds of fools, and—" Sometimes I would pick up just then, before the tirade. Suddenly butter could melt in his mouth. "Oh, hello, there! Is this my Queen? You must be out playing royalty, or being chased down by your boyfriends. Queen Catherine of the Goobydigobblins! Heee heee hee!"

Then he would spin off talking. It was hard to resist his entertainment, the life epic he would piece together in stories.

He would tell me the names of the clubs and businesses in Harlem that he had designed. I would sit and write down the names as he spoke them—Striker's, Singleton's, Rosetta's, La Palm. Then after we hung up I'd thumb through the phone directory or call directory assistance, looking for places no longer around. I imagined popping in on the way home from work to see if the walls he described were still there.

He would tell me about the set designs he did for all of Sidney Poitier's United Artist films. He cannot remember the names of the movies, but he would detail in words every line he drew. Then he'd tell me fantastic stories about hanging with Poitier in the East Village.

I wanted to believe him.

He'd charm me with other stories: "I sent Malcolm X his first Koran—when he was in the pen."

"Al Green, did you really?"

"What did I just tell you? Sure did! I knew Malcolm well. We used to argue all the time. I had convinced the mayor to give us part of Harlem—to give us some blocks to turn into poor people's housing and other things. Malcolm wanted to get some land in South Carolina—he had these bullshit ideas . . . I told that nigger, forget about the land, man. This man is going to give us *two city blocks . . .*"

I was about to call him out for lying, when he trailed back and said, "Oh, and Spike Lee got the girl's name wrong in that movie. Her name was Jackie Taylor! She was the one carried that Koran to Malcolm in the jail for me." I've never checked into that one.

Al Green would talk and talk his dreams and preoccupations with me, and truly he could convince me at times. He's a true raconteur, delivering tales, casting himself in them as brilliantly as any of the stories I raised myself on.

His past is like the lingering question of his name. Alfredo Verdene. Who needed him to be Cape Verdean? Was it Estie? Was it the art world? The mob? Was it me? For some time, it was surely him.

Some nights he would call me to talk business: I must pray for him, because the very next morning he is meeting Mike Tyson to get a video that is going to make us all millionaires.

A week later: "How much furniture do you have? You need to move right out to Vegas—Mike is going to put some money into an international boxing magazine, and he wants you to come and be the editor."

Other nights: "I need you to find me a Russian. I'm getting into the vodka trade."

"I need you to help me find some churches. We are going to start setting up enterprise loans."

"The pallet business will make us all millionaires!"

"I have a contact for an association of miners in Sierra Leone and Liberia. I am just waiting for this woman to come out of the bush with the gold."

"I have a meeting next week with the CEO at Starbucks. We are going to buy out the Ethiopian coffee market."

"I am going to send in my papers to the Choctaw nation. I have sold my last diamond. I am dead cold broke!"

He would tell me about the inheritance that awaits his children. I tried to tell him that the only inheritance I want is some photographs, a visit from him, a piece of his artwork, even the smallest things, like a piece of paper with his handwriting on it, any simple token that he wants to give me. I want the things that will make him real to me. I only want what I can trust at its surface—only the most reliable signs of some little parts of who I am. I wanted him to slow down and listen to my own ideas and stories. He and Estie both were no good at listening. I hardly got to talk about myself. They never really asked me about the life I have made or about my family and how they prepared me for it. Maybe that would be too unbearable.

Then, a few weeks later, after I'd talked to Al Green's wife, he sent me photographs to buck my complaints.

One is a high school portrait of Al Green, Jr., my oldest sibling, a man now in his late fifties, who, except for his deep brown skin, looks nearly identical to me. Today I can connect the stories: He is estranged from the family. He lives in Tennessee now; he is an executive for Nike. He had an affair with my father's second wife, and when Al Green caught them, the two of them skipped town. Al Green threatened them with such violence (they knew he was capable of it; didn't he put his first wife through a plate glass door?) that his wife never returned for her children.

There is a beautiful sepia photograph from what I'd guess is the 1920s of a man in a three-piece suit, gold pocket watch on a chain, with an impressive, graying mustache. His hair is silver and close-shaven with a tiny side part, and his skin is dark. His beautiful, narrow, very sculpted face is centered by a nose as long and straight and commanding as a rifle barrel, with nostrils flaring at its end.

I remember his story: He is the Right Reverend E. T. Green, my great-grandfather. "A Black Prince," my father says. "The first Black man to vote in Richmond, Virginia—well, he's a Black Indian, really, Choctaw and African. His mother was a full-blooded Guinea African. He was a graduate of Harvard Divinity School (there is no record he attended, though—I checked), and he was a holy hell-raiser when he wasn't preaching. He owned a dance hall not far from his church. He used to wear a light tan Hamburg hat."

There is a picture of a man in a beautiful gray suit in front of a rambling Victorian. He looks like Al Green, his right foot propped up in the open door of a shining Ford as if he's hiding his high heel. It is the only thing that might disrupt this portrait of otherwise unassumed ease. But he is too light-skinned to be Al Green, and his silver box-cut afro had me calculating dates again. This would have been the 1950s.

I called Al Green to ask him if the photo was of him. "Oh, no, that's my father. That is Ernie Delaney." Now this man could not disown my father if he tried; they look that much alike. But I have written to the Virginia Department of Vital Statistics, and the birth certificate they sent me says Wyatt Green is his father. Al Green was so pleased that I'd done this; he choked up with tears as he explained to me that it's a record he's never had—which led him to another story: "My mother was sleeping with her sister's husband. She put Green down when I was born to protect herself, but everyone knew I was a Delaney. My mother was the fashion plate of Richmond, Virginia. She was Black and Choctaw and Cheyenne. Her people came from Florida. She was a masterful cook; she owned a restaurant. She owned two houses. She used to tend to pregnant women. But she was more like a mob woman. She ran liquor and the like. (The story I got later from others in the family is that his mother ran prostitutes.) She had a terrible temper and was a dangerous human being." He told me that he lost all of his mother's keepsakes after he quarreled with her side of the family—a loss for us all and the end of my wish for even relics of a Black maternal legacy.

Also gone are all the photos of his childhood, which had remained in the Delaney family house on Putnam Avenue in Bed-Stuy Brooklyn that his cousin (and half-brother) inherited. A year later I went there in search of evidence of his stories, like this one: "I was stolen by the nuns. I had two long braids, and they dressed me in velvet knickers, and they took pictures of me. The pictures said, Please Give to the Children's Orphanage. They raised over $300,000. I wish I had that money today."

At the house on Putnam Avenue I found only a man who looked so much like Al Green it almost made me cry for all of them. Before he died, he would answer the door, and I might stand there admiring him in his three-piece suit and fancy hat. As the door swung open wider, I might see a suitcase next to him. "I'm just on my way to Downtown Brooklyn." Then I'd smell the ammonia of urine and remember that he often wasn't wearing any underwear or pants. If the nurse let me in, he'd explain again that it was Alzheimer's and pretend not to see that I'd held my shirt up to my nose as I walked around looking for the remains of the Greens' and Delaneys' lives.

It was nearly Thanksgiving. The man who answered the phone spoke to me in a voice that trembled with age, in the way only folks from another generation, with one foot still in the country, do. "No, Sabine's not home just now," he said. "She teaches school, you know. She gets out at about two forty-five. Then she picks up the kids—she should be home ten past three or so, unless Sadiyah has her dance lesson today. No—dance was yesterday. Who may I say is calling? Can I have her to call you?"

Sabine Busby. My sister. Thirty-three. A schoolteacher. With kids. Lives with her father? A Black Southern man.

Just two days earlier, Ann Kendry had called. "I've found her!" she said. "Sabine Busby. I backtracked a bit. I wanted to try to get the story straight. She was born in Boston; her adoption took place in New York State. I'm not sure why. I can't find her in any listings, but her adoptive parents are Theodore and Chloe Busby. I have information for two T's and one Theodore Busby in Brooklyn, so I think we should start there."

And there it was again: "My source said that there is reason to believe that there were other births, but we'll just take this one step at a time." Of course. One step at a time.

My head was churning. *Estie and Al Green had a baby named*

Sarah Khan. Twice? Three times? Four? Did Estie have children with another man, someone she married? Were there truly never twins?

I already knew that it didn't matter so much anymore. I had a sister named Sabine Busby. Someone who came before me, who had the same two wild birth parents and an adoption history. I knew that I would try one time with Sabine, but I would not go any further. I could not search for anyone again. I decided to make this one last call for myself, in hopes of getting my One Good Thing.

I called the numbers Ann Kendry had given me, but none of them led anywhere. So I called a friend who sat at a data engine in a big law firm.

Within minutes, she had Sabine Busby of President Street in Brooklyn on her screen. I lived less than ten blocks from President Street. Ten blocks. We had different zip codes, and my friend and I sat trying to figure out if she lived in the mostly Italian and Irish blocks between my neighborhood and the shipyards along the Harlem River, or in the Caribbean and Jewish blocks of Flatbush and Crown Heights separated from me by Prospect Park.

I'd asked Estie much earlier how she would feel about my searching. "Oh, I would like to know her," she said, and she even offered to make some of the agency calls. But I knew that she had never actually picked up the phone. I had called her when it seemed Ann Kendry was getting closer to knowing something. I told her that I knew the information could come at any moment, and I was thinking about what I would actually do with it. I wanted Estie to think about how she wanted to play her part, because I knew that if I made a call, and this sister wanted Estie's information, I would give it to her. Estie had said, "Oh, my God, oh, my God. I can't handle this. But, yes, I want to know her." This was Estie all over again: wanting it, not wanting it; alternately certain and hesitant; ultimately relieved to have her cover blown.

Now I was worried about how to handle myself and about Estie's shifting emotional world. It was such unmanageable work to deal with the changes in her feelings. But I was also deciding to take the more encouraging cues. I knew that she could not stop me from searching. She could only make me amend tactics. Only Sabine herself could have stopped me. And in an odd way, I was taking care of Estie; she trusted me to take care of everything.

I kept asking friends how I should go about it, and they kept saying, *Just tell Estie what you're doing and then call her, girl.* When I had Sabine's telephone number, I picked up the phone to call her several times, but suddenly I was afraid of diving back into Estie and Al Green's wreck. I was afraid of what I'd find. After I got up the nerve to talk to her father, I decided to wait awhile, to just take it slow, but later that night, as I made my way home from Manhattan, I felt sick from the pressure of excitement, and I stopped at the phone booths in the subway station. The A train was roaring in the tunnel below, and the men hustling in the station were swooping toward me, circling back and swooping again, saying "Nice girl," "Mami," under their breath, nearly touching me. I stood facing out of the phone booth, giving them a hardened, angry stare, while the phone rang.

"This is Sabine," a woman said, and I choked out my introduction. Before it was all out, she was shouting. "Catherine, tell me you're not lying, tell me you're not lying! Catherine, tell me you're not lying! Jesus! Good Lord Jehovah! Praise God!"

This is a religious woman, I thought. My fantasizing was about to kill me again. We didn't get very far in our conversation. We were both overwhelmed, and the noise from the tunnel was too loud, and she had the baby in the bathtub.

"Please call me back. In an hour! Catherine, please call me. Don't lie to me, Catherine. Please don't lie to me," she kept repeating. I could tell she was crying.

As I made my way home, my body was shaking with excitement. *My sister is happy to hear from me.*

When I called her again, she picked up yelling, "Hey, little sister! Girl, I've been calling all of my people to tell them that I *finally* have some news about my mother!"

She started to ask me questions about Estie and how I had found her. I felt my gut drop a little. I felt like an envoy, a pitiful messenger.

But I understood her. I was probably never in her imagination. And it was like Estie and me and the pictures—we had each quickly sorted them down to the ones that showed where our passions lay. I tried to answer her questions—*Well, why didn't she call me? When did you meet her? When did you find out about me?*—tipping around the edges. I muttered something about Estie wanting me to call first, in case Sabine might not welcome the call. I suggested that we wait and talk in person; then I could show her photos and tell her everything.

She lived just two subway stops away, on the other side of the park. "Do you know that health food store near Carroll and Seventh?" she asked. "Meet me there tomorrow at 5:00."

We met just like that, like sisters hooking up in the neighborhood after work. I knew who she was right away, before she was halfway down the block, because she had Estie's stamp on her face. As she came toward me, she looked every bit the schoolteacher, almost matronly at first glance, in a gray tweed overcoat, open on a light green sweater that matched a paisley skirt, and green colored stockings pulled over strong and well-shaped Khan legs. But a bright orange crocheted hat, which raked her head dancehall style, was mixing up the signs. We hugged each other awkwardly, and then she stood in front of me and quietly studied my face.

"Come on, I need to get my head bad! I can't stand this!" she said, tugging me toward a bar a little way down the block.

As we took off our coats and settled into the booth, I watched her: the gold Chai pendant at her neck (how Jewish could she be?); a wrist full of bangles—that badge of West Indian womanhood; the reddish dyed, latest finger-curled Latina hairstyle. I took in her face, her hands, the gestures she made while she talked. The traces of Sarah and the Greens and I were unmistakable. She had Al's broad face, a chin and eyes like Sarah's and mine, and skin like Sen's. But the way she used her hands, and her laughter, and way of talking made her seem most of all like Estie, caught between three or four racial and cultural geographies. Suddenly, I felt this rush of affection for her; the part of me still hungry for my mother rose up barking again.

Sabine shouted at the bartender, "Yo, we need drinks! I just found my sister! We never met until about a minute ago! Don't we look alike? Don't we look alike?" She was kind of standing up, getting others into the scene. When she sat down again, and looked at me, turning up her face the way Estie does, I saw tears in her eyes. "Oh, my God! Oh, my God!" she said, in a Brooklyn Jewish voice, as people commented from the bar.

Sabine told me her story: She had been in foster care in Massachusetts for almost a year, and then she was adopted by a Jewish family. Then, during the first year with that family, her adoptive mother had a heart attack, and Sabine went back into foster care. When she was almost two, Theodore and Chloe Busby, who had been wanting to adopt, found their way to her. They were Southern transplants, living in Brooklyn, who were nearing forty and had given everything to their careers. Theodore Busby was a postal clerk and worked a second job as an embalmer—two coveted professions for Black men of his generation. Chloe Busby was the first Black surgical nurse in New York. They were the first Black family to integrate their mostly Lubavitch block in Crown Heights, buying a big, fancy house just around the corner from where Gavin Cato was struck down, igniting the Crown Heights riots in 1989. Sabine told me that her mother had died four years earlier. When Sabine had divorced her husband—a high school boyfriend—and she and her two daughters had moved back in with her father. She taught middle school math at a nearby school.

We sat for a long time, sorting through the pictures I brought for her as I tried to tell her about Al Green and my year with Estie. In just a few days, Estie and I would mark our first anniversary. What swift, incredible turns I'd encountered in such a short time. I tried to explain the inevitable questions: when I'd known about Sabine, and how I'd looked for her, and what the hell was it with the name Sarah? I tipped around Estie's emotional problems, hoping the outline of facts would say enough. I wondered if she could hear what I was telling her. She was probably taking it in the way I had when Mary Steed had first talked about there being "problems." It was too hard to integrate with my fantasies. I wondered how it would feel to be Sabine, never anticipating her younger sister would be calling. As I talked, she stared at a photo of Sarah and Estie while she spun the ice in her empty glass. "Your mother never got over me," she said.

As she sifted through the photos again, she betrayed her desires the way we all had; she barely glanced at the photos of me and of the McKinleys, and she threw aside the Green family pictures, saying, "I don't care about no Al Green and his kids!"

"But these people," she said, tapping a photo of Leo and Toby, "they are first on my list. Mission #1! My social worker told me that I went home with Estie for eight days, and when the family saw how dark I was getting, they called Jewish Family Services."

I flashed back through all of the stories of Sarah Khan's birth. Did it fit? Was it true? The tones of Estie's deceptions and her choices, her parents' racism, were changing again.

I suddenly felt this enormous sorrow sitting there with her. I felt like the messenger, lost again in someone else's story, the catalyst for remembering so much pain. I was sad about Sabine losing so many parents, and I was unprepared for her anger, unready for the consequences of what I had pursued.

Sabine ordered another drink, and we sat in silence while she finished it. Then she was suddenly happy and lighthearted. "Come on, let's go back to my house! I told the girls and Papa I was going to meet you, and they were begging to come," she said. She held my hand as we left the bar, and I recovered some of my own excitement by the time we climbed into her fancy Ford 4x4. The truck was filled with tools and building supplies. "You know I have a side business—it's called 3 MTs—as in Mother Truckers. That's me and the girls! I do remodeling, renovations, lay floors. Hell, I do it all. Lately I've been trucking ladies from the church back down South—they're all about to die. You say I look like your mother, but I bet I've got a whole lot of Al Green in me!"

As we drove through Sabine's neighborhood, I looked in the windows of the grand old houses. I could see the Hebrew-lettered signs on many doors, the large portraits of Hassidic men through the uncurtained windows of houses. A few Black and Latino children raced along the sidewalks on bikes, weaving between throngs of Hassidim who, at each intersection, would step out into moving traffic to cross the street, fiercely tapping the hoods of cars as they cut across their paths. They didn't smile; they stared at the drivers in a way that seemed hostile. They expressed such a complete ownership of the neighborhood, lining the rows of shops and businesses and places of worship with their mission-decorated RVs and community ambulances and security vehicles. Hassidic children moved freely, played along the sidewalks in a way you rarely see children in New York do. The West Indian and African American and Latin people moving among them seemed strangely shunted in comparison, disconnected, like unwelcome visitors. For a long time, I had traveled in and out of the eastern end of this neighborhood, visiting and shopping for the grandmother of a friend I'd made in Jamaica. The roach-infested apartments, the grinding poverty were so different from this area, even with its evidence of long-decaying wealth. This was a different Crown Heights.

I wondered what it was like for Sabine growing up there in her striving Black Southern family, knowing she had a Jewish mother—looking so Jewish, but probably recognized as part of several things that being Jewish didn't figure in. As she drove along, she talked about the neighborhood, moving between a Brooklyn Jewish voice, fluent Spanish, and a Jamaican accent. "I like to keep people guessing, like to play with their minds, you know. Ching chow wow, daughtah," she said.

I felt as if I'd soaked up all of what I imagined were her discomforts, and the collision of feelings that that neighborhood provoked. The homogeneity of dress, the orthodoxy, at least the appearance of easy congruence of that religious community stirred my resentments. I began to feel this seething anger—in the way I'd felt in Jamaica, in Ghana, in Attleboro—over that sense of hegemony and at the feeling of being shut out of something I could never belong to in more than tiny increments. Sabine's story of being taken home by Estie and then rejected by Toby and Leo, and later being relinquished by her Jewish adoptive family, had made me furious. How had Sabine felt growing up with some of that knowledge in her head, unrecognizable to the community she lived in? And then her Blackness was ambiguous to many Black people, too. It would have taken so much work to find a way in on either side—and yet—much more than I could say about my own childhood, she already *was* in.

We parked in front of a beautiful, old, three-story brick home. From the foyer I could see her father's embalmer's certificate on the dining room mantle, photos of Chloe Busby, with her pretty, kitten-like face under her nurse's cap. Her uniform, stiff with starch, and her white-stockinged legs, pulled me right back to the nursing home. I could imagine her powdered skin, the smell of her body caught in her nylon clothes.

Sabine led me into the room. "That's Chloe Busby! Isn't she bad? She is your mother, too. If she had known, she would have adopted you in a minute. Chloe Busby would have taken good care of you." She spoke with a fierce love and loyalty that made me want to take the photo and put it in my bag. I wanted to steal Sabine's Black mama. The house seemed exactly how Chloe Busby must have left it, with the plastic covers on the couches, the 1970s velvet furniture. But it was clear that Sabine was running things now. I was envious of what she had. It was the same anger I'd flashed on since highschool. When would that anger end?

I heard the stairs creaking as Mr. Busby made his way down to greet me. He was tall and thin and straight as a building edge, with a handsome moustache and big, feeling eyes. He was nearly as light-skinned as Sabine and me, and that contrast with Chloe's dark brownness reminded me of the dynamics of Henri's adoptive family and the way color somewhat covered the story of her adoption. Mr. Busby hugged me warmly and then sat down on the couch and just stared at us. Then Sadiyah and Ina and Trouble, a big rottweiler, came crashing in from outside, and I found myself in an excited embrace of arms. The kids were calling me "Auntie Catherine" and jumping wildly. I almost couldn't stand it—I looked at Ina and saw a child that looked so identical to Sarah that it seemed like a mean joke. Their ages were less than a year apart.

I stayed at the house with them for a while, trying to keep up with everyone's questions, until we were all too overwhelmed. Then Sabine drove me home, taking me slowly back through the neighborhood, pointing out her friends' houses, her children's babysitter's house, their schools, before she peeled Eastern Parkway with her truck. The radio was turned way up, and we rode singing along with Lil' Kim. When we turned onto my block, she got excited. "This is so deep! My co-worker lives on this corner. I was waiting to see where you lived before I said anything. Do you know, she and I carpool almost every day? I've rode down this block every morning for *years!*"

We sat in front of my house for a while in silence while the radio filled the truck. "Thank you for finding me, Sister," she said as I gave her a hug goodnight.

Estie had backed out on the deal. I shouldn't have been surprised, but I was. She had told me that she was ready; it was okay for Sabine to call. But after three days, she was still in hiding. Mac kept taking messages, and Estie kept refusing to pick up her phone.

The avoidance was so obvious. It hurt me down to my heart. Sabine was furious; she called me, cursing Estie and crying. I tried to ease the hurt, explaining what I had learned about Estie again. "This is not about *you*," I begged, as if that was something I could make her understand.

We talked for a long time that night, and I woke up in the morning sick with the feeling that I'd made a bad decision. But by the afternoon, Sabine called me sounding very different. "Can you take the day off tomorrow? I want to go to Boston and see your mama. I just got off the phone with her. We had a really short conversation. I was surprised that she answered the phone. We talked a little—it was cool. I told her I couldn't wait to meet her."

"I can't wait to meet you, too," she said, copying Estie's sometimes deadpan way of talking.

"I said, 'Good. Because I'll be in Boston tomorrow morning.'"

She told me the truck was cleaned out and packed. She'd borrowed a video camera. The kids and Papa were ready. "I'll pick you up at 5:00 A.M., so we can be in Boston by breakfast." I couldn't believe Estie was going for this, but Sabine was reading me Estie's directions to the house.

"I'm not going, Sabine. I have had my reunion; this one is yours."

I thought about how long it had taken Estie and me to approach a visit; how long it would take for Estie to explain things again to Sarah. "Take your time. Why don't you wait a little while and get to know her over the phone. Take time with Estie so you can get the best of her. And remember that Sarah is a kid—"

"I'm thinking of Sarah the most," she said. "Don't you think she'll be excited to know her oldest sister?"

I started to tell her what I really thought—that she was acting crazy and running straight for trouble—but I could tell that she was already close to fighting with me for refusing to go with her, so I wished her good luck.

In the photos and the video I saw a few days later, I watched Estie and Sarah come out of the house in their nightclothes to meet the Busbys. I saw Estie trying on Sabine's purple shearling coat. I watched all of them, even Mac, pile into Sabine's truck for a drive. (Sabine told me that Mac finally broke down at the end of the day and said, "What the hell, Estie? Is there going to be a new child showing up every year?")

In each frame, Sabine looked open with delight. Estie's eyes showed that she was completely absent, even as she was smiling. Sarah looked scared and apprehensive under her own smile. Every time she appeared, you could see her body pulling away, while Sabine, with Papa and the kids flanking her, pushed in triumphantly.

As soon as Sabine returned from Boston, she called Al Green. Whatever she lobbed at him, she reported that he had warned her, "Don't try and be cute with me. I can be a devil of a human being."

"Well, I'm the devil's spawn!" she shouted, hipping him to something.

Al Green, not to be outdone, switched channels. He called to his wife and said: "It's the missing link! Lord, my children have finally come home. We looked for you, you know, but Catherine just had a little better luck than we did."

Then he handed the phone to Linda. "She just kept saying, 'The circle of your father's life is now complete. Yes, now his life is complete.' What's *wrong* with your people?" Sabine asked.

The next day, Sabine took her photos and copies of photos I'd given her to school and tacked them all up on the bulletin board in her classroom. All day her students and co-workers came to look at them. And for several weeks, each time Sabine called me, her home-girls, their children, her boyfriend, her ex-husband and many friends, people from her church who had stopped by the house to wish her well, would get on the line to say, "God bless you. This is a wonderful thing. You have really made Sabine happy."

All the while I felt as though someone was advancing with a rope; but this was not a rescue. I was bound up in bigger unhappiness.

The phone became a lottery machine; answering it was playing with high stakes. Anyone could be on the other end with any kind of news.

One morning it rang and I took a chance and answered it. "Hi Catherine! This is Lisa. I'm a producer at Talk Show B here in New York City. Girl, you are so fine! I'm sitting here with photos of you—your sister Sabine just left. She came by with them and a copy of the videotape..."

Lisa told me how Sabine had called her a few years ago when she was beginning to search for Estie. She hoped that maybe a show with millions of viewers and a hotline would help her to make some head-way. Lisa had thought they might be able to do something, but time passed, and Crown Heights had become less of a hot spot—they'd lost their angle, and in the meantime, they'd done another show on "bi-racial" children. "But now Sabine has found you all. We're really touched by the story—how she went to the rabbis in her community, and how they tried to help her in Boston. We think this is such a wonderful example of Black and Jewish cooperation. And the *Sarahs!* That is a story!"

They were willing to fly in Al Green and Estie and Sarah, and maybe some of the other children, so that we could meet our father at last, and the Sarahs could be reunited. Live and direct. The Al Green and Estie Khan and the Half-Breed Sarahs Show.

Lisa was a white woman, talking "Black," who had taken a quick look at us and was trying to serve me what she thought was a good appeal. I asked her if she was joking, but it was too obvious that she wasn't. She let me know that she'd already gotten the go-ahead from everyone except Al Green and me.

Al Green was not going for it. "That girl, uh, uh—your sister—what is, uh, her, uh, uh, what is her last name again?" he asked me when I called him.

"Her name is Sabine. Busby, Al."

"Well, I don't know what she's up to. Why would she want to go on and do something like this with a damn talk show? What happened was a family *tragedy.* It is something—*that*—*never*—*should*—*have*—*happened.*" His voice was breaking; I thought he might be crying. "It is a family disgrace, and I am not going to go on some fool show to tell people business that *never should have happened!*"

There he was, not tripping on the edges of blame. Acknowledging how we were all hurt. Calling a bad thing what it is. The man was becoming a little bit my hero. I had tears in my eyes.

"And besides that, I am known by the heads of at least three African states. The paramount chiefs! The queen mothers! In Ghana, in Liberia. I am known! Anyone can say the name Al Green, and people will know who I am. I was the talk of Africa! When I left Sierra

Leone, they sent thirteen fighter jets off with my plane! I was made a chief—and they got American TV over there. They watch CNN in the damn bush. I am not going to be made a fool of!" he stormed.

Everyone was storming now. I called Sabine and told her quietly that I was not going to do the show. I could not find the words to explain. She used every argument with me—how we could show the world "how splendiferous we've become" despite this mess; how we can meet our father, who surely won't figure out another way to get to New York. "C'mon girl, they are going to fly everyone in for the tap-ing, put us up in a nice hotel."

"Sabine, we live in New York. Are they going to take us up over Manhattan for drinks?"

I decided to let Al Green do battle with her and hung up.

But she called and called again and again, trying to cajole and trick me, guilt me on my answering machine. I called her back and told her *No, No, No,* as if it were a word I'd just learned.

"No, no way. I cannot believe you would even think of doing this crap!"

"You fucking owe this to me!" she yelled.

The next day another call came in from Lisa. Al Green and Sen, who was back in Vegas, were coming after all. ("Well, it would be an opportunity for us to get together," Al Green said when I asked him why he had changed his mind. "It's a free trip. And who says we have to make it to the show?")

Estie and Sarah were coming. ("I asked Sarah if she wanted to be on TV, and she said yes. And it is so important to Sabine. But I don't really want to do it," Estie told me, breaking into tears.)

"Don't you want to come and meet your *father?*" Lisa asked me.

"Don't you want to see your family reunited?" I reminded her that I had found each and every one of them.

"You don't have to worry, you know. Our host has bi-racial children," Lisa said, as if that should put my heart at ease.

She had one last ploy. "Catherine, what about an *off-camera* reunion. You could just come by the set. It's off-camera—*off-camera*." she said.

But all of the wrangling was soon over. Al Green couldn't come; he couldn't cross state lines. "I have a gun charge in Pennsylvania," he told me. "I went to get Sen out of school one day, and the security guard stopped me when I was coming in the building and told me I had to show him my ID. I pulled out my gun and told him, 'This is my fucking ID.' Hell, I've been a law man since the 1960s!"

| Aftershock |

Winter 1997

After everyone (the ones I had found, not the ones still missing) was known to me, I began sitting shiva for them. I cut myself off from everyone and gave in to grieving.

When someone asks me now what it meant to search, I can say that it was an act of self and an act of mourning.

I had been born into loss. People were lost to me. My personal and racial history, my link to communities of people who so much defined my experience in the world, were blotted out. No matter who stepped in, no matter what they gave to me, there was still always this fact of someone missing, this fact that there had been no language for, no structure, no recognition of that immense grief.

I had called all of my ghosts to the table. They had sat with me and feasted. The party had run on for days, until we all took a good look at each other, wiped our mouths, and got up from the table, kicking open an exit through the door marked Grief.

I had disrupted who I was. No one could have prepared me for the confusion of that or for the reservoir of intense feeling I'd collected over those years. I will try to explain what those days of Post-Family felt like, but some part of it stands on the other side of words.

At first, cutting off from all of them left only a dull ache. And then there was a moment of liberation. I remember Estie and Mac and Sarah's last visit to Brooklyn. Sarah and I took our rollerblades and raced around the park while Estie and Mac walked behind us. It was a beautiful day on the tail of bad weather, the kind that brings everyone out. Sarah and I covered several loops of the park, then we sat down for a while on the edge of the road, resting and watching people, before we circled back to find Estie and Mac. They were sitting on a bench near the softball fields, watching the women's teams play. People I knew from years of socializing in Brooklyn were out there on the field. Couples I knew strolled over. Friends with new babies. A woman with whom I had taken a writing class a few years earlier, who had been working on a book that had become a sudden success, came up to say hello. When I introduced her to Estie and Mac and Sarah, this anxiety rolled over me.

"This is—?" I felt so adolescent.

"This is my family?" Suddenly they seemed as much of a prop as Mattie had been.

I had stopped everything else to have them. I had been on my way to being a woman—working hard and having love and ambitions and friends and trying to make the kind life I wanted for myself—and somehow, believing I was enlarging that, I had cut off from myself. It was as if I'd made an odd claim on ex-communitas.

When I let go of all the Greens and the Khans and Busbys, I felt remarkably free. I was trying to get on with the business of living my own life and remaking my world. But then came the slow draining of certainty.

I had tried to reckon with my loss; I had received some important answers from Al Green and Estie, from my sisters. What I had was not at all what I had imagined I'd find, but it was probably *enough*. That feeling settled into quiet contentment, and I embraced it as the core of my search. So for a while, I felt a rush of confidence and excitement about resuming my life. But soon, that feeling started to recede. I felt my old depression—the feelings I thought my search had resolved—rolling over me again. It seemed like the feeling part of my search had really just begun.

I tried to explain this to a friend—a Latin-born, Florida-bred, Sephardic Jew. It was Yom Kippur, and he had invited me to spend the holidays with his family, and I was telling him how cut off I felt from Judaism. "You must somehow feel contaminated by this," he said. It was an odd thing to say. *Jewish. Contamination.* Later I felt a little set up. What was he looking for me to say? But in that moment, I felt myself saying *Yes,* as all of my self-loathing surfaced.

Contaminated fantasies, imagination. Contaminated bloodlines, culture. Contaminated by ill parents.

I was becoming so afraid of my melancholy. I felt so exposed and sensitive, so raw and open to everyone. When I stood in front of my students, I felt weak-minded, on the verge of tears, vulnerable to their challenges and their general boredom. And I started to feel violent toward myself again. I started having this recurring dream that someone had pierced my skin with sewing pins. It was supposed to bring on healing, like some newfangled acupuncture. But instead of letting the doctor remove them, I would push them in deeper, grinding them into the bone. And as I hit lows I didn't think I could emerge from, I became afraid that I was destined to be some part of Estie's emotional self.

I decided that I needed to protect myself, to slowly build myself up again. And for a good part of the following year, I withdrew even further. I restricted my life to home, work, and therapy, and spent time with only a few friends.

I took a Polaroid picture of myself every night and put the series near my bed. When I woke up, I would look at them and have a conversation with myself. "This is who you are. This is what you've accomplished. You are good in these ways. You struggle in these ways. This is your future and all the things that are possibilities." And what kept me going were those images and my feeling that I wanted to love the person in them.

Sometime in the thaw of my depression, I realized that the McKinleys and I were slowly coming around to each other. There was no obvious evidence, no great epiphany—none of us really changed how we acted as family or got any better at talking. But there was a new ease to our conversations; we were a little more generous with each other. It was subtle. I could barely discern it, but it was there.

Spring 1998

I had a final request for Mary Steed. I called her to ask whether I might see my files now that there could be little legal argument for withholding them. I was curious to check them against everything that I had learned. It was a way to try to finally reconcile some of the imperfections of Estie's and Al Green's and the New England Home for Little Wanderers' different stories.

Mary Steed told me that the records could be released, but I would need Estie's and Al Green's agreement. I wrote to them both, explaining what I wanted, and I included permission letters I typed for them that they only needed to sign and have notarized. I made out return envelopes and even put the stamps on them, and I sent them off, knowing how impossible the whole thing might be.

Even through my period of retreat, Al called me regularly. He didn't seem to mind too much when I ignored his calls. We were beginning to talk easily now, and he had taken to calling every week or so to catch me up on his business plans and family stories. I had told him that I wanted to see my files and explained what I needed him to do. "Of course! Anything for my little Peanuthead!" he said, laughing. "But I hope your detective work is done. Those social rambles ain't restful—who said that? Satchel Paige!" He was 100 percent spirit, but I had a little less confidence about him getting organized enough to see it through.

Estie and I were down to cards on the holidays; we never spoke. My occasional letters, the books I sent to Sarah, were never acknowledged. Now I wrote Estie a careful letter, worried that I might set her off in some way, and angry about needing something that put me at the mercy of whatever she might be feeling.

I didn't hear from her after I sent the letter. For more than a month I didn't hear from her. And then I wrote to her again. I tried to imagine what she might fear about what I was asking; for a while I worried that there might be some other unmentionable bit of history in those records. I knew that Estie was the only one who was truly vulnerable to what I was asking. Probably the only reference to Al Green was as my "alleged father." However, the files might say anything about Estie's difficulties, and they would hold more of her history than even my own.

Then, not long after I sent the second letter, Mary Steed called and surprised me. She had been holding both of their letters and was expecting to hear from me. She seemed anxious about turning over the file, anxious about discretion and sending it through the mail. We talked about what she was sending, and how she could get it to me securely, and then a few days later a short stack of xeroxed pages arrived.

She'd added a warm, simple note. She wrote that she had looked back over my letters to her and realized that it had been eight years since I'd first written to her. Eight years. For this long, Mary Steed had been a powerful authority, withholding from me what often felt like my only bid on a sane life. At the same time, she had been a witness where no one other than the FMN girls stood, and she had been kind somehow, within her limits. I had spent eight years—more than eight years really—piecing together a fragmented history, a fragmented-feeling self. Now she was standing witness once again, as I closed an era.

At the end of her note, Mary Steed had written her home address. She said that she would be retiring soon. She knew that I would write about this experience one day, and she hoped that I would share with her whatever I created because my story was in some small way her story, too.

I read her note again and leafed through the pages of records. The start of my life, the reconstruction of my life by social welfare—it was all there in less than twenty sheets. There were medical records for *Sarah Khan, illegit. Mixed racial ba. Girl.* There were intake studies made by social workers, obstetrical summary sheets, doctors' reports. I noticed right away that none of the doctors' names matched the ones in that first birthday card Estie had sent me. There was my original birth certificate, where I am *Sarah Khan, Female, Colored.* There was an adoption surrender form with Estie's signature in her same neat near-calligraphy. It looked as though she had signed with a strong hand. The name appeared, as in her letters to me, curiously at the farthest edge of the signatory line, but it did have an assurance to it; it was not the mark of someone about to slide away. Then, on the line just below, I saw Sarah Arnold, the witnessing hand of the three Sarahs' namesake. In an odd way, I took pleasure in those two signatures, and I suddenly felt a little bit freer of Estie's hurts.

After the first few sheets, the pages were headed: *Catherine McKinley (Adopted Bristol County Probate Court).* I was listed on one sheet along with *Baby girl, 5–29–63, Adopted—N.Y.C. through Jewish Home and Family Services at fifteen months of age.* There was Al Green, my *Negro, Prot., Putative father, married, Roxbury, Mass.* There was the name and address of my foster mother—Bernadette Carroll. I wondered who she was? She was my mother for the first months of my life. I had such a powerful urge to thank her.

There were liner notes: *Mother presently at Massachusetts Mental Health Center. When mother became aware of her second pregnancy, she attempted suicide by taking an overdose of barbiturates, and was then admitted to the Massachusetts Mental Health Center. Mother is depressed and suicidal. Worker recommends the intake study be closed and that a division worker not visit her.*

There was a "Problem at Referral" report for me: *Jewish Family & Children's Services is referring the placement of the child to Department of Child Guardianship as they are unable to provide a home for a mixed racial baby. Mother does not plan to be designating the child's religion as Jewish.*

I flipped back through the pages and I found myself sobbing. I was no longer the social welfare system's hostage. They had no hold on me. Everything that was written in those files seemed so innocuous now. There were no enormous secrets, just details that imperfectly corroborate the many things that had been spoken and remembered in pieces as I searched. Anything that was left out—about other children, or a marriage—can remain a mystery. I knew that Mary Steed had been a friend to me at times when I could not see it. She had told me in time-released capsules much of what was there. In some ways, her slow and careful disclosure of details had protected me. But what a price I paid. *Eight years.* What does it say about a system that exacts so much for such simple truths?

September 1999

"I'm Al Green, the nigger with the six-foot arm. I'm the nigger with the golden fist. I was a sheriff. I know the Queen of England. The President. And the King of Africa," proclaims Jasmine, my oldest niece, imitating Al Green's limping gate. This sends the other children into a riot of laughter, and they tear down the street.

We are walking the City—Sabine and Song and their five daughters. The three of us, sisters, have formed a kind of fragile union. We are not good at our relationship yet, and we disappoint each other in myriad ways, but sometimes we find ourselves like this—relaxed and comfortable together, grateful for each other. My early struggles with Sabine do not matter. We have done some fighting and some reckoning, and we have become friends. I am beginning to love her wildness, her wide open heart, which reminds me of Al Green's best self, and a sensitivity to people that comes at totally unexpected moments and makes up for how she can sometimes overwhelm me. Song is a bright, very beautiful woman, with intense, expressive eyes and sharp features, the coal black curly hair, and dark brown skin, which make her look like the Choctaw-African maternal ancestor we all imagine. She is Al Green's favorite child, his own reminder of a mother who was distant from him. She is the one who made good on his talents — who survived the chaos of his parenting and abandonment by her mother when Song was only nine — and got herself a degree in design. Song is just eleven years younger than Estie. She remembers when Estie came into their home, just as her mother left. She recalls Estie in the way I imagine her: rebellious and scared and needing Al Green's refuge. She has already given Sabine and me more memories of Estie and Al Green than they themselves can share. Song and Sabine and I are practically strangers; we've spent less than a week's worth of days together in nearly two years. Nevertheless, we are bonded by our witnessing of Al Green, what we feel we've lost of our mothers, and this shaky little promise of sisterhood.

Song has told us stories of our father that echo what I've heard from Estie and from others, stories of a man who was neglected by his family until that lack of care bled into violence. She has told us stories of the damage he has done to his children and to others, somehow always coming off clean. Stories of his mob life. Stories of how he kept his family moving from place to place, sometimes squatting, sometimes on the street and how the children learned to save themselves with his girlfriends' kindnesses.

I asked Song what her best memory of growing up with Al Green was, the best thing she got from him. "His creativity," she said. "And then I remember going around to political meetings with him, being around the gallery. He was so handsome and charismatic, and he could talk to anybody. He could find his way into any circle. I got to see a lot—I met a lot of people who made me aware of a lot of possibilities. I think I got inspiration, too, from some of his dreaming." She was quiet for a while, and then she said, "I guess he also taught me that it is easier to ask a person for $1,000 than a $1. Now that's confidence! That's what I got from him."

Just a few months earlier, I learned that I had won a Fulbright grant to spend a year in Ghana, doing research for a novel about the indigo trade. In the midst of all of these changes, indigo had sneaked in and become my obsession. In less than a month, I would be leaving. I knew that I wouldn't be coming back home during this year, and I had a sense that I might stay on there longer. I was single, and I was funded. I was packing up my apartment, putting everything in storage, and saying goodbye for a while. I was feeling an enormous freedom to do my work, and I wanted to experience Ghana and other parts of West Africa much more deeply than I had in the past. I wanted to return to places I'd visited a little more settled about who I was, a little more intellectually mature and less romantic than I was in the past. I wanted to experience myself unattached to home—to its commitments and to the language here and assumptions about identity. It was a convergence of many freedoms that I hadn't imagined I could have all at once.

So I was saying goodbye to everyone. A few weeks earlier, Sen and her mother had called me and Sabine. They had taken the bus from Vegas so that Linda could visit her parents in Pennsylvania. They wanted to come up to the City for an afternoon. Sabine and I met them at the Greyhound terminal, and three hours later, they were turning around to catch the bus home to Vegas. But they were happy just to be in Greenwich Village, one of Al Green's old stomping grounds, and to spend time with us. Linda was the same woman I'd encountered on the telephone—quiet and sweet, enormously devoted to Al Green, content with the smallest things.

She and Sen had asked me a thousand times when I was coming to Vegas. In two years, I hadn't made any move to see my father. And he had not moved to see me. "You really should come," Linda said. "He's eighty. And his health is bad. And you're going so far away, for a long time. God forbid, but you wouldn't want to see him for the first time at his funeral."

Now Sen and Sabine were echoing Linda, calling up this specter of regret they were sure I would feel. It was exhausting to explain the rationale of my decision. I tried to tell them how his life, his choices, his violence sickened me. And given the fact that he had not made much effort and I had worked pretty hard for the relationship that existed, I felt that I deserved absolution from regret.

The truth was that it bothered me a little that I could not organize myself to see him. I had offered to send him a ticket, but he wasn't keen on traveling, and I imagined that he would probably disappoint me and cash in the fare. He was a genius for spoiling anything having to do with money. I imagined that if I traveled to Vegas, he wouldn't show up; he would be too busy with his lotto or his hustles. I knew it was possible because Sabine went to see him soon after she met Estie, and he had dropped her at his house and spent a good part of the weekend "taking care of business," trying to win entertainment money at the Seven Eleven nickel slot machine.

I was afraid that he would break my heart with all the ways that he himself is broken.

The script in my head was something like the meeting my Afro-German friend Faustie experienced with her father. She flew from Germany to Illinois after a year of warm letters and phone calls. She rented a car and drove the rest of the way to the appointed meeting place. Her father left her waiting for three days in a hotel room halfway between Chicago and the town where he was living. He kept calling her at the hotel with promises. Then just a few hours before she had to return home, he arrived. She said that her English was bad, and she could not always understand him, but she felt he was almost flirting with her. He was unwilling to engage in any kind of meaningful talk. She felt like a woman left pining, wanting something of him she had no right to ask for, like she was begging him to just please the Old Girl, give her a little of what she needed. It was a tragicomic lovers' routine.

Al Green and I had talked often about dates, but each time that I could travel, I chose not to go. Now Sabine and Song were circling me with understanding, but they were working down my resolve.

When I told Al Green about my fellowship, he had said, "Girl, you're going to Africa, and you can't make it to Vegas? Now you could just take your money and put it to some real use and come on out to Vegas if you want to see a bunch of cosmetic people!"

You keep disappointing me. You know, this is why I can't do business..."

"What am I supposed to do for you, Al Green?" I asked, truly wondering.

"What is it you are supposed to do? Well, if you don't know that—shit, you're going to Ghana? Oh, forget it!" he raged and stuttered.

"C'mon now, how are things with you all?" I said, trying to calm him down.

"Things are fine here except you niggers—all of you—my—children—can't—be—relied—on—and—I—am—here—trying..."

I could feel him teetering toward the edge of where he goes off cursing and talking about how he's been betrayed by his children, who are worthless and weak and don't know loyalty, and how he's so mad he could knock all of their damn souls into next week. Somehow I have managed to stay on his good side, and he has treated me like the special one, his last hope. I have heard him talk about his whole family in this way, and I have been amazed at the violence he can work up in himself. The only thing that tempers it is that I know he is a failing man, a tiger without teeth.

But that day I wasn't having it; I hung up the phone in the middle of his tirade. I had come close to fighting with him. The only thing that stopped me was this feeling that it would be a useless thing—it would be like an argument with a mad person. I tried to forget all of his abuses. I turned to the one remarkable thing: this was the first time I had been called a "nigger" with conviction, in the true-blood, family, my people kind of way.

The first thing he did was put his cowboy hat on my head. I don't know if we hugged. We must have hugged. I only remember walking off the plane into the Vegas airport and being locked in his smile and the warm grip of his hand at my elbow. I have it in a Polaroid picture that Linda took. The photograph tells it all—what his grip felt like, how wide our smiles were, how much I am his child. It is all there in the eyes and dimples and the bridge of our nose—my membership in his sprawling Gang of Family. His arm, stretching across me, ready to hold me, is my own. It has the same wing-like curve of the bone. He took my hand in that moment and fingered the turquoise ring on my pinkie, the silver Navajo cuff that I inherited from my Arizona settler great-grandmother by way of my mother's abandoned jewelry. He wore large turquoise rings on his own hands and a wrist-cuff set with a bear's claw in a circle of turquoise stones. A thick, wavy silver pony-tail hung down his back from beneath a ten-gallon cowboy hat. "You see us, Peanuthead? We both got our Indian on today! Hee hee hee!" he laughed.

"You got your mama's legs," he said, standing back from me a lit-tle, squinting for a closer look at me. "But you're a Green. You look like your brother Al, only he's not mixed. And you look like Song a lit-tle bit, too. Don't look at all like that boss of ours!" He could only mean Sabine.

As we walked out of the airport, I tried to match the rhythm of my steps with his, catching the pause between one foot's landing and when he'd swing his hip out with this powerful kind of grace to get force behind his shorter leg. I was aware of people staring at him, try-ing in this town of spectacles to make sense of his long, broad torso, his long arms and strong, wide hands that hung well past his hips. His khaki pants and light blue pullover were neat and unassuming, but the black faux alligator loafers he wore—one with nearly six inches of narrow, stacked heel, which I knew he built into the shoe himself—looked like showbiz. I watched people struggle to hide their expression when they realized his Little Richard-esque effect was because of injury and not fashion. I didn't think Al Green could have that much fun with himself.

Vegas was looking like it might be a good time when we pulled out onto the highway in my father's borrowed Toyota. "The limo is in the shop," he said, with not one bit of irony. (I knew that just a month earlier his house had been repossessed, and he and Linda and the kids had moved to a temporary apartment.) The sun was setting, and everything had a pink blush of light over it and was much more beau-

tiful than I ever expected. I felt relaxed and happy there with him and
Linda, something I had not imagined I would feel. We drove down
the strip, and Linda called out the names of the hotels as we passed
them like a proper tour guide, telling me what each place was like,
decoding the elaborate signs in people's dress and what it suggested
about where they might be staying, and the many ways they might
entertain themselves. "You know a lot about this town, Mummy. How
do you know so much about this place?" Al Green said, squeezing her
thigh.

I saw them in the same moment he did, just before his head shot
out of the window. "Hah! Lezzies!" he said loud enough to qualify as a
shout, with the same predatory excitement of young men cruising
women from their cars. "Did you see that, Mummy? They were holding hands! And they fat, and one of them is *Black* and has the nerve
to have blond hair."

I stopped breathing. Stopped thinking.

He had placed his hat on the seat next to me, and I had been fingering its snakeskin band, playing with the rattlesnake tail ornament.
I realized I had just smashed it in my hand. Linda said, almost apologizing, "Oh, leave them alone. So what? You know this is the strip..."

I sat there, ashamed of my silence, paralyzed by too many feelings
running together. Sabine had made it her business to let all of the
Greens know that I was "funny," and she'd reported happily that Al
Green wasn't going for any of that, but it had never come up any time
that he and I talked. I was simply never much of a focus of his conversations. Was he baiting me now? I started to review my exit plans,
in case my twenty-four-hour jaunt turned out to be too long.

When we got to my hotel, Al Green disappeared with Linda into a
suit shop while I joined the check-in line. But soon I heard his voice

not far from me, telling Linda, "That's my heart beat there. I have my daughters. Now I have everything." He made a big ceremony of calling the concierge, and when we got to my room, he inspected everything and tipped the man in coins.

"Sit down, Babygirl. Let me fix you a drink," he said, and he served us each a coke on my bill. And then he told me to close my eyes and put out my hands while he pulled two gold women's watches from his pocket. "These are for you. I need to take them to get new batteries tomorrow, but—look now, this one has a diamond chip! They aren't new, but you'd never know it," he said fastening them both on my wrist.

We drank up and went out to make the most of my night in Vegas.

We drove out to the far edge of the city, so that I could see their new apartment. I expected to see chaos—five people and a dog in a hastily found one-bedroom apartment—but the order to the place, its homeyness, with framed pictures and knickknacks and furniture in sets, told me something else.

Right away, Al Green pulled me into his bedroom and sat me on the bed. "I have a hat for you here," he said, handing me an ice-gray cowboy hat with a band of green and gray and brown feathers fastened by a plume of longer white ones at the back.

"They'll love this in Ghana! They like feathers and country music and all that over there, and it will be good in all that heat!" he said. "It's a shame you're going so soon. You could just stay out here in Vegas now that we're all together."

I sat there wearing my hat as Linda pulled photos out of a closet, handing me pictures of their twenty-fifth anniversary, when they renewed their vows, of the kids, of their history of cars, of Al's art. Al

Green was pulling suits from another closet at the same time. Talking over her.

"This one is from England! This one is I-talian, right, Linda? Hey, Peanuthead, that's Lindarooskie of the Goobygoblins! Ain't you, Linda? Hey, Peanuthead, I've got belts!"

Then he pulled out his briefcase, showing me letters on FBI stationary, dated in the 1960s, attesting to his character, to his employment with the bureau. He stood up and lifted his shirt and pulled down the waist of his trousers. "You see this scar? It runs clear past my knee. You know I've had some aneurysms with this damn leg. I won't show you. You'll lose your appetite, and we've got a dinner to go to! C'mon ladies!"

After we left the apartment, we drove out toward the hills. He instructed Linda to stop at the end of a cul-de-sac in front of enormous cookie-cutter brick homes that looked like they were straight from the celebrity pages of *Ebony* magazine. "This is a five-acre lot. This is the one we're going to make an offer on, right Linda? Five acres! That's enough room for horses. I just wanted to show you what you will come home from Ghana to. Now let's go eat!"

We ate dinner at a typical strip mall buffet place and drove around town again for what seemed like hours. "Cheap entertainment!" my daddy says.

It was nearing midnight. I had been in Vegas less than six hours. I sat in my hotel room after they dropped me off, exhausted by even that little time together. It already seemed like enough. But I felt oddly satisfied. Al Green was giving me everything he had. I didn't want to push my luck. I was kind of dreading how we would spend the next day, but I was happy that I had come. In just those few hours

I'd lived a whole chapter of Al Green. Suddenly, I was feeling anxious to close out my period of ambivalence and start living my truly post-search life. I was thinking about things at home—my packing, the things I had to do in the two weeks before I left for Ghana, the visits I would make to my family, the ones who were truly mine. I put on my new cowboy hat and sat for a long time in the three-way, lighted mirror, tracing Al Green and Estie's faces in my own, feeling a little sad, but strangely content.

I woke up worried that he wouldn't come the next day. But by ten o'clock, he and Linda and Frankie—my arsonist brother, once on the FBI list for mob work—found me at the pool. They settled into chairs next to mine, happily chatting with me and checking out women.

By afternoon, we'd done some gambling. Al Green and Frankie showed me how to work the machines, and Al made "Six for me, one for you; all for me, none for you" jokes as he counted out tokens. Then we were sitting in the car, in the garage at Caesar's Palace, passing a bottle of cheap wine. "I bought it to celebrate," Linda said. "To hell with your Indian blood! Al and Catherine, you better have a drink today!" We suffered some of its sweetness, and then we rushed Linda off to work and headed out to the airport.

My plane was delayed, and Al Green and Frankie and I sat together for nearly two hours, sharing hot cinnamon rolls he bought me, complaining all the while how expensive they were and then going back for seconds. We sat mostly in comfortable silence.

"Peanuthead, I have something—" Al Green said as he pulled out his wallet. It was leather, worn almost to paper, filled more with business cards and paper scraps than money. It reminded me of the old men at the nursing home where I worked all those years, whose wallets were still essential to them, still an important part of dressing them, important to their sense of power, long after the cash was out of their hands.

He pulled out a business card for a used car dealer and handed it to me. My number at the writers colony in Seattle, where I had stayed the summer before, half-expecting him to show up with his Hell's Angels friend, Bill, en route to make a coffee deal with Starbucks, was written on the back of it. He had spelled my name "Catchy" above it.

"That's yours, Peanuthead," he said, letting me know he'd had me in mind all along. He handed me his old 1976 Massachusetts driver's license. "That's yours, too." I sat with him in silence again, fingering the edges of the cards until it was time for me to board my plane.

"I hate good-byes, so, please, go now, okay?" I said.

"Ah, girl, I wanted to give you some money now, before you go to Africa, but..."

"Oh, Al Green, don't worry. You've already given me these beautiful watches," I said, pulling back my sleeve.

He looked hard at my face, and then he hugged me. "Okay, Babygirl. I'm leaving you now."

| Epilogue |

The punchy smell of *indigofera* leaves permeates the atmosphere. The first time the cloth enters the dye pot—when it is submerged below the thick, foamy, oily head of the treacly blue bath and quickly released—it emerges a thin, dirty yellow that deepens as it is exposed to the air. With each subsequent submersion, and each infusion of oxygen, the cloth changes from the yellow hues of skin, through a spectrum of greens, into blues that progressively deepen to the purple-blueness of black. This is the quirky alchemy of indigo—the bath of fortune and toil.

Indigo is the color of my tie-dyed print Danskin suit—my third-grade "African" dress; of the cloths Mattie sold, captured at the edge of her photo; of the worn, soft denim of my mother and father's farm clothes; of the mohair coat my grandmother wore to work at her elevator company in Long Island City that I now donn, living a part of her New York life; of the bedspread Estie and I share. As I play with the dye, design, and stitch the cloth, I feel a bit of Al Green's artist life in me. It is a Yoruba *adire* cloth, intricately hand-painted in a design that is protective, and prophetic in meaning: "My head is correct." The cloth is the gift of a beloved teacher, a Nigerian, who saw how I was struggling to understand and measure the people around me through my book reading and urged me to see the line between the imagination and people who perhaps live in the world more complicatedly.

Indigo is the color of the deep, druglike haze of melancholy I once lived in, and of the cloth that became a balm.

I left New York City for Ghana, with traces of mourning still in me. I established a base in Accra, and then over a year and a half I journeyed through nine West African nations—from Nigeria to Benin, Senegal to Niger—in search of blue-stained women's hands, tracing the routes of trade, the stories of women whose once powerful dye economy, spread on bicycles and steamships and lorrys, stretched across half of a continent. I spend my days traveling, exploring the mysteries, the cosmology of the dye pot that, because I am outside of language and uninitiated I can never wholly learn. Each blue cloth, with its complex pigment, its unique feel, and smell, and design, has the depth of a narrative I want to enter with my own knowledge. I spend my days seeped in blue, decoding, searching again.

Whenever I return to my base in Ghana, I become "obruni" again. Who I am, who I'd just become—the daughter of the parents who parented me, and of Al Green and Estie Khan—is inscrutable to those around me. At the end of my search for self-definition, I have become a rich, white woman. A stranger. Entertainment for many as soon as I step outdoors. No one asks much about me; such inquisitiveness is considered rude. If I offer explanations—that I am African American—people respond with comments that betray their sense of the incongruity of my Blackness. It is as incongruous as the Blackness of the permed and gold washed models in the proliferation of Dark & Lovely hair ads. If I say that I am Jewish, it means little to this world of Muslims and traditionalists and Christians outside of the Old Testament, or a brother or cousin who got as far as Israel trying to reach the States. At the end of all my explaining, people say, "Ah, but we like you as a European lady!" This simply means "white." None of what matters to American social sorting, to one's identity at home, counts for much here. I remember eight years back to Rhea's suggestion: Against this moody, depleted, intoxicating landscape, I sit down in someone else's paradigms and try to figure myself out. (After all those years of letter writing; Rhea, now bitter, her optimism beaten down, lives just down the road from me.)

And then, strangely, slowly, as I became a citizen of Accra, something more of my humanity was affirmed. My belonging was predicated on how we shared a meal, the quality of how we passed the days together, how I participated in children's lives, and in too many burials, and the bit of domestic work "obruni" couldn't foul up. Soon I was being brought deeper inside. My triumph was when someone declared, "Ehhhh? Obruni! I've never seen some like you before! You are truly part of us." I am more deeply immersed in a community of Black people than I've ever been—I mean the daily life within a city more society than metropolis, with a Black nation. There are many limits to my descent, but I'm not barred by the particular entanglements of American race and color suspicions. Slowly, I am learning the art of Accra communitas. I practice patience, and self-forgiveness, and belonging in measures I didn't know I had in me.

But I also know that I remain outside. The Akwapim woman from the hills who married a Ga coastal man and has raised five coastal children is an outsider after twenty-eight years, so how much further outside am I? When we lay outdoors on the cooling cement of her yard one night, surrounded by sleeping children and dogs, with the roar of the Guinea Sea reaching over the sounds of night traffic, almost naked to the heat, she asked me about *The Book of Sarahs.* I had read from it that night to an audience at the U.S. embassy. I was aware of how incongruous this particular kind of memory work and self-revelation is outside the West. And that sense was intensified with my friend, as I struggled to communicate with her across my one, and her four, languages. After a while she said, "Catherine, don't be sad. This is our star." And she told me a story about herself. "You see that you like indigo. It is our cloth of mourning, and it is the one we use to welcome birth. Tie your cloth to my cloth ('join me') and forget." She knotted the edge of our wrappers together, and we sat quietly together until it was time to retreat into our rooms, hoping the ovenlike holding of the day's heat had eased.

Next to my bed, I have a family photo that I took just before I left. It reminds me of an earlier photo I have from the family files, in which I am eight and William is standing next to me. He is wearing a bright plaid shirt and a clip-on tie. His arm is wrapped around me with an odd paternalism—where did he learn that? One hand is planted on his chest, as if he's making a presentation of me. I am shy, awkward-looking. My arms are folded protectively across my middle, with my chin tucked almost to my chest. In the recent photo I am standing next to my brother. His arm circles me warmly, and that old affection is still there. There is an ease in my body now. My brother's wife, Ana, and their two daughters—the Filipina branch of the McKinleys—surround us. My parents stand together to the side. I like the picture. I like the people in it.

Time has become a perfect balm for all my pains. I feel it now in simple things: the ease from crippling doubts, the way I've begun to enjoy my parents, and to feel the freedom of forgiving them, the way I feel that I am beginning to know just who I am. There is no longer a question mark at the end of the tricky line of my identity. WASP and Jew and Choctaw and Africa mark me with ferocity. I've lined up photos of my other families, bearing the faces of these different tribes, all estranged from each other, with little reason to connect. I am in the center of each photo. When I look at myself there, I feel membership in all; in none.

Estie and Sarah and I have not had any meaningful contact in five years. I know, however, that we might meet again in a better place. Al Green reaches out only sporadically; I broke the bond of his affection, his telephoning constancy, by traveling. And his life has become more troubled by poverty and the constant upheaval it creates. He is in his early eighties, and he is failing. Sabine and Song and I still intersect, but familyness is not automatic, and our differences are great.

I have all of the imperfections of my family—and the steady love and clear memories of those who raised me. I can see that I had a childhood unnecessarily complicated by my parents' choices and circumscriptions. What I got were parents who, in their own way, put raising their children first, who valued independence, and integrity, who were not afraid to take risks, and who didn't express their love in words or easy affection. But their emotional steadiness, the compass pointing to Attleboro, and later to a Vermont farm, was a bedrock as I wavered and grieved. My parents gave me the tools to go forth and figure out an American Black woman's life. My bond with them is as simple and as automatic as love; as vexing and as intractable as our distances.

I know that these longings and pains can surface again: as my parents age, with death, with some of the old disappointments that remain, with my own questions about parenting. But my life can never return to what it was, and I'm grateful for the distance between who I was Before Family and who I am now.

I am at the end of mourning.

Acknowledgments

For my parents who parented me, and for William: Immense love for you! And with deep gratitude for: Gabriella, Carlina, Sabina, Toshi, and their parents, who have helped me to look again at the hopes and choices I was raised on. My agent and friend, Charlotte Sheedy; Neeti Madan, who helped to give this book a start; and Jack Shoemaker, Dawn Seferian, Trish Hoard, and the Counterpoint team for the very best publishing experience. Chris Jackson, Charles Flowers, Jane Vandenburgh, Miss D, Jacqueline Woodson, Gloria Fisk, Carolyn Ferrell, Nikky Finney, Jan Clausen, and Jane Lazarre, who each read incarnations of this book and helped to shape a critical departure. Kai Jackson-Issa, Hawley Fogg-Davis, and all the Yellow Girls I've met along the way who have been so much fun and trouble. Del Hornbuckle; David Unger; Judith and the Tuesday night girls; Sherry B. Bronfman; Gwen Kelly, Deadria Farmer-Paellman, Jennifer Hunt, and Shay Youngblood, for kind support and friendship. And a supreme "Oyiwaladonn" to my beloved Vida Saforo, Adolaye Mingle, Lady Diana, and Quansah, Ceci, Naa Ode, Korkoi, and Adakou

Crentsil, Bruno and Tsuishito, and the area people of Osu, RE who gave me shelter and the ultimate balm.

Early grants from the New York Foundation of the Arts, the Audre Lorde Estate, residencies at the MacDowell Colony and Hedgebrook, and a desk at the Writers Room gave critical support and put "more grease to the elbow."